MIMESIS
INTERNATIONAL

HASEKURA LEAGUE INTERCULTURAL STUDIES EDITIONS
n. 5

IMAGES, PHILOSOPHY, COMMUNICATION

Aesthetics and Thought in Japan and the World

Edited by
Christopher Craig, Enrico Fongaro,
Raffaele Milani and James Tink

MIMESIS
INTERNATIONAL

This book has been subjected to a peer review process.

www.mimesisinternational.com
e-mail: info@mimesisinternational.com

Isbn: 9788869773303
Book series: *Hasekura League Intercultural Studies Editions*, n. 5

P.I. C.F. 02419370305

TABLE OF CONTENTS

Foreword 7

IMAGE AND THOUGHT

Comparative Aesthetics 13
Raffaele Milani

Silence and the Speed of Human Perception 27
Luca Cesari

The Aesthetics of Ma (間) in a Comparative Perspective 43
Laura Ricca

IMAGES IN MOTION

Landscape Paintings through the Traveler's View 63
Nakama Yūko

Rembrandt and Japanese Washi Paper: Toward an Aesthetic of Black 79
Ozaki Akihiro

Images, Thoughts and Words on Disease in the Works of Michelangelo 93
Manuela Gallerani

Sandro Botticelli's Primavera and the Bridal Mysticism of the Song of Songs : The Flower Symbolism of the Bride and the Gaze of Love's Arrow 111
Nakama Aya

IMAGES AS BRIDGE

Toward Intercultural Thought: Steps between European and Japanese Aesthetics 127
Marcello Ghilardi

Kire-tsuzuki and *Shōji* : A Pictorial Analysis of the "Flower" as Image of Dis/Continuity between Life and Death 143
Alberto Giacomelli

The (Original) Nature of Images: The Beauty of the Place of Origin 165
Raffaele Milani

POP AESTHETICS

Images of Beautiful Bodies in the Internet Era: The Heritage of Old-School Bodybuilding 177
Federico Farnè

The Changing Image and Role of *Oni* in Japan: *App Oni Kara Denwa* (Call from an *Oni* App) 189
Kyōko Itō-Morales

Style Negotiated: Transformations of the Visuals in Manga-to-Anime Adaptations 201
Olga Kopylova

STUDENT PAPERS

Abanindranath Tagore and Okakura Kakuzō: A Brief Comparison on Biographical, Technical/Methodological, and Theoretical Grounds 223
Luca Contardi

Beyond Metaphor, in The Making of Poetic Word: A Comparative Analysis between Heidegger's, Bashō's and Kyoto School Aesthetic Perspectives 241
Giacomo Barbini

FOREWORD

Images, in the broadest sense suggested by the term, describe both a means and a consequence of the human interaction with and struggle to apprehend the world. It is natural that a metaphor based on sight, the most fundamental and immediate of senses, should come to hold a rich variety of meanings of such tremendous importance to the human experience. From its most literal sense of the brain's recodifying of light information into a comprehensible picture of the world, through its association with humanity's creative potential and its crucial role in the synaesthetic endeavours of rendering reality into aural language and aural language into written syllabary, the centrality of images, their reception, and their production of human consciousness is clear.

Questions concerning images and their place in human history, art, and consciousness abound. How do we perceive images and attach aesthetic value to them? How do images become embedded in culture and what insight can be gained through comparisons of the different aesthetic structures that are built around them? How do images, symbols, and narratives migrate across cultures, media, and space? In what ways does language function as a metaphor and how can we understand the relationship between signifiers and that which they signify?

The present volume is dedicated to exploring these and other issues under the rubric of a philosophical analysis of human work as expressed in arts, poetics, and techniques within the framework of the history of Japanese, East Asian, and

Western civilizations. The chapters that follow are based on presentations prepared for the Hasekura League Symposium: Images, Philosophy, Communication, held on November 11-12 in Bologna and hosted by the University of Bologna and Tohoku University. Over the course of those two days, scholars and students from Europe and Japan presented research and engaged in a discussion that approached images and the host of philosophical problems connected to them from a variety of disciplinary orientations.

The book is divided into five sections. The first of these, entitled "Image and Thought", gathers three works concentrating on analyses of human interactions with images and the ideas that inform aesthetic traditions. Raffaele Milani examines the synaesthetic nature of the sensory consumption of images and other artistic products and conducts a detailed survey of the thought and theories created to explain this nature. Luca Cesari moves in a different direction, engaging in a detailed discussion of the ideas of the eclectic artist and philosopher Gillo Dorfles in order to explore the roles of speed and of intervals of silence in the chaotic press of sensory input that forms the backdrop of life. The concept of the interval is also a central consideration in Laura Ricca's contribution, which examines the importance of intermediate spaces and pauses in Japanese aesthetics and searches out points of comparison in Western aesthetics.

The second section is titled "Images in Motion" and contains research pertaining to different forms of movement associated with painting. Yūko Nakama places her focus on the movement of artists themselves, conducting a close analysis of the influence on the ink painter Sesshū's landscapes of the artist's experiences during a two-year posting in China. In Akihiro Ozaki's study, it is the materials of the artist that move in a similarly focussed consideration of the influence of Japanese paper on both the production process and aesthetic sense of the Dutch painter Rembrandt van Rijn. Manuela Gallerani takes up movement of a different kind, examining the ways in which the physical ailments that afflicted the Italian sculptor and painter Michelangelo in his later life found expression in his art and writings. Aya Nakama explores the movement of story and symbol in her examination of the migration of narrative and symbolic elements from the biblical *Song of Songs* to Sandro Botticelli's *Primavera*.

The third section, "Images as Bridge" is comprised of works concentrating on the potential of images to forge conceptual links across time, space, and states of being. Marcello Ghilardi undertakes a philosophical consideration of the artistic traditions of Japan and Europe and proposes images and aesthetics as a means of establishing an intercultural mode of thought. In his study of the place of cutting and continuity in the Japanese aesthetic tradition, Alberto Giacomelli explores the idea, image, and symbol of the flower as a bridge between life and death. Finally, Raffaele Milani's second piece in this volume ruminates on the relationship between image and nature and discusses the role of art and aesthetic production in linking past, present, and future.

"Pop Aesthetics" is the title of the fourth section, which brings together works considering various permutations of images and aesthetics in aspects of contemporary pop culture. Federico Farnè's chapter discusses the changing aesthetics of male beauty as seen in the culture and sport of bodybuilding. Kyōko Itō-Morales focuses her attention on the evolution of the image of the monstrous *oni* from its mythological roots through its current incarnation in a smart phone application used for disciplining children. Olga Kopylova provides a detailed examination of the stylistic considerations that emerge in adaptations between the media of manga and anime and the connections of these considerations to ideas of authenticity among the consumers of these products.

The final section of the book presents two of the student papers presented at the Bologna symposium. Luca Contardi examines the relationship between the Japanese scholar Okakura Kakuzō and the Indian artist Abanindranath Tagore and the meeting of aesthetic traditions occasioned by their association. And in the final chapter, Giacomo Barbini engages in a complex analysis of the German philosopher Martin Heidegger's encounter with and interpretation of the work of Japanese poet Bashō and his conception of the aesthetic meaning and nature of words.

IMAGE AND THOUGHT

RAFFAELE MILANI[1]

COMPARATIVE AESTHETICS

In our century, synaesthesia and the similarities between the arts have gained increasing influence from a creative, ideational point of view and from a participatory, receptive one. They reflect the condition of contemporary sensibility continually stimulated by the evolution of the mass media, the decline of compositional conventions, the abandoning of expressive specificity, changes in techniques and materials, and by the fall of the system of fine arts. The 20th century witnessed the exasperated conflict of the shock effect as the dominant aesthetic quality against tradition. Within this contrast, the arts and the senses refer to and affect each other obliquely, not directly. It has long been observed in fact that a form of art does not correspond to only one sense: there are no absolute, univocal relations between painting and sight or between music and hearing because the other senses are involved by nature, depending on the case and to a varying degree. However, the situation concerning the arts and the senses is rapidly changing on the basis of a vast range of gradations and possibilities, resulting in an endless exchange between the aesthetic results of these new means and the elitist production of art.

It can be said that the similarities among the arts are in a way parallel to sensory correspondences. The theme of isomorphism (immediately apparent in the verbal and visual arts) enters into this picture echoed by a freer interplay between the senses. Parallelisms can be noticed which present different modes according to our historical outlook on past centuries. Clearly,

1 University of Bologna

these themes, though intrusive or prevalent in the 20th century, originated in a remote past. The relationship among the arts has been treated since ancient times when, however, they were all characterized by their conformity to the canons of classical tradition. In the Stoics and in Plato, one finds references to the relationship between poetry and painting, but prior to that, the motto *ut pictura poesis* (Simonides), to which Horace and Plutarch were to return and which was to be taken up again during the 5th and 6th centuries, should be recalled. This was analyzed by Giorgio Agamben in order to underline the connection between image and idea, between the philosopher and the painter in the sense of a realization of art.[2]

In more recent times, the debate over what is common to the different arts has gained increasing prominence. There are those who argue that the unifying element is ingenuity, while others claim that it is imitation; although one should not forget that, especially in the works of Mannerism and Rococò, the rhetorical figures can be interpreted as important means of passage or of translation from one art to another. To cite more recent examples, we may recall that for F. Schlegel architecture is congealed music, and for Schelling, theater, as the art of words corresponds to sculpture because it shows the object from all sides. For his part, Schopenhauer posited the relationship between music and sentiment in melodic development: sadness is associated with "minor" keys, while happiness and serenity are associated with "major" keys. Recently, Levi-Strauss[3] has traced a number of analogies underlying literature, painting, and music, starting from the principle of double articulation. Clearly, the examples, including those from the internal plane of art as the use of allegory, metaphor, and analogy in a strict sense, are numerous. Traces of these parallelisms may also be found in craftwork. In Kashmir the woof of the carpets is made according to an order of threads and colors that seems to reflect a criterion typical

2 See Giorgio Agamben, 'Immagine', in *Stilo*, 9 (1986).
3 Claude Levi-Strauss, *Regarder, écouter, lire* (Paris: Plon, 1993).

of music (whatever Etienne Souriau, who had established this relationship in his comparative studies, might say[4]).

If we turn to primitive societies in order to find the cultural roots of the human mind regarding the themes of the symbolic arrangement of the senses, Chatwin[5] seems to be the most reliable guide. In his journey across Australia, he developed the theme of nomadism, of the wayfarer who charts the songlines. Through these trails the wayfarer becomes the trail, in other words, the place he has sung of. It is necessary to cite these songlines because they represented the organization of social life through the description-imagination of the territory. These trails (reversed) resemble the ancient Art of Memory in which the various aspects were represented by places (loci), with a system of correspondences the systematization of which is sometimes found in complex architectural designs. But in Australia we are not faced with a mental construct, as the events of the Time of Dream have always existed there. There is a link between the land and song which can be explained by the aboriginal myth according to which every Man of ancient times, moving from the beginning of time, names the things and beings surrounding him with his every step. It is an intertwining of rivers, rocks, mountain ranges, and men. According to these trails, which are ultimately instructions and laws, there is a bond between man's soul and a particular point of the landscape. Certain trails and Times of Dream regard generation or being generated. Along these trails, which can be seen and heard only by the initiated, there is also a song of taste and smell.

Let us return to sensory correspondences proper and to the making of art. These events become charged with evocative cross references, structural equivalences, metaphorical suggestions, purely synaesthetic experiences, and combinations. They are enveloped in an aura of magical indeterminacy or calculated symmetry. If we exclude the work of artistic creation and limit

---

4 Etienne Souriau, *La corrispondenza delle arti. Elementi di estetica comparata* (Firenze: Alinea, 1988). See also the 'Introduction' by Raffaele Milani, pp. 13-53.

5 Bruce Chatwin, *Le vie dei canti* (Milano: Adelphi, 1988).

ourselves to common behavior, we feel that it is natural that the different sensory spheres are not equidistant and are to a certain degree homogeneous. Sensory arrangements should be viewed in the light of the language system which acts as a mediator. Defining a sensation with words in fact often entails recourse to another sensory sphere; for example, we may describe the taste of wine as round or soft, a color arrangement as strident, or sounds as soft. In this game of transference, synaesthesia refers to or reveals a unitary code. It seems that our mind immediately acts synaesthetically.

Let us attempt to understand the functioning of the perceptual apparatus better. According to Merleau-Ponty's analysis[6] (in particular the chapter entitled 'Feeling', pp. 283-325) perception is not a state or a quality, nor is it the awareness of a state or a quality. Instead one must understand color and sound in a certain behavior because in each act of perception there is a global adherence to the world. We detect sensory excitation on muscle tone and these reactions are integrated into an overall situation. Perception is in relation to movement in space. Sensations and "sensible qualities" reveal a motor physiognomy, a conduct; they are wrapped in vital meaning. It is in this light that the subject of the sensation should be placed, no longer intended as a thinker who describes a quality or as an inert being with respect to the sensation, but as "a force which arises together with a certain context of existence or synchronizes itself with it".[7]

The subject empathizes with the qualities. Perception is in all respects communion or coexistence. The sensation linked to a color, the identification of its *quale*, is intentional, it does not consist of itself like a thing, but is extended and signifies beyond itself. In other words, it is an exchange between the subject of the sensation and the sensible; the sentient and the sensible go together. The spectacle of sensible *qualia* is not pure being, but a moment of my personal history. Thus "perception is perceived in me". I can no longer say "I perceive" because in perception

6 Maurice Merleau-Ponty, *Phénoménologie de la perception* (Paris: Gallimard, 1945).

7 Maurice Merleau-Ponty, *Phénoménologie de la perception*, cit., p. 388.

there is always a sensation which entails the seed of a dream or of depersonalization connected with an "original acquisition". This acquisition shows the sensation as the mode of a general existence. As for the unfolding of the senses, their unity or diversity are truths of the same order, to put it as Merleau-Ponty would. Sensory facts concretely pose their being moments of a global configuration.

It is in this perspective that we consider the synaesthetic experience within which there is no longer any reason for claiming that vision is given by a visual *quale* and sound by a sonorous *quale*. Scientific knowledge removes experience. Instead it is necessary to find again the body and the life of the senses which communicate with one another, opening up to the structure of things. We thus discover that perception does not bring together our sensory experiences, as science does, by separating them. In this respect the qualities, the given of the different senses, in relation to each separate sense and each manner of modulation, communicate with one another and are united in a single mode.

> The form of objects is not their geometrical shape, but it has a certain relationship with the nature proper to them and, while it speaks to the sight, it speaks to all our senses. The form of a fold in a piece of linen or cotton shows us the softness or the dryness of the fibre, the coldness or warmth of the fabric.[8]

The pivot is the phenomenic body which projects a certain "environment" around it; its receptors are arranged in such a way as to make the perception of objects possible through synergy. The body, which Merleau-Ponty considers "the coagulated image of existence" is a synergic system whose functions are linked in the general movement of being in the world. Insofar as it adopts behaviors, the body is that object which uses itself as a general symbolics of the world thanks to which we can experience and understand the world itself. Following this line of thought, we understand that the unity and diversity of the senses are truths of the same order, that of sensory experience as a form

8 Maurice Merleau-Ponty, *Phénoménologie de la perception*, cit., p. 308.

of existence. There is a strict relationship between synaesthesia and movement. The senses act together with movement, which must not be understood as objective movement or as movement in space, but as a project of movement or "virtual movement". Movement thus becomes the basis of the unity of the senses. Merleau-Ponty specifies that

> ...it makes sense to say that I see sounds and hear colors if vision or hearing is not the mere possession of an opaque quale, but the experience of a mode of existence, the synchronization of my body with it. The problem of synaesthesia moves towards a solution if the experience of quality is that of a certain mode of movement or of a certain conduct. When I say that I see a sound, I mean that I echo the vibration of the sound with all my sensory being and in particular with that part of myself assigned to the perception of colors.[9]

On this basis not even words or the acts relating to corporeity are subsumed "under an ideal meaning", but the word is exchanged with the gesture and the gesture with the word in a communication through the body that in actual fact is revealed to be a system of equivalences and intersensory transpositions. "The senses translate each other...without having to pass through the idea".[10] Following up Herder, Merleau-Ponty goes on to say that man is "a perpetual common sensorium which is touched now by one part, now by another". The unity of the body is also the unity of the senses and the unity of the material and cultural object. The body thus becomes "the common texture of all objects" and, as a result, the instrument of my understanding of the world. Synaesthesia leads us to the original layer of feeling which we can find again, provided it coincides with the act of perception and we abandon our critical attitude. "I experience" - he says – "the unity of the subject and the intersensory unity of the thing, I do not think of them as reflective analysis and science will".[11]

In the light of these considerations, which bring synaesthesia to the fore, we will briefly deal with some aspects of colored

9 Maurice Merleau-Ponty, *Phénoménologie de la perception*, cit., p. 313.
10 Maurice Merleau-Ponty, *Phénoménologie de la perception*, cit., p. 314.
11 Maurice Merleau-Ponty, *Phénoménologie de la perception*, cit., p. 318.

audition. Levi-Strauss[12] analyzed the well-known *Voyelles* arguing that Rimbaud poses some analogies between differences. It would be mistaken to see each vowel separately in relation to a color. According to his interpretation, it is not the sensory correspondences perceived immediately that reveal the architecture of the sonnet, but the relationships that the intellect (*entendement*) unconsciously establishes between them that shows this architecture. From a historical and problematic perspective of the sound-color relationship, he cites Rousseau's *Essai sur l'origine des langues* in which a homology between the melody-harmony opposition and the design-color opposition is suggested. In his comment, Levi-Strauss reiterates that both colors and sounds may exist independently on the basis of the number of vibrations and in reference to an order of pure sensations. Painting and music consider both things and the relationship between them. Rousseau and Diderot had gone a step further than Batteux, who, bound to the concept of imitation, had prefigured but undervalued abstract art because he believed it to be an interplay of blots of colors, pure pleasure to the eye, but unable to involve the mind.

From the studies on physiology conducted by Lussana (who was against the thesis of a common sensorium), Tornitore[13] relates a framework of correspondences. The starting point is color seen as vibration to which different sensations and ideas are linked and which arouses excitations. In it, cases of homology between a given color and a given sentiment are also described. But in the specific case reported by Lussana, two brothers perceive the tones of voice (not the sight of letters) in relation to colors (red - acute and soprano voices, black - low voices). I have mentioned a parallelism between sounds and feelings. This is where the symbolism of color comes in, which can regard strictly transcendent aspects, common behavior, or certain linguistic constructions (alongside

12 Claude Levi-Strauss, *Regarder, écouter, lire*, cit., pp. 134-135.

13 Tonino Tornitore, *Storia delle sinestesie. Le origini dell'audizione colorata* (Genova: Facoltà di Lettere e Filosofia, 1986).

synaesthetic metaphors). As Paul Souriau[14] has already argued, the correspondence between colors and sounds can intertwine and imply the correspondence between colors and feelings due to the influence of evolutionary force. With respect to the *qualia* and feelings, we take into account mythological and religious considerations and implications. In the museum adjacent to the Shiva temple of Minakski-Sundareshuara in Madurai (Tamil-Nadu, India) there is a table of correspondences between colors and feelings: dark red - sensuality; grayish blue - fear; bright blue - pure religious sentiment; grass green - falseness; bright green - a communion of ideas and feelings; lemon yellow - the intellect; pink - unselfish affection. In Far Eastern culture and generally speaking in esoteric thought, correspondences are the structure of a whole system of representation of man and nature. In their range of action, we also find analogies with acute and obtuse angles, fragmentary or curved signs. A thick web of references is disclosed between the plane of emotions, feelings, forms, and senses that involves the organs of the human body, the seasons, astrological symbols, mythological tales, numbers, and directions, as Grasset has pointed out. In yoga, for example, we find, as Eliade[15] indicated, a map of similarities among chakras, colors, shapes (mandalas), sounds (mantras), the elements (earth, water), and the senses. However, we must not forget that also our tradition, from scientific and artistic treatises (not only in the 5th and 6th centuries), has envisaged a rich pattern of correspondences.

In observing an aesthetic life increasingly bound to factors of intersensory perception and an artistic evolution heavily conditioned by comparative research (homologies, exchanges, etc.) - the most famous cases come to us from Scriabin, Kandinski, Rimskij-Korsakov, Klee, Boulez, and Veronesi - the need for a comparative aesthetics arises. In other words, an aesthetics aimed first of all at studying these conditions of contemporary sensibility, thus renewing the project and theoretical efforts

14 Paul Souriau, 'Le symbolisme des couleurs', in *La Revue de Paris*, (1895).

15 Mircea Eliade, *Lo yoga. Immortalità e libertà (1954-1967)* (Milano: Sansoni, 1991).

of Etienne Souriau.[16] But the task of comparative aesthetics cannot be reduced to the analysis of the 20th century because the intersections and synaesthesias may also be viewed retrospectively and historically on the experimental terrain of analogy, allegory, symbol, and metaphor in singling out and highlighting procedures, materials, and compositional aspects. What differentiates our comparative analyses from those of 18th century aestheticians? Also, in the 18th century, when aesthetics became established as an autonomous philosophical discipline, the resemblance or affinity between the arts was debated. The main difference lies in the importance given to form today, rather than to the subject, imitation, and the hierarchy of the arts. Besides, in our age, as has already been pointed out, the new media place direct and indirect intersensory aspects in the foreground.

Etienne Souriau sees comparative aesthetics as a positive, scientific study based on a rigorous language of what is common to the various arts, an analysis of the structure of simile including the examination of a comparison between technical and aesthetic factors. It is a search for the similarities and differences between works belonging to different fields of expression. It aims at a careful and deep analysis of the mechanisms of translation from one art to another. The intention is to ascertain the appropriateness and the legitimacy of "borrowed" languages (for example, what it means to speak of a painting in terms of a symphony in white or blue major). This leads to an exploration of a phenomenological kind that shifts our attention from the material plane to the thematic and compositional one of inspiration. For Souriau, however, there exists an absolute moment revealed in the highest unifying manifestation of art by the elusiveness of the work of art. The latter consideration prevents him from examining the dynamic force of radical avant-garde movements. Souriau excludes the poetics of provocation, of the negative, of "aesthetic" annulment, which instead are strictly connected with the evolutionary processes of the new techniques of reproduction,

16 Etienne Souriau, *La corrispondenza delle arti. Elementi di estetica comparata*, cit.

as Benjamin has explained. Moreover, his division of the arts into presentational (for example, literature as pure prosody, an arabesque of consonants and vowels) and representational (literature as description, a reproduction of states, things, situations) does not respond to the needs of our age and might not be supported by historical study.

Within the framework of comparative aesthetics, we must not forget the work of Munro,[17] who has left us a broad vision of artistic diversifications. The debate on specificity (with a criticism against the priority of sensible *qualia* established by Souriau), the different meanings of art and its ambiguity, artistic genres, the relationship between art and the arts; philosophic classifications; materials; means of expression; techniques; the nature of aesthetic form; spatial, temporal, and causal organization; combinations; typologies; and styles are the fundamental points of a systematic interpretation that, as the author himself declares, can only formulate vague, provisional hypotheses to be modified, integrated, and updated in line with the mode of the creative and receptive planes.

Within the framework of artistic theories, Schaub-Koch[18] perfected an experimental comparative method that traces a parallelism between technique and expression. Although his work is unsystematic and too heavily influenced by the painting-sculpture relationship, it interprets the value of style and manner, the law of beauty as the law of proportions and as the product of technical and industrial civilization, and the suggestions of the pictorial and the linear along the lines of Focillon, Ghikha-Woefflin. Art and organic life are seen as poles apart, in that in art the form of creative thought, of thought as reality, is elevated; this concept of form makes way for immaterial, psychical space. For Schaub-Koch, comparative methods, situated between the ideal and the real, are instruments for stimulating the imagination.

In a broader perspective and more deeply rooted in philosophical thought instead, we find the comparative

17 Thomas Munro, *Les arts et leurs relations mutuelles* (Paris: P.U.F., 1954).

18 Émile Schaub-Koch, *Valeurs des rappels d'estétique comparative* (Lisbonne: International Institute of Art and Letters, 1958).

aesthetics of Pandey.[19] With great theoretical and historical effort in a constant and precise comparison between Indian tradition and Western one, he closely examines a set of fundamental and intermingling motifs: the theory of imitation, imagination, catharsis, the arousal of feelings and emotions, art as activity and work, the transfiguration of natural phenomena into mythological phenomena, contemplation, illusion, idealization, symbolism, the classification of the arts, verisimilitude, concretizing, invention, sensibility, reflection, sacredness, the priority of poetry, and drama. The course he charts is one of concordances and comparisons developed around thematic issues, not temporal axes. We thus find side by side the ideas of Aristotle, Descartes, Leibniz, Kant, Hegel, Schopenhauer (to whom he unfortunately and, strangely enough, devotes only a few pages), Croce, Bharata, Ananda Vardhana, Abhinavagupta, Bhatta Nayaka, Prattibha, and Mammata. There are also his observations on the single arts; in architecture Pandey finds similarities between the dictates of Vitruvio and those of Manasara. As for some of the principles of aesthetics mentioned above, invention in the Platonic sense of the divine inspiration of the poet is compared with the power of Sarasvati and in a rationalist and classicist sense (Boileau) with the Rasa (in Bharata and Dhananjaya); while for the Sublime, a connection is noted between the sublime and Adbhutarasa. As regards the sublime in architecture, Pandey's analysis of the fear of greatness proves interesting: it is not a question of "delightful terror", but of "astonishment". Also important is the discussion on the chakras and music, as well as that on the concentration of the mind on music in order to attain liberation. The latter consideration leads us back to the sensory correspondences from which we started.

A reflection on artistic and intersensory correspondences aimed at offering a theoretical solution necessarily calls in question a framework of structural relationships. This framework must be able to contain essentially the guidelines of the arts and

19 Kanti Chandra Pandey, *Comparative Aesthetics* (Varanasi: Chowkhamba, 1956).

techniques, of materials and procedures, of ideas and sensory bodies. Its importance is obvious, otherwise we are at the mercy of the impermanence and elusiveness of metaphor and of the psychological given. Etienne Souriau perfected a system for pinpointing and highlighting correspondences between music and the arabesque based on algorithmic notation. This may immediately suggest valid parallelisms with other arts: architecture, painting (especially abstract art), literature, the art of weaving and decorating, and so on. This system is not metaphorical, symbolic, or esoteric; it is a rational writing, and rational writing is certainly an indispensable tool for understanding synaesthetic and interartistic factors. On the aesthetic and scientific plane, Souriau made a choice we must take into account since he adopted spatio-temporal individuations proper to systems of mathematical description; although, by so doing, the field of aesthetic elements is inevitably narrowed down. If we in fact abolish the references of metaphor and symbol as the direct suggestions of synaesthetic perception, the field of observation is greatly reduced. But Souriau also points to the choice of a theoretical solution following a rational method with the purpose of a better understanding of the phenomenon in general: the comparison between the arts, the comparison between the senses through which we may discover an underlying law. We might ask ourselves whether there is actually a law at the basis of these phenomena, a verifiable and constant hypothesis. Here lies the theoretical and problematic crux: finding primary connections. It is not a question of enclosing the variety of aesthetics within a system, but of singling out the essential points from which such phenomena originate.

Bibliography

Thomas D. Albright, 'Color and the integration of motion signals', in *Trends in Neuroscience*, 14-7 (1991).

Giovanni Anceschi, *L'oggetto della raffigurazione* (Milano: ETAS, 1992).

Gabriele Baroncini, 'Colori e suoni tra Newton e Goethe', in *Giornale di Fisica*, 30-1/2 (1989), pp. 77-92.

Harold Bloom, *Western Canon. The Books of the Ages* (New York: Harcourt, 1994).
Louis-Bertrand Castel, *L'Optique des couleurs* (Paris: chez Briasson, 1740).
Daniel Charles, 'Sur quelques problèmes d'esthétique comparée aujourd'hui', in Grazia Marchianò (ed. by), *Le grandi correnti dell'estetica novecentesca* (Milano: Guerini, 1991).
Jean Claviere, 'L'audition colorée', in *Annuaire Psychologique*, 5 (1899).
Ananda Coomaraswamy, *The Transformation of Nature in Art* (New York: Dover Books, 1934).
Richard Cytowic, *The Man Who Tasted Shapes* (London: Abacus, 1994).
Eliot Deutsch, *Studies in Comparative Aesthetics* (Honolulu: Univ. of Hawaii Press, 1975).
Louis Favre, *La musique des couleurs* (Paris: Bibliothèque des Méthodes dans les Beaux arts, 1901).
Ivan Fonagy, *La ripetizione creativa* (Bari: Dedalo, 1982).
Marcel Granet, *Il pensiero cinese* (Milano: Adelphi, 1987).
Terence McLaughlin, *Music and Communication* (London: Faber and Faber, 1970).
George Lausing-Raymond, *Proportion and Harmony of Life and Color in Painting, Sculpture and Architecture, an essay in Comparative Aesthetics* (New York: Putnam, 1909).
R.E. MacLaury, 'From Brightness to Hue: An explanatory model of Color-Category evolution', in *Current Anthropology*, 33-2 (1992).
Friedrich Mahling, *Das Problem der Audition Colorée* (Leipzig: Akademische Verlagsgesellschaft m.b.H., 1926).
Karin v. Maur (ed. by), *Vom Klang der Bilder. Die Musik in der Kunst des 20. Jahrhunderts* (Stuttgart: Prestel, 1985).
Alan Merriam, *Antropologia della musica* (Palermo: Sellerio, 1983).
Victor Segalen, *Les Sinesthèsies et l'ècole symboliste* (Montpellier: Fata Morgana, 1981).
Karel Teige, 'Manifesto del poetismo', in Karel Teige, *Arte e ideologia* (Torino: Einaudi, 1982).
Tonino Tornitore, 'L'origine delle sinestesie. Mersenne, Kirker e le corrispondenze tra suoni e colori', in *Intersezioni*, 1 (1987).
Giuseppe Tucci, *Teoria e pratica del Mandala* (Roma: Ubaldini, 1969).
Boris Andreevich Uspensky, *Isomorfismo delle arti verbali e visuali in teoria della letteratura* (Bologna: Il Mulino, 1975).
Luigi Verdi, *Alexander Skrjabin tra musica e filosofia* (Torino: Passigli, 1991).
Jean Wahl, *Essence et phènoméne. La poèsie comme source de philosophie* (Paris: C.D.U., 1958).

Luca Cesari[1]

SILENCE AND THE SPEED OF HUMAN PERCEPTION

In an elegant book titled *Anche Harry Potter fa bene agli scienziati* (*Even Harry Potter is good for scientists*, 2014),[2] Gillo Dorfles writes as follows regarding the great scientist Galileo and the great German philosopher Kant:

> We are surely amazed to learn that they were not entirely immune to having "illuminations" that transcended their normal rationality, but it is vital to understand that there does not exist a unified mental structure that is totally impervious to interactions with materials other than those it normally uses.[3]

This represents a crucial situation for the scholar since it affirms the probable non-uniformity of mental activity as a whole, including thinking, which has almost always been interpreted as a synthesis or unity of divergent trajectories of cognition.

Therefore, among "scientific thinking, imaginative thinking, and artistic thinking there exist indissoluble links that are more often than not ambiguous",[4] quoting once more from the 2014 publication. At any rate, we can also find similar assertions in earlier works by Dorfles, starting with *Nuovi riti, nuovi miti* (*New*

---

1 Academy of Fine Arts Urbino

2 Alongside Marco Ciardi, *Galileo & Harry Potter. La magia può aiutare la scienza*? [Galileo and Harry Potter. Can magic help science?] (Rome: Carocci, 2014).

3 Gillo Dorfles, *Anche Harry Potter fa bene agli scienziati*, in Gillo Dorfles, *Estetica senza dialettica – Scritti dal 1933 al 2014* [Aesthetics without dialectic – Writings from 1933 to 2014], edited by Luca Cesari (Milan: Bompiani, 2016), p. 2559.

4 Gillo Dorfles, *Anche Harry Potter fa bene agli scienziati*, cit., p. 2559.

rituals, new myths, 1965),[5] in which the author acknowledges the multiplicity of the human mind's manifestations, which are not totally different from one another but contain elements rejected "by almost all the 'rationalist' thinkers of our times", because they are thought to have a degree of irrationality, which is incompatible with the legitimate "lucid and limpid analyses offered up by the institutionalized and self-conscious languages".[6]

Dorfles goes on to say that herein lies the blunder of not realizing that it is possible "to establish a normal and rational discourse even with respect to elements that appear not to be rational", and the error of not comprehending that such an "irrational component [...] serves as a safety valve for the human imagination"; he argues for the establishment of "a mythic-symbolic element" [...] "even in sectors that are apparently more rationalistic, for instance, science, politics, etc.".[7] Without being a sociologist, an anthropologist (or much less, a historian), Dorfles looks critically at myth and uncovers new opportunities for re-examining the many questions that still revolve around the principle of symbolism, which he studies closely in the writings that come after *Nuovi riti*.

In other words, consistent with the core issues explored in all his books that come before, and paralleling the increasing pace of unstoppable consumerism that intrudes into all our activities, it is the case that, due to the increasingly intense flow of visual, acoustic, etc., agents of conditioning, "the symbolic element [...] reasserts itself in the most typical moments". In *Oscillazioni del gusto* (*Oscillations of taste*, 1958)[8] and *Simbolo comunicazione consumo* (*Symbol communication consumption*, 1962),[9] this same reassertion is connected with the "technical and sensorial transformations" that also explain the insistence on

5 Gillo Dorfles, *Nuovi riti, nuovi miti*, in Gillo Dorfles, *Estetica senza dialettica*, cit.
6 Gillo Dorfles, *Nuovi riti, nuovi miti*, cit., p. 1061.
7 Gillo Dorfles, *Nuovi riti, nuovi miti*, cit., p. 1057.
8 Cfr. Gillo Dorfles, *Estetica senza dialettica*, cit.
9 Cfr. Gillo Dorfles, *Estetica senza dialettica*, cit.

the "relationships between aesthetics and psychology, especially the psychology of perception" ("Preambolo all'estetica di Rudolf Arnheim") ["Preamble to the aesthetics of Rudolf Arnheim"].[10]

These brief preliminary comments apply as well to the next phase (and collection of studies), which relates to the discussion of sociopathic expressions, for example, the one to which the most noteworthy essay of the entire pentalogy is dedicated, inaugurated by *Simbolo comunicazione consumo* (comprising as well *Nuovi ritmi, nuovi miti*, *Artificio e natura* [*Artifice and nature*, 1968],[11] and *Dal significato alle scelte* [*From meaning to choices*, 1973]).[12] We can say that, from the time of its publication, *L'intervallo perduto* (*The lost interval*, 1980)[13] introduces a new theme or ur-form for the entire development of Dorfles' later reflections on the controversial cognitive problem that he attempts to define (such as in *Horror pleni* [*Fear of full spaces*], subtitled *La (in)civiltà del rumore* (*The (in)civility of noise*, 2008).[14]

L'intervallo perduto describes a condition that is harmful to our sensory apparatus, in a state of emergency that can be identified by changes in behaviours made more acute by the excesses of an epoch that, unavoidably, is the one in which we live. We could also align the argument of the book with the notion of *labilità temporale* (ephemerality of time) that encapsulates concepts that Dorfles frequently confronts, but whose exceptional import perhaps adds to phenomena that are de-familiarizing in different ways, even with important epistemological and cultural connotations of oriental derivation.

For an adequate understanding of the viscous, undeniably epochal, phenomenon, we need once more to go back in time, not only to previous manifestations of phenomena that are certainly

10 Gillo Dorfles, *Preambolo all'estetica di Rudolf Arnheim*, in Gillo Dorfles, *Itinerario estetico. Simbolo mito metafora*, edited by Luca Cesari (Bologna: Editrice Compositori, 2011), p. 204.

11 Cfr. Gillo Dorfles, *Estetica senza dialettica*, cit.

12 Cfr. Gillo Dorfles, *Estetica senza dialettica*, cit.

13 Cfr. Gillo Dorfles, *Estetica senza dialettica*, cit.

14 Cfr. Gillo Dorfles, *Estetica senza dialettica*, cit.

at the root of current degenerative manifestations related to the perceptiveness of our consciousness, but back as well in the chronology of Dorfles' writings to find an antecedent whose importance is concealed. This would be an article that appeared in the journal *La Nuova Europe* in 1945, one that offers the reader a rich interpretation of Paul Valéry's *Cahiers* (*Notebooks*).

Studying the notebooks,[15] Dorfles uncovers leitmotifs that run through the entire 30-year period of meditation on the part of the poet; among these, he finds one whose importance is more apparent if it is related to the correspondence between the artificial and the natural. I refer to the concept of *récusation de l'enthousiasme* (rejection of enthusiasm) that, due to the specificity that Valéry attributes to it, describes the lost solidarity with the Platonic myth in much of European twentieth-century poetry. Yet, despite this, the peremptory tone with which the poet declares, "L'enthousiasme n'est pas un état d'âme d'écrivain" ("Enthusiasm is not the writer's state of mind"), we need to wait for dialogues like *Eupalinos ou l'architecte* (*Eupalinos or the architect*, 1923), *L'âme et la danse* (*Dance and the soul*, 1925), *Dialogue de l'arbre* (*Dialogue of the tree*, 1942), and the unfinished *Mon Faust* (*My Faust*, 1946), in order to clarify the essential evolution of Valéry's most important philosophical ideas.

If we are dealing with the "rejection of enthusiasm", and if, as Dorfles cites in several texts of 1919, "Je trouvais indigne d'écrire par le seul enthousiasme" ("I found it unworthy to write solely on the basis of enthusiasm"), the concept of "enthusiasm", nonetheless, entails a daemon that generally, in the form of the masks alluded to in the dialogues cited above, activates, like Plato's "lodestone", the infinite investigations of the creative act, which is the same as that "of nature which continues in man":

> In the very heart of the shadows where fused and confused are what pertains to our species and what pertains to our living matter, what pertains to our memories and our secret strengths and weaknesses, and what is the

15 Cfr. Gillo Dorfles, *Valéry e la 'recusation de l'enthousiasme'*, in Gillo Dorfles, *Estetica senza dialettica*, cit.

indistinct feeling of not always having been and having to cease to be, resides in what I have called [...] the INEFFABLE".[16]

The ineffable is that which veils "our powerlessness to express, that is, to attain freedom through words", as we understand from the statements directed at Tityrus and Lucretius (*Dialogue de l'arbre*), in the copy edited by Sereni, which is cited here. If, therefore, the correction of "enthusiasm" with the "drama of the intellect" expresses the substitutability of the "fire of inspiration", the "dance" symbol (which inspires the other dialogue) conveys the image of a twinning with the light of the flame, which is the synthesis of the creative act: a synthesis that conjoins the cosmos and time, the highest and most comprehensive manifestation of the "plant" (understood in the Goethean sense), the "organized mystery", exemplar of forces, laws, and "duration".

With the reference to "duration", or to the problems related to the concept of time, the book introduces a new level of questions, as it contemplates the problem of "temporal alienation" and

16 Paul Valéry, *Eupalinos preceduto da L'anima e la danza e seguito dal Dialogo dell'albero* [Eupalinos, preceded by Dance and the soul, followed by the Dialogue of the tree], translation by Vittorio Sereni, introduction by Enzo Paci (Milan: Mondadori, 1947). The theme of the ineffable associated with the meaning of the word appears often in the writings of Dorfles. For example, in 'La parola come segno dell'ineffabile' ['The word as sign of the ineffable'], *Aut aut* 66 (1961), where Dorfles, some twenty years later, makes some rather discordant observations: "Today when we begin to look with a certain amount of suspicion at some too rigid illustrations of fixed and unbreakable links (We know by now, from different branches of 'semiotics', what are the relationships between sign and meaning, or as Carnap would say, between sign and *designatum*, or as Morris would say, between sign and *denotatum* [...], we listen with renewed interest to a sentence such as that of Merleau-Ponty: 'Cette sorte de cercle qui fait que la langue se précède auprès de ceux qui l'apprennent s'enseigne elle-même et suggère son propre décryptement, est peut-être le prodige qui définit le langage'. This statement, in fact, informs us that *le langage* (in this case language in the strict sense, the spoken idiom) as well as the different artistic languages are in reality only in part institutionalized 'sign systems' [...] There does not exist a meaning (*Bedeutung*) that can be identified with meaning (*Sinn*) and it is the word that tells us that which it itself does not know how to signify [...] As we can say that the act of perception is always 'creative', similarly we can talk of the word's creativity beyond the will of the person who uses it".

the auditory and visual degradation of messages, or that of re-balancing certain necessary chrono-aesthetic elements aimed at restoring the psychological distance that allows us to valorize the vitality of our sensory apparatus. These represent two opposing sides of Dorfles' theorizing, which is already rich (from preceding texts) in human manifestations that reflect a convulsive absence of the "interstitial element"; and these same manifestations compel the author to pursue an inversion of tendency that might justify the existence of a sensoriality exercised creatively, which the new theoretical direction seeks to pursue, to achieve a "coherence between social structure and aesthetic expression".[17]

Contributing to the development of this new direction is a notable prohairetic tendency in Dorfles' choices (which is unfailingly present in his work after a certain date) and in direct relationship with the corresponding period, which assumes the form of a premise to a concept of extensive time on which depends "to a large extent the possibility of recovering many conditions [...] that are today changed", in every sector of human existence, of "our very way of thinking, *Erleben*, and judging".[18] Along this path are interspersed the heterogeneous situations that emerge from his knowledge of aesthetic and psychological motifs, which can be found everywhere, in every social or anthropological sector, and by virtue of corrections aimed at bringing about an axiological assessment of the phenomenon, perceived to be a menace.

In essence, this is a hope that culture can regain a form of existence that has been lost on account of our sensory disposition, which is by now damaged (if not atrophied) by the excess of stimulations that cause an inevitable cancellation of temporality. From this comes the warning of the negative limits associated with such a loss of the "feeling of duration", which (according to Dorfles) even a major contemporary writer has pointed out for

17 Gillo Dorfles, *Dal significato alle scelte*, in Gillo Dorfles, *Estetica senza dialettica*, cit., p. 1622.

18 Gillo Dorfles, *Dal significato alle scelte*, cit., p. 1622.

us in a poem that is touching with its exquisitely colloquial tone, one that conveys a personal experience of temporality.[19]

His analysis, in fact, is not on a level too different from the one that uncovers, albeit within the particularity of poetic expression, an appeal to something that is so decisive to the formation of our expressed extensive "rhythm", as Handke sings in the face of the chrono-aesthetic "pandemonium" of our quotidian sense of time that casts doubt on habitual "chrono-topological" alterations. These are the increasingly "abnormal", "hypertrophic" stimuli of "interstitial urgency" to which the modern individual is to be subjected.

These last features recall the example of phenomena that are, frankly, impactful on our sensory apparatus, which Paul Valéry identified with such prescience, not only in the area of demythologizing "enthusiasm" but, at the same time, in the area that is more directly connected with the sociopathic destabilization of our perceptual apparatus and the analogous blunting of our sense of time, which interfere with the psychological and physiological conditions of *Erlebnis* and *Dasein*.

Indeed, we cannot avoid mentioning many observations in Valéry's *Regards sur le monde actuel* (*Reflections on today's world*) that lavishly illustrate such profoundly altered perceptions of our anthropology, produced by our awareness of technical transformations and by mass communication media, which is all the more surprising if we consider the epoch in which they were written. These are reflections on the situation of our contingent time that, by virtue of their prophetic nature, constitute the substance of reflections on history, on which is based the last

19 The reference is clearly to the Austrian writer Peter Handke, author of an extraordinary poem titled "Gedicht an die Dauer" ("Song to duration", 1986): "How often I have sensed duration / in the first signs of spring at Fontaine Sainte-Marie, / in the night wind from Porte d'Auteuil, / in the summer sun of the Carso, / as I walked at dawn toward home after an embrace! / What was that sense of duration? Was it a period of time? Something measurable? A certainty? / No, duration was a feeling, / the most elusive of all feelings, / often more fleeting than an instant, / unforeseeable, uncontrollable, / ungraspable, unmeasurable". (Translation by C. Federici)

philosophical work of Karl Löwith, dedicated to Paul Valéry[20] (*Grundzüge seines philosophiscen Denkens*, 1971).[21]

On the one hand, the reflections are concerned with the perception of the "loss of duration" that, for Valéry, defines an epoch; and by duration the poet means the affirmation of the speed of technological progress, which clashes with the idea of a more profound sense of permanence, in other words, a "lastingness" in the face of pragmatic activities, customs, and scientific discoveries that reduce everything to the ephemeral effects of shock and the "excitement of the moment".

On the other hand, they are concerned with the "rejection of duration", which perhaps implies a more serious degeneration of human nature: "The era of the provisional is now upon us", writes Valéry, "the time required for a surprise is our current temporal unit". If we accepted the idea that "La poursuite des perfectionnements exclut la recherché de la perfection" ("The pursuit of improvements excludes the quest for perfection"), it would be like saying that transformations will increasingly reduce the possibility of a different "cataloguing of the imagination". Valéry writes:

> Modern man has blunted his senses; he puts up with every kind of noise [...]; he puts up with [...] violently contrasting or insanely intense lighting [...]; he feels the need for brutal stimulations, strident sounds [...]. He tolerates incoherence; he lives in mental disorder [...] The more we advance, the more the methods of symbolization and rapid depiction multiply. *Their aim is to do away with the effort of thinking* [...] Our modern world is entirely engaged in the increasingly effective and extensive exploitation of natural resources. It does not search for them

20 Paul Valéry, *Sguardi sul mondo attuale* [Views on today's world] (Milan: Adelphi, 1994).

21 Karl Löwith's *Paul Valéry* (Milan: Celuc Libri, 1986) was translated into Italian by Gianni Carchia who, in the Introductory note observes (p. 9): "Karl Löwith's last book, *Paul Valéry Grundzüge seines philosophiscen Denkens*, 1971, dedicated to a philosophical dialogue with Valéry's 'non philosophical', if not 'anti-philosophical', theories, and virtually ignored at the time of its publication in a spiritual climate that was certainly averse to accepting the author's bold provocations, today appears to be the best key to free ourselves from the historiographic conventions that have accumulated on his work".

> or use them only to satisfy the infinite needs of life, but instead it wastes them and is excited to do so, to the point of creating every kind of unheard of need [...] For the enrichment of others, we are injected with tastes and desires that are not rooted in our deep physiological life, but are the result of psychological or sensory excitation deliberately inflicted on us. Modern man is drunk on dissipation. Abuse of speed, abuse of light, abuse of tonics, of hallucinogens, of stimulants ... Abuse of frequent impressions; abuse of novelty; abuse of resonance; abuse of ease; abuse of wonders; abuse of these prodigious means of deactivation whose immense artificial effects are put into the hands of children. Today's life is inseparable from these abuses. Subjected each day to increasingly new mechanical, physical, and chemical experiences, our body, in the face of these forces and rhythms inflicted on it, behaves roughly the way it does when it is in the grip of *insidious intoxication*. Each day it finds the dose to be insufficient.[22]

It is difficult to find a remedy for such an insidious intoxication, created by mechanical, physical, and chemical experiences, especially because, in Valéry's time, such abuses, such excesses, seemed inevitable. Even more difficult is the task of adding something that is more precise or as effective, so forward looking; the exhaustive codification of this repertoire leaves no room or possibility of development except for the attempt to add a "balanced judgment of the ethical, aesthetic, anthropological situation of our civilization", such that it guides individual choices for our future toward a mode of the being (and choosing) of future generations. Perhaps, in some way, the resuscitated need for relationality, already stated elsewhere by Dorfles, could signal the sensory re-equilibrium we seek in many of our actions and events, and bring about change ("We find ourselves in a historical period where, more than in many that came before, man is expected to 'make his choices', and the future of humanity will depend precisely on these choices" – writes the author in *Dal significato alle scelte*).[23]

A rebalancing of our actions and events, preceded by the space for "choices", seems to anticipate the concept of the "interval" (of an *in-between*) that the condition of ideological, social, and psychological

22 Karl Löwith, *Paul Valéry*, cit., pp. 147-48.
23 Gillo Dorfles, *Dal significato alle scelte*, in Gillo Dorfles, *Estetica senza dialettica*, cit., p. 1617.

coercion, in the stated situation of speed and acceleration, tends to annihilate. And if we are not wrong to say that the meaning of many of our choices "is tied to a constant that we could define as 'freedom of choice' and that allows us to visualize in man the presence of a prohairetic quotient on which our actions and events depend, thus eluding every form of predetermination", it will be the case as well if we antedate this insight of such an interval of semanticity to many years before 1980, as regards Dorfles, to the research on the Baroque that Italian aesthetic studies produced in the years following the Second World War.

With respect to Eugenio D'Ors' essay *Del Barocco* (*On the Baroque*), in the Anceschi edition, Dorfles writes in the journal *Domus* ("Attualità del Barocco" ["The Topicality of the Baroque", 1946]):

> In a certain sense, it can be said that – as in music, where real music resides in the interval between two sounds – real architecture resides in the space enclosed by the surfaces that delimit it. The architecture that we see and perceive is merely the material element of the primitive structural essence, immanent in the controlled space. The day when we succeed in perceiving the sound of music in the silence of the interval, the motion of architecture in the empty space underlying the edifice, we will truly understand the harmony of the spheres; we will dwell in the house of the gods. On that day, we will realize that what seemed to us more or less attained, more or less impermanent in the constructions of mankind was only the empty shell left by the mollusk, the carcass from which the spirit exited.[24]

We can therefore see the importance that a certain type of feature receives from the remotest times, in which the concept is present in embryonic form, and precedes the emergence of the diastematic clash that continues be an indicator of our ontic situation. We can also see how some profound constants became the way they are today ("The day we succeed in perceiving the sound of music in the silence of the interval"!).[25] The pause, too, like the image, has an extraordinary autogenetic capacity that

24 Gillo Dorfles, *Attualità del Barocco*, in *Estetica senza dialettica*, cit.
25 Gillo Dorfles, *Attualità del Barocco*, cit.

is sufficient to account for the historical importance of such a premonitory expression.

We can, then, consider *L'intervallo perduto* to be the "continuation of that socio-anthropological research", begun with a series of earlier essays, according to what the author writes, although we note the greater prohairetic emphasis along with a diminished attention, than appeared to be the case, to the absolute innovations that are now juxtaposed to our knowledge of the evolving mind and interest in the civilizations of the Far East, which explored a contentious subtlety of the senses.

A sensory subtlety that is as real as the word that manages to say "that which it itself cannot mean"? This too is a legitimate question that occurs with the academic respectability of the classical discipline, by virtue of the many forms of knowledge of all the "selective" and "creative" functions of the sensory system ("active in each of its sectors"), which is not always within the scope of what current science can analyze. It is true that the void, silence, and the sense of hearing that detects even beyond the audible datum, are interesting points of reference that can be noted from the first lines of the book:

> The abrupt jolt – right in the middle of sleep or in the act of falling asleep caused by a truck passing along via Aurelia, a few paces from the villa where I lived during the summer, is by now replaced by a continuous, incessant hum of traffic that never stops. Despite the irritation of this unending buzz, the view that I had in the past of the single interruption that destroyed complete quiet, absolute silence, was even more unpleasant and disturbing. As the condition worsened, therefore, the loss of the interval of silence between two noises would seem to be an improvement. However, it also represents the definitive erasure of the condition of complete peace that exists by virtue of the minute and discontinuous interruptions of the same. This condition of continuous noise, of constant motion, of endless becoming, by now pursues us everywhere and at every moment. The forces with which we fight against this situation are increasingly weak and tired. Many have already surrendered in this battle; they have lost the awareness of the meaning of stasis and the pause, the emptiness of an interval. Losing the interval (and especially the awareness of the interval) means blunting our sense of time and approaching a situation where our chrono-aesthetics is obliterated.[26]

26 Gillo Dorfles, *L'intervallo perduto*, in Gillo Dorfles, *Estetica senza dialettica*,

As is evident from such a narrative opening, the interstitial experience is the funnel into which flows the ontic situation outlined above on the basis of relationality and information, both of which are now called upon to configure an interstice within which relationship comes into being rather than sink into the condition of "noise". This means that relation extends to all the forms of sensory experience and is not limited to describing a sectorial experience, but every kind of contemplative or reflective reality that is part of the aesthetic whole, which is indivisible from the naturalness and the temporality of "being in the world".

This need for interstitial time is, therefore, interdependent with judgment that stimulates the socio-anthropological synthesis and uses the prohairetic norm as consciousness of a self-directed choice on the part of the individual, in "the search for an aesthetic quotient that might cause man to valorize his nature so as to allow its appropriate development".[27]

This is how, in order to repair the damage of the "too full" and the uniformity of the acoustic and symbolic hypertrophy of the aesthetics of the day, the "loss of the interval" (which has choices as a corollary) engenders a severe repudiation as well as the scrutiny of some elements that are necessary for the interpretation of the period in which we are living. This is a period that spans the excesses of a civilization (or un-civilization) of communication (once it has become a cultural fact that is totally a part of the quotidian language), on the cusp of an historical epoch hurtling toward the future, on the one hand, and the manifestation of some progressive changes that "allow us to see a reversal in trend" (still quoting Valéry), injecting a positive "diastema" into the flow, on the other hand.

And what is "diastema"? Dorfles informs us that it is a "Greek" word that more convincingly than the word "pause" suggests "that aspect of separation", "capable of highlighting certain elements"; and it may indicate something unusual or new, for the

---

cit., pp. 1881-82.

27 Gillo Dorfles, *Artificio e natura*, in Gillo Dorfles, *Estetica senza dialettica*, cit., p. 1368.

reasons stated above, although it "always appears spontaneously in different epochs". It is, therefore, that which "separates two events, two objects, two notes (in the case of music)", from which emerges a perhaps disconcerting experience due to the interstitial disconnection from the action of incessant stimulations. It is a creative act, therefore, even without attaining an artistic result, as it deviates from the paroxysm of acoustic, verbal, and visual images (*Horror pleni*), and functions as a harbinger of reacquired imaginative and intuitive qualities blunted by the absence of the "imaginative pause":

> I contend that it is indeed a case of a-diastema or anti-diastema, of interstitial absence, against which we must react [...]. It is, instead, this element that has frequently proven to be defective in our age, for a variety of reasons that are difficult to pinpoint, but such as to cause or have caused much of the psychological, sociological, and aesthetic damage by which we are victimized, but as well many of the oddities of some of the most typical creations of our times.[28]

Psychological, motor, auditory, rhythmical, visual, etc. distance represent the many possible ways to describe the pause we are considering as it still presents itself, as the condition of *in- between* ("what lies between") and not only in the sense of an effective perceptual "specialization", of the aesthetic kind.

It is rich in subtlety and formativeness, and it is to be thought of as the attainment of an intuitive vacuity, not too different from a sort of pause in being, sheltered from the damage of the "too full" and the "damage caused by the civilization of consumerism"; therefore, it entails the safeguarding of a beneficial "void", a "silence" beyond the "frenetic word-generation" and the familiar stimulation of *noises* and *signs*.[29]

---

28 Gillo Dorfles, *L'intervallo perduto*, in Gillo Dorfles, *Estetica senza dialettica*, cit., p. 1879.

29 The theory of the "lost interval" developed by Dorfles in the homonymous book (Turin, Einaudi, 1970) corresponds to what others call "duration", speaking of John Cage's "silent composition" *4'33*" (Leonardo V. Arena, *La durata infinita del non suono*, Milan, Mimesis, 2013). From the philosophical standpoint, the theory cannot really be attributed to any specific author. We may find echoes of it in a number of anthropological and psychological

For Dorfles, this is where is located the indispensable re-evaluation of typical conditions in which we find "the absence of a chrono-aesthetics of the occidental type", as occurs in ancient and Far Eastern civilizations that confront "the void as a condition that is necessary for appreciating relative fullness", a vaccine against the "unhealthy mania" of our social life (of "flowing into fullness" in our daily lives). Examples of other forms of "mythic a-temporality" include "Buddhist a-temporality, understood as awareness of the will to alter the flow of time" (accompanied by the examples of the haiku lyric genre and other aesthetic-religious concepts of the Far East), along which we could mention the most recent considerations of a scholar like Grazia Marchianò, concerning the opportunity to counter our excess of expressions by having recourse to that which opposes them through the sensory experience of the "brullo" or the "barren".

From these brief remarks we see that what is at stake is the confirmation of the ethical, temporal, and sensory role that the "diastemic pause" plays with respect to every "temporal-spatial" instance of *Dasein* as it struggles to create a space from which its own creative "authenticity may emerge".[30]

---

comments on myth, religion, and ancient Chinese and Japanese thought found in the writings of Alan Watts. However, to identify something very similar to Dorfles' concept of "diastema", we could cite aspects of the pragmatist-naturalist philosophy of Alfred North Whitehead (who, in the context of his organicist system, discusses the meaning of "relationship" by using the term "infra-ity", which is to say, the actual connection among things, in *Adventures of Ideas*, New York, Free Press, 1967); or we could mention Charles Sanders Peirce, who had already spoken of the "interval". It is also possible to connect this idea to Valéry's reflections in *Regards sur le monde actuel* (Glimpses of the modern world, 1931), where he states, "the rejection of duration defines a world epoch", or "modern man's senses are blunted; he tolerates noise … violence and maddeningly intense lighting. […] Modern life as a whole is inseparable from these forms of abuse. With each passing day, our body is increasingly subjected to […] psychological or sensorial stimuli deliberately inflicted on it" (See Karl Löwith, *Paul Valéry*, cit.).

30 Grazia Marchianò, 'Spiritualità: l'esperienza del brullo' ['Spirituality: the experience of the barren'], in *Rivista di Psicologia Analitica* 90 (2014), edited by S. Carta and R. Madera. Marchianò writes: "The title of this article contains the gist of what I mean by the spiritual dimension and experience: as regards excess, the use of spare words; as regards the relationship between spirituality and religion(s), rejection of the notion that the two terms are

interchangeable, as is usually believed; as regards the possibility that a spirituality in the secular sense can avoid being misunderstood is improbable. What remains, nonetheless, is the aim of illustrating the unadorned, bare, and worldly holistic nature of the spiritual experience, examining its aspects from a transcultural perspective, to which I am accustomed […] Hence the barren! In relation to the repertoire of images that flood the mind: the spare, the ascetic, the frugal, the neutral, the absorbed, the austere, and the silent may be evoked" (pp. 167-168). The author of *La parola e la forma* [Word and form] (Bari: Dedalo Libri, 1977) has produced a series of transcultural studies on aesthetics that are very broad in comparison to the monolithic enlightenment and romantic European tradition. Also noteworthy is her important contribution in terms of theory consisting in the article 'Verso una nozione plenaria dell'estetico e dell'estetica' ['For a plenary concept of the aesthetic and aesthetics'], in *Oltrecorrente* 7 (2003), where we read: "On the formal level, the philosophies and aesthetics of the Orient and the Occident have in common a conceptual lexicon, a dialectical structural argumentation, and a body of texts, Hence, it is not only appropriate but necessary to trace out a map of aesthetic thinking that incorporates not only the Mediterranean basin, Europe, and the Anglo-American world, but all of Eurasia. The most unbroken expanse of land between the Atlantic and the Pacific is, in fact, the place where, in the last five millennia, the forms of knowledge at the root of the process of human civilization were developed in a systematic way and preserved in written records. Beyond the physical geography, then, we are talking about a mental continent that is partially submerged, the unseen portion being analogous to the *cathédrale engloutie* (the sunken cathedral) described by Debussy, whose spires can be seen and the sound of whose bells can sometimes seem to be audible beneath the water surface. The ways of thinking of the peoples of Eurasia provide us with important keys with which to enter the sunken cathedral of the aesthetic feeling. On the theoretical level, these keys are comprised by a body of specific texts dealing with literary compositions, poetry, and the arts as a whole, but they are also keys that can be found in a vast exegetic, ritualistic, cosmological, and religious literature that indirectly, but substantively, sheds light on the cognitive abilities and the creative resources of the human mind […] From this stems the importance of re-contextualizing not only aesthetic theory but philosophy as a whole – with its privileging of Euro-Asian thought – in the expanded field of ethnophilosophy, a new discipline with a bright future" (pp. 42-43).

Laura Ricca[1]

THE AESTHETICS OF MA (間) IN A COMPARATIVE PERSPECTIVE

In order to understand the importance of the concepts of intermediate space, interval, pause and suspension in Japanese culture and aesthetics, and to undertake a comparative reflection on these categories as they pertain to Western aesthetics, we must begin with the more celebrated linguistic-aesthetic category of Japanese sensibility, namely *ma*.[2] The notion entails a dense web of meanings, starting with its figurative structure as an ideogram: 間.[3] In the ideogram 間 the component 門 represents the pictographic and semantic reference to a "fixed" architectural element, the *mon* that marks the boundary between the exterior and the interior, the inside and the outside of a home area, the sacred and even the urban, thus depicting the interval in its spatial dimension. But at the centre of *mon* we find the ideogram *nichi* or *hi* (日), which means "day" and "sun": a second figurative element, opposite to the first, of the movable temporal type, indeed the very measure of time, incarnated in the solar star. It is the sun seen from inside the house through the door. This mobile element is set precisely "between" the two pillars of the door: this is how, in a strictly pictographic sense, the prepositional value of the character *ma* that combines spatial and temporal values originates.

---

1 University of Bologna

2 A fundamental work on the concept of *ma* is the volume edited by Luciana Galliano, *Ma, La sensibilità estetica giapponese* [*Ma*, The Japanese Aesthetic Sensibility] (Turin: Edizioni Angolo Manzoni, 2004).

3 For such analyses see Francesco Lizzani, *La quindicesima roccia. Stazioni di un viaggio in Giappone* [The Fifteenth Crag. Stages in a Journey through Japan] (Rome: Castelvecchi, 2016), p. 23 and ff.

The character's primary and most elementary meaning, when it is not used in conjunction with other terms, is that of asemantic functional element equivalent to the preposition "between", pronounced *aida*. In no other language is such a simple particle capable of generating a series of meanings so rooted in the sensibility and in the history of the art of a civilization. In a general sense, the character means both "space" and "time", according to the expressions to which it belongs. This is however a time and a space seen not as abstract categories but rather in the sense of "the right and appropriate time" similar to the Greek *kairós*.

Moreover, in a more specific sense, we enter the semantic spatial and architectural field, where the *ma* acquires the meaning of "room". It may seem odd, but the room in the traditional Japanese architecture is nothing more than a mobile interval within the home space, a provisional space determined by the opening and closing of mobile walls that carve out a larger space, as it appears evident in the following image of the Katsura Imperial Villa (Katsura Rikyū, 桂離宮):

Figure 1
Katsura Imperial Villa (Katsura Rikyū, 桂離宮)
© Laura Ricca

It is significant that in all Japanese architecture the space is conceived in terms of pause, interval, in a perspective that cannot be separated from the temporal plane. For example, the word *tokono-ma* (床の間), where our character assumes a prominent place in its final position, rather than a space abstractly conceived, indicates an interval cut out in the perimeter of the room that houses it; one might even call it a perceptual, and therefore temporal, interval, considering the pause with which the eye lingers in the contemplation of the calligraphic scroll (*kakemono*) and of the *ikebana* composition in the niche that represents the most intimate and sacred place of the Japanese house. *Tokono-ma* is a kind of architectural pause in the heart of the traditional Japanese house.

When we say *pause*, however, we know that, even when it is used in conjunction with other characters that have a full lexical function to mean "space," the word "between" has a range of chrono-topological denotations that cannot be reduced to Cartesian space, which is considered an abstract geometric system. We are dealing, instead, with space in time or space-time, in other words, a narrative time that is both physical and virtual (architectural or diegetic). For example, it is the space-time of the *kaiyūshiki* (回遊式, "gardens in motion" or "stroll gardens") where natural and artificial elements are not arranged so as to be taken in as an overview, but to be revealed progressively to the gaze as it proceeds temporally into the space (like an effect called *inken*, 隠顕, or "appearance and disappearance"), as occurs when we walk along the meandering *roji* (露地, "dewy ground"), a path of large, irregularly-shaped stones leading to the tea house.

Remaining in the context of architecture, the *engawa* (縁側), or deck projecting out onto the garden, is a transitional space that, even if the character does not appear in the word, represents perhaps the most apt architectural illustration of the category of *ma*: a spatial but also temporal diaphragm, of pause, which separates the outside of the house from the inside. As *margin*, the focal point of the transition, it emphasizes both passage and pause; the threshold, in this sense, is by definition a place of mediation, as well as other spatial diaphragms that dominate in the Japanese environment.

Figure 2
Engawa (縁側)

It is the case, for example, of the *genkan* (玄関), a ground level atrium where shoes may still be worn and which modulates the passage into the house or the temple; it is an intermediate space functioning as a welcome area that reduces the contrast between interior and exterior.

Figure 3
Genkan (玄関)

The intermediate spaces not only characterize the structure of the living space; they are also evident in the urban morphology. They are real areas of "suspension", within the fabric of the city, which we can find in the heart of the most central and populous *ku* (区) of Tokyo, where one can see areas of primitive nature that can be of spectacular size (such as the Meiji-Jingū, 明治神宮, buried like the shrines of Ise (伊勢神宮) in a forest of tens of thousands of trees, a veritable sacred forest that is like a *ma* among humans and the divine, or the abyss of emptiness created by the imperial residence in the centre of the city, which so impressed Roland Barthes), shattering the very topographical continuity of the urban fabric.

Figure 4
Tokyo: the green bubble in Yoyogi Park between Shibuya and Shinjuku, with the Meiji-Jingū

Figure 5 The "empty" centre of Tokyo

We can now interpret all the foregoing examples as manifestations of that aesthetics of the void that informs not only Japanese architecture and space, but the other figurative arts as well, and all the Japanese arts: the *sumi-e* (墨絵), or black ink painting typical of Zen, where the void-pause occurs in the spaces between the lines, in their allusive "incompleteness", in the pauses between white and black; the *karesansui* (枯山水), or dry gardens of stones and gravel, where the intervals of void between the individual rocks create compositional balance; the *ikebana* (生花), where the gaps between branches generate the spatial field; the *shodō* (書道), the art of calligraphy, where the brush does not "fill" the void of the white background, but generates it with its irregular and spaced lines. It is clear, therefore, that interval (*ma*) and void (*kū*, 空) overlap; in this sense, Japanese art "builds" the void, which plays a fundamentally important role.

It is the perceptual equivalent of that "nothingness" (mu, 無), understood as emptiness, which is the philosophic cornerstone of Zen, the Buddhist current that, from the thirteenth century onward, has exerted an increasingly important influence on all the Japanese arts, not only the figurative ones, including those that, not by coincidence, we call martial "arts". This is because, from this perspective, art is in essence a subtle practice that, taking different "paths" (道, *dō*: whence *sadō* (茶道), or "way of tea", *shodō*, or "way of writing", *kyūdō* (弓道), or "way of the bow", etc.), "produces", as it materializes, that "poietic" void wherein its meditative goal is realized.

In this respect, particularly illuminating are the theories of the greatest exponent of Nō theater, Zeami Motokiyo (世阿弥元清, 1363-1443). His treatises contain important reflections on the value of the pause, understood as a complete suspension of the scenic action, a veritable absolute void, in which *ma* assumes all its temporal meaning:

> What is interesting is the *non-interpretation*. It is a concentration of the mind that, the moment you stop dancing or singing or in any other situation during a pause in the text or in the mimesis, causes you to remain alert and

> totally attentive. The emotion (created by) this mental concentration [...] constitutes the interest.[4]

The word "pause" (せぬ隙, *senuhima*) is used here by Zeami to indicate a purely temporal void that plays an explicitly encoded syntactic role, as it does in other ways, in traditional music and dance. This is a very clear confirmation of how the Zen artistic culture as a whole has found the lifeblood for its expression in the concept of *ma*. In any case, even in the few examples cited above, it is evident that the topic of the pause attains an absolutely central importance in the Japanese arts, forming a relationship that seems inverted relative to our Western categories, as if empirical reality, fullness, were used to construct the void, seen as a goal and not as a means; in the West, on the contrary, the void and the interval are means of segmenting and constructing empirical reality. A final synthesis of this concept is presented to us by one of the greatest works in Japanese art history and world art, the garden of Ryōan-ji (龍安寺), attributed to Sōami (相阿弥, -1525), and dating from the late fifteenth century.

Figure 6
Ryōan-ji (龍安寺)

4 Zeami Motokiyo, *Il segreto del teatro Nō* [The Secret of Nō Theatre] (Milan: Adelphi, 2002), pp. 178-9.

In this extraordinary figurative masterpiece, which appears to antedate Western abstract art by four centuries, space seems to expand indefinitely as an effect of the intervals separating the fifteen rocks that the artist has placed within the frame of sparkling white gravel, from which they emerge. It is the void itself that assumes here a tangible form due to the tension that separates the rocks: a tension we could contrast with that of another great rectangular space of the Laurentian Library, designed by Michelangelo, where, on the contrary, the plastic elements of columns, windows, shelves, and balustrades seem to compress spasmodically each spatial interval, almost causing space itself to implode.

Figure 7
Laurentian Library, interior

Figure 8
Laurentian Library, stairway

Figure 9
Laurentian Library, detail

We are at the polar opposite of the conception of space that I have been attempting to delineate here, and to which a comparative study can contribute a deeper understanding and corroboration. Western art, from that of the Greeks onward, has certainly not neglected the topic of the interval, the pause, and segmentation. The Greek word *kosmos*, "cosmos", "universe", incorporates the concepts of beauty and decorum, as indicated by the word "cosmetic", and at the same time the ideas of order and regularity, and therefore rhythm, division into parts; so much so that the verb *kosmeo* also indicated the division of the army in ranks. The Doryphoros, literally "lance-bearer", by Polykleitos, offers us an exemplary image of these basic concepts of Western aesthetics as this is an ideal male figure that is standing, but constructed on the basis of a "chiasmus" that juxtaposes flexed and relaxed limbs, producing an inverted relationship in the form of an X.

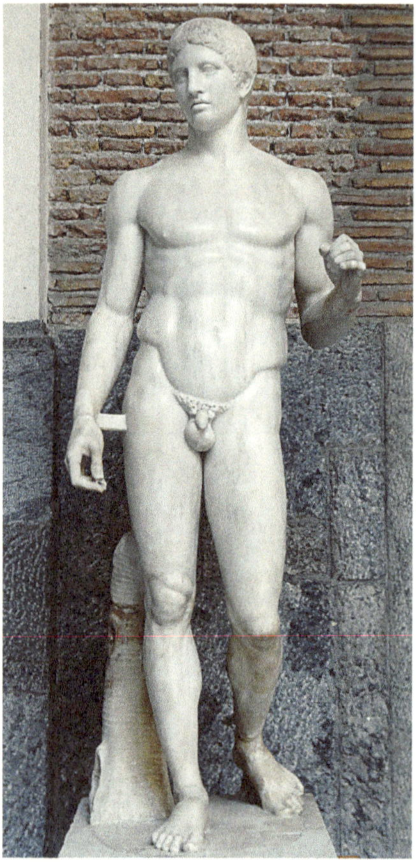

Figure 10
Polykleitos, Doryphoros (Spear-Bearer)

It is obvious that this is not a simple visual symmetry, which would be monotonous, but an actual inverted alternation of strain and rest, action and pause, arsis and thesis. Due to this alternation, to which the slight rotation of the head also contributes, any impression of stillness is denied, and the figure is permeated by a contained movement that animates it and renders it "natural", in comparison to earlier, severe styles of sculpture. In this way Polykleitos indeed inaugurates the "classic" style of Western art, a word that in Latin is not by coincidence derived from "class", group, subdivision. Classic is what is well distributed, ordered, subdivided, and, therefore, it presupposes intervals. Polykleitos is also the author of a treatise, the "Canon" or "Rule", in which the proportions of the figure sculpted in the Doryphoros are theorized, and the word came to be identified with the statue itself, taken as a classical model, that is to say perfect, of the human figure. Echoing the title of a famous essay by the literary critic Harold Bloom (1930-2019), we might say that the Doryphoros embodies the "Western canon" of aesthetics: proportion, naturalness, balance, harmony, and symmetry. This is, of course, a baseline that has many variants in the history of Western art, but that remains the main line of development and articulates a conception of the interval very different from the Japanese one: a pause that serves to divide, subdivide, order, and not to "empty", "open", or bring the void to the foreground. So, whereas, the Japanese art of Zen is oriented toward rarefaction, Western art has historically always been inclined towards the opposite, namely, the multiplication of intervals, divisions, and subdivisions, in a word, "complication", "filling up". This trend re-emerges periodically throughout the history of Western art, and we see that as Hellenistic follows Classical art, Gothic follows Romanesque, and Baroque comes after Renaissance. Throughout its history, Western art has tended toward the *horror vacui*, the "fear of emptiness", precisely the opposite of the trend in Japanese art. Even in the historical avant-gardes of the twentieth century, this dynamic continues to manifest itself, though in a completely new way. Futurism, Cubism, and Dadaism, have shattered forever the norm of the orderly division of space and time, and introduced compositional principles based on simultaneity, contemporaneity, interruption, and decomposition. The interval returns in a guise that is the opposite of the traditional one: no longer as a connective-disjunctive, but as an allotropic, alienating, even provocative, element. In the painting *Glass and Bottle of Suze* (1912) by Picasso, we note the use of the newspaper that breaks into the picture plane as a breach of external reality that has nothing to do with the already disassembled subject of the painting. We also note, in a form that is quite new, the same tendency toward the *horror vacui* discussed above: it is as though the Euclidean surface of the canvas were shattered to accommodate a multiplication of spaces much greater than the frame can contain. Once again, Western art expresses its horror of the void. But in the face of this return, in the same avant-gardes re-emerges the opposite tendency of Western art, the classical one that tends toward balance, modular design, ideal order based on intervals. Any painting by Mondrian illustrates this point:

Figure 11
Mondrian, *Composition with Large Red Plane, Yellow, Black, Gray and Blue*, 1921

Yet, perhaps for the first time, something new happens: the interval seems to emerge here as protagonist, as rarefaction, emptiness, the elimination of every element indicative of "fullness". We are not far from the atmosphere of the Katsura Imperial Villa:

Figure 12
Katsura Imperial Villa (Katsura Rikyū, 桂離宮)
© Laura Ricca

Figure 13
Katsura Imperial Villa (Katsura Rikyū, 桂離宮).
© Laura Ricca

Along the path taken by Mondrian, we find a spiritual and mystical trend and, perhaps because of this approach, it seems that the distance between Western art and Eastern Zen art is being eliminated. In any case, in the art of the late twentieth century, the interval becomes the main feature of artistic languages in both forms we have seen, that is both as provocative and as mystical rarefaction. Both tendencies express the great rebellion in contemporary art against the "excessive fullness" of neo-capitalist consumer society, the pervasive nature of advertising, and the constant background noise of radio and television.

From the dry referential language of the nouveau roman, to the slit canvases of a Fontana (*Spatial Concept. Waiting*) or even the white canvases of a Rauschenberg (*White Painting*), "intermediate space" becomes the protagonist and the subject of artistic creation, as an expansion of the useless, laceration, or even absolute void.

Rauschenberg's white paintings seem to suggest that the task of saving us from death by inflation of signs in the contemporary world is now left to art alone. In the field of music, we finally find what can perhaps be considered the most blatant provocation in this regard: sixty-nine years ago, in 1952, John Cage "writes" the revolutionary score 4.33 "for any instrument". The work, however, consists in not playing any instrument at all, of course, in the presence of a musician or an orchestra duly assembled and equipped. The provocation of the musician during the first legendary "performance" aroused the indignation of the audience, which roared and rose to leave, while pointing out that absolute silence itself does not exist: there are always noises that emerge, within and outside the room, including the heartbeat in an extreme case, if we were to find ourselves enclosed in a soundproof room. Silence needs to be interrupted in order for it to be "heard"; the void needs space in which to occur, and the nothingness of being to be thought. Silence cannot be but the interval, and here the interval is absolutely the protagonist. In the figure of John Cage, two opposing pathways, that of Western art and that of Japanese art, seem to have finally and consciously converged, to the point where the two elements we first took to be separate, namely, the mystical and the provocative element, are fused: this fusion is, in fact, characteristic of certain events in Zen, such as the *kōan* (公案). It is not a coincidence that Cage, as well as other members of the Beat Generation, referred explicitly to the East and to Zen.

While the echoes of Zen culture in the Occident tend to be translated into conceptual abstractions that are typical of our rationalism, in Japan, Zen continues to influence, directly or indirectly, modern artistic experiences on an essentially aesthetic level as, in the literary field, the stories of Nagai Kafū (永井

荷風,1879-1959) illustrate, where the void, the interval, the *ma* assert themselves like a natural punctuation of Japanese expressiveness.

Nagai Kafū, a great Japanese writer active during the early twentieth century, remains little known in the West, at least among non-specialists. As Edward Seidensticker (1921-2007) wrote in a brief profile of Kafū and Tanizaki (谷崎潤一郎, 1886-1965), the reason why the former had a smaller following in the West than the latter is perhaps only the fact that "Tokyo is essential to his [Kafū's] work as no other city has been for Tanizaki; and, therefore, what can this city represent for all those who do not know it?".[5]

The leitmotif of the story "Kumo" (雲, "Clouds", 1908) is aimless wandering punctuated by digressive "situations." The opening lines are important in this regard:

> At the end of the workday at the Imperial Embassy in Paris, the diplomat Koyama Teikichi, would pass the gate and head for the corner of the Avenue des Champs Elysées. Arriving at the usual intersection, that day he came to a stop, as though suspended in a vortex of thoughts: how was he going to spend the rest of the day? Proceeding to the right along the gently uphill sloping west side of the broad avenue, past the Arc de Triomphe, in the vicinity of Place de l'Étoile, was the boarding house where he lived; continuing to the left downhill on the east side of the end of the Avenue des Champs Elysées, he would arrive at Place de la Concorde, which was connected to all the most frequented places of the city.[6]

We, therefore, find ourselves immersed in the place of choice of the Japanese urban space and of Kafū's narrative, namely, the street. In this case, however, it is the "capital of the twentieth century" to which Walter Benjamin (1892-1940) dedicated important pages in his reflections on modernity. We are at the centre of that universal model of modern urbanism that has inspired Japan, from the height of the Belle Époque to

5 Luisa Bienati (ed. by), *Nagai Kafū, Al giardino delle peonie e altri racconti* [Nagai Kafū, At the Peony Garden and Other Stories] (Venice: Marsilio, 1989), p. 13 and p. 14.

6 Nagai Kafū, *Nuvole* [Clouds], trans. by Laura Ricca, in *Pagine Meiji* series, *Quaderni giapponesi* 2 (Rome: Bulzoni, 2009), pp. 219-51.

the Meiji period of Tokyo's history, and that represents the exact opposite of Tokyo's traditional "logic of space" and its rejection of the linear and totalizing perspective vistas symbolized by Haussmann's Paris. We have, instead, a street layout that is quite different from the reticular one of the old Edo that Kafū loved and that struggles to survive in the Tokyo of his day. The protagonist of the tale, however, behaves in exactly the same way he would if he were on one of the narrow streets of Shitamachi (下町); he is suddenly transfixed at an *intersection* and experiences a dilemma that suspends him "in a vortex of thoughts"; in fact, it seems that the intersection itself gives rise to the vortex. This is because, it appears that, in the place of an intersection of major boulevards where the gaze can scan the surroundings without obstructions, the character stops at the kind of intersection we find in the labyrinthine road network of Tokyo, where "two-thirds of the intersections are not crossroads but dead ends."[7]

In the same way, the character feels the gravitational pull of the transitional and liminal zones of the urban space, which create vanishing points of disturbing depth for a Japanese person. Here is an illustration of this effect:

> Where the city of Paris ended, beyond the iron grates near which was a garden, a road started the end of which could not be seen. To the left, the dense Bois de Boulogne, his destination, stood solemnly in the late autumn afternoon. The area seemed unusually vast. The street was dirty and noisy. The men and women walking idly in the mud had a rather mysterious appearance. Beyond the grates, through the dense, dark-grey fog, you could glimpse the express train to Versailles crossing the countryside and spewing dark smoke from the chimney of the oil-burning motor. The gloomy suburbs had completely extinguished Teikichi's boldness. He stood motionless at the exit of the subway and did not have the courage to take a step toward the mud in front of him.[8]

This is another spatial caesura that functions as an internal blockage and a suspension of the action, as well as a *ma* in the

7 Augustin Berque, *Le sens de l'espace au Japon: vivre, penser, bâtir* (Paris : Éd. Arguments, 2004), p. 75.

8 Nagai Kafū, *Nuvole*, cit., p. 229.

diegesis. Once more, we see how the grand urban perspective of Paris, which is far removed from the reticular, closed space of Japanese streets, hypnotically draws the character's attention into a genuine contemplative haze that once again suspends the progression of the story:

> The Arc de Triomphe looming in the distance, behind which the sky of the setting sun was dark red, appeared so dark and foreboding that it struck fear into you. The Avenue des Champs Elysées, the principal artery of Paris, which is wide and slightly uphill extending right up to the Arc, was jammed with a seemingly endless and dizzying row of coachcs and vehicles. It was a scene Teikichi was used to seeing every day, but, though he intended to get home as soon as possible, he stopped to contemplate with amazed eyes the sight of that animated and luxurious neighbourhood that only Paris can offer. What power, what depth in the echo of the carriages and the hooves of the horses that made the ground shake noisily! In the image of carriages filled with men and women he seemed to hear the voice of destiny that caused human beings of an infinite variety of races, professions, social status, ages, without exception, move blindly. Due to the mass of humans, horses, and the evening mist, everything appeared hazy. In contrast to the movement of the people and horses was the silent stillness of a thicket with dense, delicate foliage flanking the avenue. The trees numbered in the thousands, all of the same height, forming a stream of colours, ranging from the green of the thick foliage of the nearest trees to violet and dark blue, creating something like a long black line of clouds that receded into the distant evening horizon.[9]

Striking is the stark contrast, generated by the internal perception filter, between the perspective of the broad, busy avenue and the view of nature that the observer captures in the row of trees lining the street, transforming it into a "thicket" on one of those natural islands that can appear unexpectedly even in the heart of Tokyo and that, here too, expresses the typically Japanese proclivity for this kind of imagery in an objectively very different context. No western writer would have picked up on this perspectival contrast of a tree-lined street that opens up like a void, a *ma*, in the diegesis, similar to Zeami's "non-action," and similar to the voids that can appear in the urban fabric of Tokyo.

9 Nagai Kafū, *Nuvole*, cit., p. 244.

Bibliography

Fujiwara Shigekazu 藤原成一, 'Ma—Nihon bunka no kihon shisō' [*Interval: The Basic Thought in Japanese Culture*] 「間ー日本文化の基本思想」, in *Bulletin of College of Art*, 41 (2005), pp.77-92.

Kenmochi Takehiko 剣持武彦, *"Ma" no nihonbunka* [The Japanese culture of *Ma*] 『「間」の日本文化』 (Tokyo: Kōdansha 講談社, 1978).

Kenmochi Takehiko, Nishiyama Matsunosuke 西山松之助, Seike Kiyoshi 清家清, Ogura Rō 小倉朗 and Kimura Bin 木村敏, *Nihonjin to "Ma"-Dentōbunka no gensen* [The Japanese people and *Ma*, the origin of a traditional culture] 『日本人と「間」–伝統文化の源泉』 (Tokyo: Kōdansha, 1981).

Sue Toshimitsu 末利光, *Ma no bigaku-Nihonteki hyōgen* [The aesthetics of *Ma* and Japanese expression] 『間の美学–日本的表現』 (Tokyo: Sanseidō 三省堂, 1991).

IMAGES IN MOTION

Nakama Yūko 仲間裕子[1]

LANDSCAPE PAINTINGS THROUGH THE TRAVELER'S VIEW

1. *Sesshū, a Travelling Ink Painter*

Sesshū Tōyō (雪舟等楊, 1420-1506), a Japanese Zen monk of the Rinzai school (臨済派), was the most admired of Japan's medieval ink painters. As such, six of his paintings, including *Landscape of Autumn and Winter* (fig.1), *Splashed Ink Landscape* (fig.2), *Landscape of Four Seasons* (fig.5-10, 12), and *View of Amanohashidate* (fig.19-20) are designated as national treasures in Japan. Sesshū's identity as an ink painter is the result of his two-year mission to China during the Ming dynasty from 1467-1469 (fig.3).

Figure 1 Sesshū, *Landscape of Autumn and Winter.*
Late 15th century to early 16th century, Tokyo National Museum
Figure 2 Sesshū, *Splashed Ink Landscape.* 1495, Tokyo National Museum

1 Ritsumeikan University

Figure 3 Attributed to Sesshū, *Picturesque Scenery of China* (唐土勝景図巻) [detail, near Zhenjiang], 16th centry, Kyoto National Museum

During the time of Sesshū, which was called the Muromachi period (室町時代, 1336–1573), attachment to Chinese art culminated in the production of ink paintings. The collection of Shōgun Ashikaga Yoshimitsu (足利義満, 1358–1408) became the basis for modal ink painting, a system of conceptualizing and commissioning paintings. Among the treasures of the collection were the ink paintings of Muqi Fachang (牧谿, Southern Song dynasty, 13th century, fig.4). These paintings had a poetic atmosphere, which was articulated by the surrounding blank space (*yohaku*, 余白) called *zanzanjōsui* (残山剰水). Moreover, they were of extraordinarily high value and influenced Japanese ink paintings for generations.

Figure 4 Muqi Fachang, *Returning Sails off a Distant Shore, "The Eight Views of Xiaoxiang"* (遠浦帰帆 [瀟湘八景図]), Southern Song dynasty, 13th century, Nezu Museum

Sesshū learned Chinese styles and used motifs, especially those of *The Eight Views of Xiaoxiang* (瀟湘八景図) and the ideal landscape of *West Lake* (西湖); however, as a whole, the dynamic touch and composition were his own. Sesshū's technique is particularly evident in the rigid architectural composition *of Landscape of Autumn and Winter* (fig.1). The perpendicular line in the center abbreviates the peak of the mountains through the mist. Thus, abstraction and representation are sublimated in a dialectical tension. Such bold intention is hardly seen in other Japanese ink painters.

Travel itself was the subject of *Landscape of the Four Seasons* (四季山水図 [山水長巻], 1486, fig.5-10, 12). This large-scale picture scroll of circa 16 m represents a special commitment, as it was dedicated to Ōuchi Masahiro (大内政広, 1446-1495), a notable *Daimyō* (大名, powerful landholding magnate) in the Yamaguchi prefecture to show Sesshū's gratitude for Ōuchi's long-time patronage.

Figure 5 Sesshū, *Landscape of the Four Seasons* [detail Spring], 1486, ©Mohri Museum

Figure 6 Sesshū, *Landscape of the Four Seasons* [detail Summer], 1486, ©Mohri Museum

Figure 7 Sesshū, *Landscape of the Four Seasons* [detail Autumn], 1486, ©Mohri Museum

Figure 8 Sesshū, *Landscape of the Four Seasons* [detail Winter], 1486, ©Mohri Museum

The landscapes are characterized by Sesshū's powerful touch through his simultaneously rough and sensitive brush work.

Furthermore, the architectonic features in the piles of rocks and the clear color variations—the green leaves, the red and white tree flowers, the pastel sea, the colorful costumes, and the dark-light gradation of ink—make the landscape appear lively and rhythmical.

This piece has been analyzed as a compilation of Chinese influences in terms of the composition and expression, especially inspiration from Xia Gui (夏珪) of the Southern Song dynasty. According to Shimao Arata, Sesshū incorporated three elementary motifs from Chinese models: rocks, trees, and ships.[2] However, it is difficult to point out a resemblance to the work of Xia Gui or other Chinese landscapes as a whole. We could hypothesize that Sesshū learned Chinese styles and used motifs, especially those of *The Eight Views of Xiaoxiang* and the ideal landscape of *West Lake*; however, as a whole, the dynamic touch and composition were his own.

In this scroll, the seasonal transformations are witnessed by a Chinese nobleman, accompanied by his young servant. They lead us on a journey through nature—from a mountainous landscape in spring (fig.5), to a river or sea landscape in summer (fig.6), to West Lake and Mountain Market in autumn (fig.7), to a landscape of a city covered with snow in winter (fig.8). Upon closer observation, tree branches serve as our guide and show us the way. The traveler is sometimes depicted as walking in different directions on winding paths that continue into the deepness of the rocky hills. The meteorological elements of rain and heavy clouds contribute to the environmental setting, making us feel that we are one with nature. At the end of the scroll (fig.9), a tree with the dead leaves of winter is followed by young pine trees, as if the latter is receiving a message from the former, and the green broad-leaved trees, which look just like the tree from the beginning of the scroll (fig.5), appear to suggest the cycle of the seasons. As stated above, the landscape motifs and the composition of the picture scroll were mostly influenced by

2 Shimao Arata 島尾新, *Sesshū no 'Sansuichōkan'* [Sesshū's Long Landscape Scroll] 『雪舟の「山水長巻」』 (Tokyo: Shogakukan 小学館, 2002), pp. 94-99.

Xia Gui. However, although Sesshū's theme was the seasonal cycle, it was not generally Xia's interest in his scrolls.[3]

Figure 9 Sesshū, *Landscape of the Four Seasons* [detail Winter], 1486, ©Mohri Museum

Technically speaking, a picture roll characterizes a specific time and space. The roll is opened from right to left by one's left hand in a repeated action based on the length of one's shoulder; the scene is a part of this movement. As Katō Shūichi pointed out, the major picture scrolls in the Heian Period (平安時代, 795-1185), namely, *The Tale of Genji Scroll* (源氏物語絵巻, c.1120-1140) and the *Shigisan-engi Scroll* (信貴山縁起絵巻, 12th century), reflect Japanese cultural characteristics by attaching importance to "the part" rather than "the whole." The viewer may choose the duration of time, just like the traveler in the pictorial space, sometimes slowing down or standing still to experience the surrounding nature or to meditate. Thus, the picture roll style allows viewers not only to be integrated into the pictorial space but also to manipulate time like a real traveler.

According to Katō, the concept of the picture roll is a chain of the "present" that is lined up equivalently. In other words, the viewer does not see the scenes as a consecutive flow of past, present, and future but is attracted to what is happening in each scene because "it is now/it is here."[4]

3 Shimao Arata, *Sesshū no 'Sansuichōkan'*, cit., p.105.

4 Katō Shūichi 加藤周一, *Nihon bunka ni okeru jikan to kūkan* [Time and Space in Japanese Culture] 『日本文化における時間と空間』 (Tokyo: Iwanami Shoten 岩波書店, 2007), pp. 90-93.

This aspect of the picture scroll may relate to the "eternal present," which contrasts with Martin Heidegger's concept of "horizontal time," as explained by Japanese philosopher Kuki Shūzō (九鬼周造):

> If we locate time in the present, we can say that his present possesses as present an infinite past and an infinite future and moreover that it is identical with a limitless present. The present is the eternal present with an infinite depth; in short, time is nothing but the infinite present, the eternal present.[5]

In contrast, Shimao, refers to the painter's act from a religious perspective on eternity: "Sesshū created a landscape scroll of eternal time, just like the world of truth told by Buddha."[6] For example, in one scene of the scroll, the nobleman is having a conversation with a man in a stone cave in the deepness of a rocky hill, isolated from the secular world (fig.10). The setting is reminiscent of Sesshū's *Huike Offering His Arm to Bodhidharma* (慧可断臂図, fig.11), which depicts a well-known Zen anecdote in which Huike asks Bodhidharma to accept him as a disciple and shows his fierce determination by cutting his arm. Although the extreme tension of that moment is lacking in the scene of the two men in the cave in *Landscape for the Four Seasons*, it does transmit the sacred atmosphere of the eremite. At the end of the scroll, Sesshū stamped his seal with the *hitsuju* (筆受) description under his name. *Hitsuju* literally means received by brush, signifying the hand-copying of the Buddhist text (sutra, 写経). Since this is an unusual description for an ink painting, we can assume that Sesshū had the intention of visualizing the Buddhist text through images.

5 Michael F. Marra, *Kuki Shūzō: A Philosopher's Poetry and Poetics* (Honolulu: University of Hawaii Press, 2004), p. 37.

6 Shimao Arata, *Sesshū: shōgai to sakuhin* [Sesshū: Life and Works] 『雪舟：生涯と作品』(Tokyo: Tokyo Bijutsu 東京美術, 2012), p. 45.

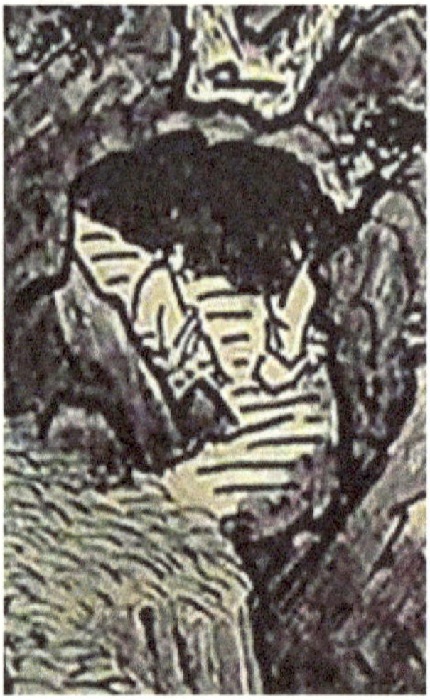

Figure 10 Sesshū, *Landscape of the Four Seasons* [detail], 1486, ©Mohri Museum
Figure 11 Sesshū, *Huike Offering His Arm to Bodhidharma,* 1496, Kyoto National Museum

In the palace-like building in the last scene of the scroll, the nobleman seems to gaze far beyond the landscape without any signs of humans (fig.12). Based on this depiction, we may ask ourselves the following questions: Could this image symbolize man's yearning for the eternal world? Is this nobleman Sesshū himself as a traveling painter?

Figure 12 Sesshū, *Landscape of the Four Seasons* [Winter, detail], 1486, ©Mohri Museum

2. *Landscape Painting as the World Landscape*

In Western art history, landscape depictions began to play an important role in 16th century as seen in *Landscape with St. Jerome* (fig. 13), which was painted by a Flemish painter, Joachim Patinir (c.1480-1524), in 1516-1517, about 30 years after Sesshū's *Landscapes of Four Seasons*. There is an eremite in a cave, which is similar to men in the cave in Sesshū's rocky landscape; however, a panoramic view is used in this painting. This landscape style is called world landscape (*Weltlandschaft*). Partinir's landscape invites us to engage in an elaborate inspection of the world. This sense of detachment, characterized by the urge to observe the world from a distance through a wide perspective, marks the Flemish world landscape as one of the most prominent expressions of the 16th century.

Figure 13 Joachim Patinir, *Landscape with St. Jerome,* 1516-1517, Prado Museum

The style was developed further by Peter Bruegel the Elder (c.1525-1569) in 1565 in the *Labors of the Months* (*Gloomy Day, Haymaking* [fig.14], *Harvesters*, *Return of the Herd*, and *Hunters in the Snow* [fig.17]) series.[7] The labors of the months had been venerable subjects in the Christian world for centuries with the seasonal cycle presented by the typical agricultural labors of each month. Bruegel's series is considered to be a successor of the tradition of well-known illuminated manuscripts *The Very Rich Hours of the Duke of Berry* (1411-1416, fig.15) by the Flemish painters Limbourg Brothers (1385-1416). In fact, Bruegel's work has been analyzed as 'heaven descended to earth.'[8]

Figure 14
Bruegel the Elder, *Haymaking*, 1565, National Gallery Prague

7 According to Fritz Novotny's research on this series, a year was traditionally composed with 6 seasons, namely *Gloomy Day* for the early spring, *Haymaking* for the early summer, *Harvesters* for the midsummer, *Return of the Herd* for the autumn, *Hunters in the Snow* for winter (the piece of spring is considered as lost) (*Puraha Kokuritsubijutsukanzō Buryūgeru to Nēderurando Fūkeiga* [Bruegel and Netherlandish Landscape Painting from the National Gallery Prague] 『プラハ国立美術館蔵ブリューゲルとネーデルラント風景画』, ex.cat., The National Museum of Western Art, Tokyo, 1990), p. 135; cf. Walter S. Gibson, *"Mirror of the Earth", The World Landscape in Sixteenth-Century Flemish Painting* (Princeton, New Jersey: Princeton University Press, 1989), p. 70.

8 Cf. T.J. Clark, *Heaven on Earth: Painting and Life to Come* (London: Thames & Hudson, 2018).

Figure 15 Limbourg Brothers, *The Very Rich Hours of the Duke of Berry* (June, Haymaking), 1411-1416, Musée Condé, Chantilly

Walter Gibson pointed out that the popularity of world landscape based on two factors: the discovery of the New World in the 16th century, which ushered in a grand platform for geography and cartography, and the Renaissance attitude regarding humans' relationship to the world. Humanists during the Renaissance period urged man to look down on the world beneath them from the position of a superior being. Gibson shared the following quotation by Marcus Tullius Cicero (106-43 BC) inscribed on the world map in the second edition of Abraham Ortelius's *Theatrum* in 1579: "Man is born to contemplate the universe."[9] This idea was celebrated by Renaissance humanists; Pico della Mirandola (1463-1494) said that God wished to have

9 Walter S. Gibson, *"Mirror of the Earth", The World Landscape in Sixteenth-Century Flemish Painting*, cit., p. 59.

some being that could admire his creation in order "to love its beauty, and to wonder at its vastness."[10] Furthermore, Erasmus (1466-1536) said, "what spectacle can be more splendid than the sight of this world!"[11] Thus, the elevated world landscape viewpoint corresponds visually to the exalted dignity of man.

The passion for maps went beyond their geographic functions. The painting-map correlation can be attested in the common use of maps as wall decorations in the 17th century in the Netherlands, e.g., in the paintings of Johannes Vermeer (fig.16). For example, the *Map of Piedmont Region* (fig.17), made by Hieronymus Cock in 1552, presents ways to navigate around buildings and through the mountains to the sea, allowing the viewer's eyes to travel through the map and offering a close affinity with the world landscape.

Figure 16 Johannes Vermeer, *The Allegory of Painting*, c. 1662-1668, Museum of Art History, Vienna

10 Walter S. Gibson, *"Mirror of the Earth", The World Landscape in Sixteenth-Century Flemish Painting*, cit., p. 57.

11 Walter S. Gibson, *"Mirror of the Earth", The World Landscape in Sixteenth-Century Flemish Painting*, cit., p. 57.

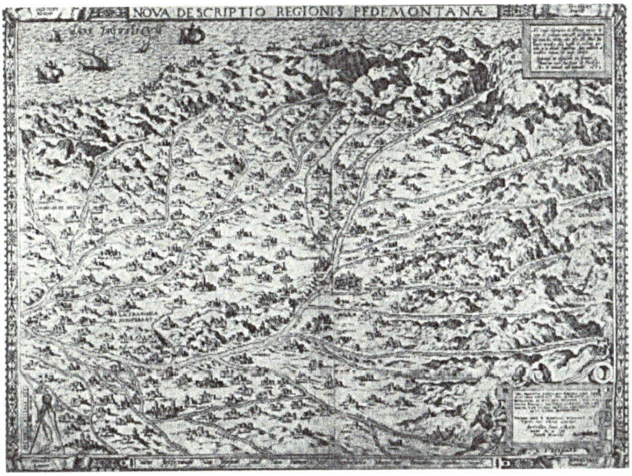

Figure 17 Hieronymus Cock, *Map of the Piedmont Region,* 1552, National Gallery Prague

Figure 18 Bruegel the Elder, *Hunters in the Snow*, 1565, Museum of Art History, Vienna

In *Haymaking* and *Hunters in the Snow* (fig.18), the panoramic view is a decisive feature. *Haymaking,* which depicts midsummer, shows peasants laboring under sunlight and a clear sky, as we saw in the illuminated manuscript. The path on which the vegetable bearers walk leads to the hayfield and then to another field, which leads to the castle on the broad river plain, and the river leads to the sea. Such a long distance indicates people's yearning to travel far to unknown regions. In *Hunters in the Snow*, the viewer sees the vast expanded landscape below, passing through skating ponds—a traditional joy of the people of the Netherlands—to reach the high mountains, which are based on the artist's fantasy and do not have any topographic authenticity. That is also the case of the giant rocky mountain in *Haymaking*. These unique staffages are possibly due to the interest in the Alps at that time; people who had travelled across the Alps would have liked to see such mountains in works by Patinir or Bruegel. Ernst Gombrich observed that, because of the Alps, a traveler was ready to "recognize in any stock image of an 'Alpine rock,' in any stereotype of an old castle or in any imaginary 'prospect' the very thing he had seen on his journey."[12] Likewise, the watercolors of German painter Albrecht Dürer, which were produced during a similar period at the end of 15th century, contain images of the Alpine region from his journey to Italy.

3. *Sesshū's* View of Amanohashidate*: Landscapes from Aesthetic and Political Perspectives*

Figure 19
Sesshū, *View of Amanohashidate*, c.1501-1504, Kyoto National Museum

12 Ernst H. Gombrich, 'The Renaissance Theory of Art and the Rise of Landscape', in *Norm and Form: Studies in the Art of Renaissance* (London: Phaidon, 1971), pp. 107-121.

View of Amanohashidate (天橋立図, c.1501-1504, fig.19) is an ink painting that is representative of Sesshū's later years. Sesshū was over 80 years old when he travelled across the region and sketched the famous sceneries of *Amanohashidate*, one of three most celebrated scenic sights in Japan. *View of Amanohashidate* consists of 20 pieces of sketches that are pasted together (*Daishitae* 大下絵, large sketch), but the complete work did not survive.[13]

View of Amanohashidate functioned as a geographic map and may have been used for military purposes by Sesshū's patron, Ōuchi. At the time of Sesshū's travels, the war between Ōuchi and Daimyō Hosokawa (細川), who ruled Kyoto, might have broken out, and this region could have been a battlefield. In this work, Sesshū provides a panoramic bird's eye view so that one can take note of the district at a glance. Furthermore, the names beside the major temples, shrines, and other important locations are written distinctly. This method strongly indicates the painter's intention to depict the landscape from both aesthetic and political perspectives.

Figure 20 Details from *View of Amanohashidate*
20-1 Chionji temple (智恩寺)
20-2 Nariaiji temple (成相寺)
20-3 Kono shrine (籠神社)

13 Shimao Arata, *Sesshū: Shōgai to sakuhin*, cit., pp. 68-71. Shimao suggests that the complete work is not only limited to a single work, but that there should be another work with precise geographical information, used only for political purposes.

The landscape features a triangle composition. On the left of the pictorial space is the two-storied *Chionji* temple (智恩寺) (fig.20-1). *Chionji* worships *Monju Shinkō* (文殊信仰), one religious sect of Buddhism. At the top of the triangle is *Nariaiji* temple (成相寺) (fig.20-2), a sacred place of *Kannon* belief (*Kannon shinkō* 観音信仰) since ancient times. On the right is *Kono Jinja* shrine (籠神社) (fig.20-3), the highest ranking shrine in the province. These three notable religious places are painted in red to pull the viewer's interest. Amid these precise geographical descriptions, Sesshū's imagination can be seen in the extremely high mountains, evoking similar examples from Chinese mountain landscapes with spectacular views and a mythical atmosphere.

Unlike in *Landscape of the Four Seasons*, in which Sesshū uses the nobleman in the pictorial space to travel through an ideal landscape while yearning for an eternal world, in *View of Amanohashidate*, Sesshū becomes a traveler in an actual landscape, using temples and shrines as central motifs depicting specific sacred places.

Postscript

Sesshū's attempts to describe uncultivated or natural landscapes with a traveler in their midst and Bruegel's attempts to describe man's labor activities in cultivated landscapes in a panoramic view are both derived from a yearning for an ideal world. The horizontal eye movement required in the picture scroll of Sesshū's landscapes and the vertical eye movement in Bruegel's landscapes are attributed to historical cultural differences of thought in terms of space and time.

The human desire to travel across borders to distant regions and follow the results of cultural intersections always provides an impetus for art production. The history of landscape painting is closely related to the discovery of or longing for landscapes as seen through a traveler's view, as evident in the Chinese landscape motifs in Sesshū's works and the long and winding paths to the sea and the heterogeneous rocky mountain motif in Bruegel's landscapes.

Ozaki Akihiro 尾崎彰宏[1]

REMBRANDT AND JAPANESE WASHI PAPER

Toward an Aesthetic of Black

Rembrandt and Japanese Washi Paper

Rembrandt did not choose to be the first artist in Europe to create his prints on East Asian paper simply from a sense of its rarity and curiosity. Groundbreaking research by Christopher White and Karel G. Boon[2] and more recent work by Kida Shō[3] and Kōfuku Akira[4] has made this clear. Japanese paper was much better suited than European paper to visually express the solid sense of time surrounding the encounter. Rembrandt made remarkable use of Japanese paper for his woodcuts and it is well-known that Japanese paper was used for a number of prints, especially from the late 1640s onward.

Indeed, as early as the 17th century mention was made of how Rembrandt used non-European papers for their artistic effects. In 1668 a certain Englishman wrote that some of Rembrandt's prints were printed on Indian paper. Roger de Piles, the renowned French art critic, known for his high praise of the color palettes used by Rubens and Titian, also reported that collectors competed amongst themselves to obtain Rembrandt prints made

1 Tohoku University

2 C. White & K. G. Boon, *Rembrandt's Etchings: An Illustrated Critical Catalogue*, 2 vols., (Amsterdam: van Gendt, 1966).

3 Kida Shō 貴田庄, *Renburanto to washi* [Rembrandt and Japanese paper] 『レンブラントと和紙』(Tokyo: Yasaka shobō 八坂書房, 2005).

4 Kōfuku Akira 幸福輝, '"Papier de demi-teinte": Japanese paper in Rembrandt's œuvre', in Kōfuku Akira (ed. by), *Renburanto Hikari no tsuikyū/yami no yūwaku* [Rembrandt The pursuit of light/the seduction of obscurity] 『レンブラント　光の追究／闇の誘惑』, 展カタログ *Rembrandt: The Quest for Chiaroscuro* Exh. Cat. (Tokyo: Nippon terebi hōsōmō 日本テレビ放送網, 2011), pp. 329-343.

on slightly reddish, brown toned Chinese papers, not those printed on white European papers. Florent Le Comte, an art critic and contemporary of De Piles, also reported the fascinating effect that Chinese papers had on the neutral color tones seen in Rembrandt's prints.[5]

What effect did Rembrandt's use of *washi* (和紙, Japanese paper), as opposed to European paper, have on his prints? As is well known, prior to that he had used vellum, Chinese papers, and others. Kōfuku Akira has made the following observation about why Rembrandt noticed Japanese paper. While Japanese paper heightened the beauty of midrange tones, the glossy paper surface itself was also fascinating, giving a soft feel to the motifs themselves. The paper was also seen to evoke all the shades of deep black, and thus effectively bringing out the expression of print details.

De Piles and Le Comte were not fascinated by the actual lines and forms of Rembrandt's prints, but rather how the prints adroitly depicted half tones. Just as the pale to dark tones found in ink painting ink give a sense of color, they were surprised at how the ink tonalities created by the paper and ink in Rembrandt's prints evoked this same sense of color.

When did Rembrandt start using Japanese paper in his prints? Did he use it throughout his career or just during certain periods? A careful investigation of his use of Japanese paper shows that he began using this paper type around 1647, and that most of his prints produced particularly in the 1650s were on Japanese paper.[6] Rembrandt's prints are not unusual in their existence

---

5 Florent Le Comte, *Cabinet des singularitez d'architecture, peinture, sculpture et graveure*,III (Paris: A Paris, chez Nicolas Le Clerc, ruë Saint Jacques, proche Saint Yves, à l'Image Saint Lambert, 1699), p. 126. Roger de Piles, *Abregé de la vie des peintres, avec des réflexions sur leurs ouvrages* (Paris: Langlois and Muguet, 1699), p. 433. Cf. Kōfuku Akira (ed. by), *Rembrandt: The Quest for Chiaroscuro*, cit.

6 Erik Hinterding, Jaco Rutgers, *Rembrandt* (The New Hollstein Dutch & Flemish Etching, Engravings and Woodcuts 1450-1700), Plates I-III, Text I-III (Ouderkerk aan den Ijssel: Sound & Vision Publisher, 2013). Erik Hinterding, *Rembrandt as an Etcher: The Practice of Production and Distribution*, Ouderkerk aan den Ijssel: Sound & Vision Publisher, 2006), pp. 112-114.

in numerous different states, representing his different work in stages on the blocks. It is noteworthy that he did not use Japanese paper on the final state of a print, but rather in the first and second states, the first half of a print's development, or sometimes on the mid-range third and fourth states. There are many examples of his using this paper type for test runs of his first states; it is noteworthy that he used precious Japanese paper for these. Unlike the image depiction found in drawing, drypoint, in which the needle draws elements directly on the block, eases intense abrasion. As a rcsult, cvcn though artists in general might use Japanese paper in test prints or early states when the print plate was in good condition, undoubtedly even at the test print stages Rembrandt knew that the prints he was producing were marketable.

First let us look at the prints that Rembrandt was making just as he began using Japanese paper. By that point in the process these prints must reveal Rembrandt's expectations regarding Japanese paper.

Figure 1 Rembrandt, *Jan Asselijn, painter*, Japanese paper, State I, Rijksmuseumprentenkabinet

Figure 2 Rembrandt, *Jan Asselijn, painter*, Cartridge paper, State I, Rijksmuseumprentenkabinet

Let us look at his portrait of *Jan Asselijn* (Fig.1-2), produced in 1647 when Asselijn, who had become a landscape painter and had been active in Rome, returned to Amsterdam. This is a rare example of Rembrandt creating a portrait of a fellow painter. Seated, with one hand on a table, the other at his hip, the subject looks out with a faint smile at the viewer. An easel appears behind, with a glimpse of an Italianate landscape. Close examination reveals that a palette, brushes, and books are placed on the table, all indicating that he is a painter.

The first state (Fig. 1) is signed and dated (with the two last numbers rubbed out), indicating that it had reached the state of completion to be considered a work of art. Rembrandt used various papers to print this first state, including Japanese paper, cartridge paper, and Indian paper. The different paper types all create visible effects in the prints. What kind of effects? Let us compare the Japanese paper and cartridge paper versions. The *Asselijn* image (Fig. 2) printed on cartridge paper has a pronouncedly neutral character, suited for its function as a record of the work. The viewer can see Asselijn's expression, his age, and information about the garments he is wearing. The print on Japanese paper (Fig. 1) is deeper yellow than that on cartridge paper and, as a result, it appears that Asselijn is floating in a sepia-toned space. The feeling is all the stronger that Asselijn has turned to the viewer as if to say something. As if cast overall with a translucent shadow, the work exudes a sense of time and spatial depth.

Thus, Rembrandt was able to confirm the effect of using Japanese paper in a portrait print. The *Portrait of Jan Six* (Fig. 3-6), who as a literatus understood his friend Rembrandt and had asked him to produce the illustrations for his own drama *Medea*, reveals all the stronger the effects of Japanese paper. Six was a member of a wealthy merchant family and his father operated a silk textile factory in Amsterdam. He was also an art collector and his collection included a splendid group of prints that Rembrandt was able to view.[7]

7 Erik Hinterding, Ger Luijten, Martin Royalton-Kisch (ed. by), *Rembrandt the Printmaker*, (Chicago: Fitzroy Dearborn, 2000), Exh. Cat. Rijksmuseum Amsterdam, National Gallery London 2000-2001, cat. 57.

Figure 3 Rembrandt, Jan Six, state I, Japanese paper, 1647, Rijksmuseum Prentenkabinet, Amsterdam

Figure 4 Rembrandt, Jan Six, state II, Japanese paper, 1647, Rijksmuseum Prentenkabinet, Amsterdam

Figure 5 Rembrandt, Jan Six, state III, Japanese paper, 1647, Petit Palais, Paris

Figure 6 Rembrandt, Jan Six, state IV, European paper, 1647, Rembranthuis Museum, Amsterdam

The *Portrait of Jan Six* shows a single picture hanging on the left-hand wall, with a curtain half shut, giving the room a dim lighting that makes it hard to identify as a specific place. Six, set against a bright window, stands looking at the manuscript he holds in his hand. The manuscript paper may function as a reflecting board, but those reflections allow a clear view of his melancholic expression.[8] Conversely, the curtain hanging at the window blocks light and becomes a prop that scatters illumination around the room from the single area that allows it in. The papers on top of the chair, a decorative frieze on the table, a sword, and a staff are all vaguely apparent in the dimly lit space.

Rembrandt took endless pains to express amounts of light, as can be seen in various changes he made in this print from the first state (Fig. 3) to the second state (Fig. 4). As if increasing the amount of light in the room, he removed the crosshatching etched across the glass window to the upper right of Six's head and removed the window shelves. Five different states of this print are known and, with the exception of the final state, they have all been handed down printed on Japanese paper. Added to his skill with drypoint and etching effects, the use of Japanese paper can be seen as a means of enabling the expression of subtle light dark gradations. Kōfuku Akira has made some superb observations about the differences in *Portrait of Jan Six* prints on Japanese and European paper.[9] Kōfuku compared states three (Fig. 5) and four (Fig. 6), relating in detail his fascination with the deep blacks created by the Japanese paper. "Viewed alone the fourth state also shows some truly beautiful harmonies. However, a comparison with the third state printed on Japanese paper shows that the fourth state lacks the fascination of an all-the-deeper black, a richer expression created by velvety, softly coiling light and dark tonality."

The points suggested by Kōfuku become even clearer when

8 Dixon considers the portrait of Six to be an image of "melancholy". Laurinda S. Dixon, *The Dark Side of Genius: The Melancholic Persona in Art, ca. 1500-1700* (Pennsylvania: Pennsylvania State University Press, 2013), pp. 107-108.

9 Kōfuku Akira (ed. by), *Rembrandt: The Quest for Chiaroscuro*, cit., p. 160.

we compare *Portrait of Jan Uytenbogaert, "The Goldweigher"* (1639, Fig. 7) and the *Portrait of Jan Six*. Separated by about a decade, the two works show subtle differences in skill level and the interest in details. However, the biggest difference between the two can be seen in the level of Rembrandt's interest in the expression of light and darkness. In the 1639 work, there is still the sense of dramatic dark/light contrast seen in *The Night Watch* (Fig. 8). At that stage the use, or thoughts of use, of Japanese paper had not yet occurred.

Figure 7 Rembrandt, *Jan Uytenbogaert*, The Glodweigher

Figure 8 Rembrandt, *The Nightwatch*, 1642, Rijksmuseum, Amsterdam

While hard to express, an interest in what can be called the coloristic, soft expression of light and dark can also be observed in Rembrandt's self-portraits. Let us look at his 1648 work, *Self Portrait Drawing at a Window* (Fig. 9-11). There are three different states extant: the first state print (Fig. 9) on Chinese paper today in Amsterdam, a second state print (Fig. 10) on Japanese paper in London, and a fourth state print (Fig. 11). Differences in details, such as the fact the second state print (Fig. 10) is signed and dated above the window frame and the fourth state shows a landscape outside the window, can be seen.

Figure 9 Rembrandt, *Self-Portrait Etching at a Window*, 1648, Chinese paper, State I, Rijksprentenkabinet, Amsterdam

Figure 10 Rembrandt, *Self-Portrait Etching at a Window*, 1648, Japanese paper, State II, British Museum, London

Figure 11 Rembrandt, *Self-Portrait Etching at a Window*, 1648, Japanese paper, State IV, British Museum, London

What I would like to note here, however, are the different impressions received from the prints made on Chinese versus Japanese paper. The shift from state one to state two shows a clarification of the shape of the desk and the creation of depth. There is denser, finer crosshatching to create shadow effects. This is especially true on the deepening of the shadow on the painter's right side. The result is an emphasis on black and a superb rendition of the mood of the painter concentrating on his work as he looks in the mirror. The black is all the more richly expressed thanks to the use of the Japanese paper. The greater importance of the black is apparent at first glance in the fourth state print produced on Japanese paper. The painter cast in tonal shadows is quietly working, his expression gentle, exuding a sense of strange, soulful radiance.

In addition to its use in portraits and self-portraits, Rembrandt also used Japanese paper for his landscape and historical pictures. Images printed on Japanese paper share a beautifully rich gradation of deep shading, indeed creating an ink painting-like effect (Fig. 12).[10] In other words, the pursuit of the beauty of black appealed to those looking for richly varying shades

10 Cf. Luc Tuymans, Yu Hui (ed. by), *The Forbidden Empire: Visions of the World by Chinese and Flemish Masters*, Exh. Cat. Brussels, Beijing (Brussel: Mercatorfonds, 2007).

of black and provides iconographic information that cannot be replicated in words, it is a means of imbuing the work with an emotive sense of immediacy.

Figure 12 Shen Zhou, *Imitating Yunlin's Landscape*, 1479 (Ming dynasty), The Forbidden Empire, Beijing

Then can we say that he discovered this interest in black thanks to Japanese paper? Of course, we cannot deny that Japanese paper spurred on this interest. However, as noted in a separate work by the present author[11], the recipient (in this case Rembrandt) must also have been in a receptive context in order to make creative works utilizing elements from the distant cultural spheres of Europe and Asia. For Rembrandt, Japanese paper was an important medium because he himself had a strong interest in black. Then we might ask, what was the connection between Rembrandt and black?

The Aesthetics of Black

Many people feel that Rembrandt's works overall, not just his prints but also his oil paintings, include broad swathes of shadow that cover sections of the composition and employ darkened palettes, as if depicting a night scene. While dark varnish is blamed for some of this effect, the painting known as *The Night Watch* tells its own story. Officially titled *The Shooting Company of Frans Banning Cocq and Willem van Ruytenburch*, the painting came to be known as *The Night Watch* around the 19th century, given its seemingly nocturnal setting.

By no means was Rembrandt alone in placing dark shadows in his pictures. The creation of shadows through the use of black rather than layered colors is said to have been spread by Titian and the other 16th century Venetian school painters. Then in the 17th century Caravaggio developed his dramatic chiaroscuro methods, which became a fashionable trend across Europe, including northern Europe. Rembrandt was likely deeply involved in this trend begun by Caravaggio, and he made expressive shading an important element of his own artistic approach.

As has been frequently discussed before,[12] Rembrandt's expression of shadow, in other words his fondness for black,

11 Akihiro Ozaki, 'Porcelain's White Gleam: Iconoclasm and Encounter between the Netherlands and Asia', in Taku Kuroiwa (ed. by), *The Values of the Other* (Sendai/Grenoble, forthcoming), pp. 25-44.

12 Akihiro Ozaki, *Renburanto no korekushon - Jikoseikei he no chōsen* [Rembrandt's collection: challenging for self-formation] 『レンブラントのコレクション一自己成形への挑戦』 (Tokyo: Sangensha 三元社, 2004), Chap. 3.

was also a means for the viewer to sense the depicted figures' souls. Self-portraits were one of the ways that Rembrandt became active as a painter. He depicted himself not only in oil paintings, but also repeatedly in print form. A typical example of this kind of print self-portrait can be seen in the image showing his face half-covered by shadow (Fig. 13-14). Covering the face in shadow makes it harder to determine the person's physical features, but more so than anything, it makes it more difficult to understand their emotional expression. Except in cases where the revealing of a person's features was not desirable, or that effect was sought, it is impossible to make a portrait out of such an image. In other words, not aiming to depict a person's features, hiding the details of emotive expression in shadow, might be seen as conversely changing them into something else. It is the expression of melancholy, one of the human temperaments.

Figure 13 Rembrandt, *Sheet of Studies: Head of the Artist, A Beggar couple, Heads of an old Man and Old Woman, Etc.*, 1632

Figure 14 Rembrandt, *Self-Portrait in a Cap and Scarf with the Face Dark*, 1633

Melancholy was seen as one of the four human temperaments, alongside sanguinity, irascibility, and apathy. Melancholy was traditionally valued as the temperament that indicated natural genius. Research on melancholia was particularly active at Leiden

University, Holland's oldest university located in Rembrandt's hometown. One study has shown that some 55 doctoral theses on the subject were submitted from the latter half of the 17th century through the beginning of the 18th century. Of those, 23 were written during Rembrandt's own lifetime.[13]

Albrecht Dürer's *Melencolia I* (Fig. 15) stimulated Rembrandt to fuse past traditions of artistic expression with that of his own age.[14] It was Albrecht Dürer who created the monumental artwork depicting *Melencolia I* as the genius temperament, a concept revived in Florence by Marsilio Ficino. The melancholic condition, in which the person's bile is black, is expressed by showing a face in complete shadow. Originally black was something that struck fear in the heart; a portent of evil in the dark of night, a world of witchcraft, but here it has been transformed into artistic genius.[15]

Figure 15 Albrecht Dürer, *Melencolia I*, engraving, 1514

13 Laurinda S. Dixon, *The Dark Side of Genius: The Melancholic Persona in Art, ca. 1500-1700*, cit., p. 51.

14 Cf. Catherine B. Scallen, 'Rembrandt, Emulation, and the Northern Print Traditon', in Laurinda S. Dixon (ed. by), *In Detail: New studies of Northern Renaissance art in honor of Walter S. Gibson* (Turnhout: Brepols, 1998), pp. 135-150.

15 John R. Harvey, *The Story of Black* (London: Reaktion Books, 2013), Chap. 6.

Rembrandt used subtle gradations to express melancholia, using black just as if it were color to express the model's inner being. The inner being is not depicted through the facial expression, but rather the evoking of a sense of those feelings in the viewer. In detail, Rembrandt created self-portraits in which his face was in shadow and his facial expressions unreadable, not only in oil paintings but also in numerous prints and drawings (Fig. 13-14). This depictive method by which the slightest visible hint gives the viewer a sense of the deepest inner workings of the model was entirely novel at the time in the Netherlands. It differed from the ordinary expression in which the image conveys a clear-cut emotion to the viewer, such as a laughing face or a crying face. Now the form appealed directly to the viewer's own subjective experiences, a means of depicting the inner, invisible elements of a person.

For Rembrandt, an extremely important issue was how to manipulate the black of shadows as much as possible in order to give it a sense of color. And it was Japanese paper that gave the widest range of potential[16], a chance to create his own unique works as a painter/printmaker whose breadth of print expression approached that of painting.

16 Akihiro Ozaki, 'The Artistic Challenges of Rembrandt as Painter-Printmaker', in Kōfuku Akira (ed. by), *Rembrandt: The Quest for Chiaroscuro*, cit., pp. 107-117.

Manuela Gallerani[1]

IMAGES, THOUGHTS AND WORDS ON DISEASE IN THE WORKS OF MICHELANGELO

Introduction

The purpose of this contribution is to present an analysis of *illness* and *disease* in its various artistic expressions, as found in some excellent and relevant works by Michelangelo.

Paintings, sculpture/statue, poems, letters, and other literary forms are examined with the intent to explore ill health as it appears in the work of the great artist Michelangelo Buonarroti (1475-1564), who created vividly paradigmatic works of strikingly expressive force.

In the *Rhymes*[2] he composes, for example, a sort of autobiography in verses, wherein it is possible to trace all the dominant motifs of his poetics: a poetics that has been increasingly evolving and changing throughout his long life. His extraordinarily original and innovative artistic style (a precursor of modern taste), rich in variations and nuances, has deeply changed the way of conceiving art in its different forms and

---

1 University of Bologna

2 Robert J. Clements, *The Poetry of Michelangelo* (New York: New York University Press, 1965); Enzo Noè Girardi, *Studi su Michelangelo scrittore*, Biblioteca di 'Lettere Italiane', vol. 13, (Florence: Olschki, 1974); Glauco Cambon, *Michelangelo' s Poetry* (Princeton: Princeton University Press, 1985); Roberto Fedi, *La memoria della poesia. Canzonieri, lirici e libri di rime* nel *Rinascimento* (Rome: Salerno Editore, 1990); James M. Saslow, *The Poetry of Michelangelo* (New Haven: Yale University Press, 1991); Claudio Scarpati, *Michelangelo poeta dal 'canzoniere' alle rime spirituali*, in: *Aevum* 77, 3, (2003), pp. 593–613. *JSTOR*, www.jstor.org/stable/20861490. Accessed September 24, 2020.

declinations. So that, through a careful analysis of his works, it is possible to bring out the close intertwining between the life of the *man*, with his thoughts on the complexity of existence,[3] on illness and death (as well as his emotions and his inner world) and the *furor* (*Genius* and passion) that moves the personality of an *artist* all immersed in the brilliant, ingenious, and imaginative artistic creation carried out mostly in a solitary way.

1. *The Representation of Illness in some Masterpieces by Michelangelo Buonarroti*

Adopting an interdisciplinary approach based on archival research, evidence from paintings, and the interpretations of art critics, philosophers, and physicians, it is possible to discover that many artists have provided a record of the ailments that afflicted their subjects. This was often unintentional, since some diseases and anomalies may not have been recognized as such by the artist. In accordance with Renaissance aesthetics, the aim of the great masters, like Michelangelo Buonarroti (1475-1564), whose perceptiveness was influenced by classicism and humanism,[4] was, above all, to understand every expression of the *soul* and *personality* hidden behind the outward appearance of their models. As a result, it is possible to identify, through their paintings and written testimonials, an ample "anthology" that today constitutes an important source of interdisciplinary (philosophy, medicine, literature, and other fields of sciences) study and research for the illnesses, as well as for the states of mind of the characters they represented.

Presently different words are used to define sickness, vulnerability, and conditions of ill-health (as it clearly distinguishes the word *cure*, being medical lexicon, from *care*,

3 Guglielmo Gorni, 'Temi platonici in Michelangelo' in *Intersezioni*, 15, 3 (1995), pp. 375-387.

4 Delio Cantimori, *Umanesimo e religione nel Rinascimento* (Turin: Einaudi, 1975); Charles de Tolnay, *The Art and Thought of Michelangelo*, trans. by Nan Buranelli (New York: Pantheon, 1964).

which means taking care of a person and ourselves in a meaning closer to the Latin notion of *cura sui*). Briefly, the word *sickness* expresses the perception of society in the face of an ailment or an imbalance and *illness* implies an ailing condition or physical and mental disequilibrium, while *disease* is the physician's diagnosis of the illness. Though these conditions of existential crisis reflect a sort of conflict, our lives are marked by imperfections, which make us aware of our weakness, frailty, and mortality and force us to recognize, respect, and accept our human condition.

In this perspective, *imperfections* (including illnesses) are, in many ways, the natural quality that gives to each person individual temper and grace, and in line with this, the life and works of Michelangelo offer, as enunciated at the beginning of the chapter, a wide range of diseases (imperfections and illnesses) in their different representations.

Regarding the representation of *illness* in an artist's aesthetic work, it is possible to observe that – in portraying the desperate cry of *Adam and Eve banished from Paradise* (Paradise lost) – Michelangelo depicts both the profound pain caused by the original sin and the tragic destiny of the humankind and the sorrow of the Creator over their betrayal.[5] The viewer (looking at the painted images) also becomes aware, symbolically, of the human projection of *grace* in a God who watches over his creatures. Symbolically, meaning that Michelangelo represents a duality of God who expresses himself as majestic, just and merciful (as he is described in the *Rhymes*), but also as a relentless and firm God towards sinners such as Adam and Eve.

Furthermore, one may discover how this artist experiments with the depth and complexity of figurative solutions (and of innovative themes, not at all fixed and ahistorical) both in frescoes – for example in *The Last Judgment* – or in sculptures, as in poems. In fact, in the figures portrayed by Michelangelo it is possible to perceive a grace understood as an *attribute* that expresses amiable qualities of the soul (sweetness, cheerfulness,

5 The *Original Sin and the Banishment from the Garden of Eden* is a fresco by Michelangelo dated around 1510, part of the Sistine Chapel ceiling in the Vatican Museums in Rome, commissioned by Pope Julius II.

affability, sense) and refined movements, but also *vigor*, strength, tension of the body,[6] and *dignity*, that is, moral beauty and self-respect (in line with the Renaissance principles).[7] Indeed, Michelangelo is exceptional in his representations of illness, particularly, in the *Last Judgement* fresco (ca. 1536-1541) on the Sistine Chapel ceiling, where he paints a self-portrait[8] of a suffering man in the skin that Saint Bartholomew holds in his right hand (referring to the martyrdom of the Saint)[9] and in the face of Saint Jeremiah shown as a thoughtful and melancholic[10] old man with rather swollen legs (excellent details of the Sistine Chapel ceiling).

At this point of the analysis it is pertinent to ask, what were the real diseases that afflicted Michelangelo? It is possible to find detailed information regarding Michelangelo's health in his own writings, especially in the *Rhymes* and much more in the *Letters*.[11]

---

6 The bodies (mostly male) sculpted or painted by Michelangelo are usually vigorous, with muscles much more pronounced than those represented by Leonardo Da Vinci, who ironicized them as seen in a sketch portraying Michelangelo's David, with grotesquely exaggerated musculature, so that it takes on the appearance of a caricature. An example of Leonardo's well-known taste for the *grotesque* and the caricature (cf. Leonardo da Vinci, *Study of Michelangelo's David*, Royal Library of Windsor, Royal Collection).

7 John K. G. Shearman, *Only Connect. Art and the Spectator in the Italian Renaissance*, A. W. Mellon lectures in the Fine Arts 1988 Bollingen Series 35, 37 (Princeton NJ: Princeton University Press, 1992); Johan Huizinga, *Il problema del Rinascimento* (Rome: Donzelli, 2015).

8 According to the Italian semiologist Omar Calabrese, the self-portrait represents a story of oneself and allows the protagonist to talk about himself talking about the painting that represents him. Cf. Omar Calabrese, *L'arte dell'autoritratto. Storia e teoria di un genere pittorico* (La casa Usher, 2010, p. 149). On the meaning of the self-portrait as a pictorial *genre* see also Jean-Luc Nancy, *Il corpo dell'arte* (Milan: Mimesis, 2014).

9 Paolo Pozzilli, 'Endocrinologia ed arte' in Gian Carlo Mancini (ed. by), *L'arte nella Medicina e la medicina nell'Arte* (Rome: Azimut, 2008), pp. 130-131.

10 Raymond Klibansky, Erwin Panofsky, Fritz Saxl, *Saturno e la melanconia. Studi di storia della filosofia naturale, religione e arte* (Turin: Einaudi, 1983).

11 Eileen Hartley Ramsden, *The Letters of Michelangelo* (Stanford, CA: Stanford University Press, 1963), pp. 153-211; Filippo Tuena, *La passione dell'error mio. Il carteggio di Michelangelo. Lettere scelte 1532-1564* (Rome: Fazi, 2002), p. 121, p. 184. In many letters, for instance, it is possible to read that Michelangelo often apologizes to people who have commissioned his works,

The *Rhymes* is a collection of poems[12] rich in metaphors, images and intellectual analogies capable of arousing real *ekphrasis*:[13] poems that represent his philosophical reflections on the meaning of life, death, art, friendship, and many other themes.

Even in poetry, Michelangelo adheres to the exquisitely Neoplatonic principles, emphasizing the substantial synonymy between *concept* and *idea*. He does so by removing the superfluous (just as in sculpture) to free the concept, that is the essential and deep meaning of life. Thus, reflecting on old age and on the connection between *pain* and *knowledge*, he proceeds from eliminating what is not needed and strives to transform suffering and tormented pain into serene knowledge. He tries to recompose the dialectic between *logos* and *pathos* to reach harmony. Specifically, he composes an anguished and icastic self-portrait in verse, in which he describes himself as profoundly saddened by illnesses and comes to a negative assessment of his life, contrasting the great pain of old age with the minimum joy (and vanity) obtained through the artistic activity (masterpieces, works of extraordinary imagination and artistic genius) to which he has dedicated his entire existence. In fact, in the Rhyme 267 (ca. 1546-49)[14] he writes:

---

because he greatly underestimated the time needed to complete them.

12 Alfred von Reumont, *Vittoria Colonna: vita, fede poesia nel secolo decimosesto* (Turin: Loescher, 1892); Pier Luigi De Vecchi, 'Studi sulla poesia di Michelangelo', in *Giornale storico della letteratura italiana* 140 (1963), pp. 363-402.

13 On these aspects see: Jaś Elsner, 'Introduction. The Genres of Ekphrasis', in *Ramus* 31 (2002), pp. 1-18; Ruth Webb, 'Ekphrasis Ancient and Modern: The Invention of a Genre', in *Word & Image* 15 (1999), pp. 7-18.

14 Michelangelo Buonarroti, *Rime*, ed. by Enzo Noè Girardi (Bari: Laterza, 1960), see in particular 267, vv. 22-26; vv. 28-33; vv. 34-40; vv. 41-45; vv. 49-55, pp. 127-128. See also the English edition ed. by Christopher Ryan, *The Poetry of Michelangelo: An Introduction* (London: The Athlone Press, 1998).

I' sto rinchiuso come la midolla
da la sua scorza, qua pover e solo,
come spirto legato in un'ampolla:
e la mia scura tomba è picciol volo,
dov'è Aragn' e mill'opre e lavoranti,
e fan di lor filando fusaiuolo.
D'intorn'a l'uscio ho mete di giganti,
ché chi mangi'uva o ha presa medicina
non vanno altrove a cacar tutti quanti.
I' ho 'mparato a conoscer l'orina
e la cannella ond'esce, per quei fessi
che 'nanzi dì mi chiamon la mattina.
Gatti, carogne, canterelli o cessi,
chi n'ha per masserizi' o men vïaggio
non vien a vicitarmi mai senz'essi.
L'anima mia dal corpo ha tal vantaggio,
che se stasat' allentasse l'odore,
seco non la terre' 'l pan e 'l formaggio.
La toss' e 'l freddo il tien sol che non more;
se la non esce per l'uscio di sotto,
per bocca il fiato a pen' uscir può fore.
Dilombato, crepato, infranto e rotto
son già per le fatiche, e l'osteria
è morte, dov'io viv' e mangio a scotto.
La mia allegrezz' è la maninconia,
e 'l mio riposo son questi disagi:
che chi cerca il malanno, Dio gliel dia.
Chi mi vedess' a la festa de' Magi
sarebbe buono; e più, se la mia casa
vedessi qua fra sì ricchi palagi.
Fiamma d'amor nel cor non m'è rimasa;
se 'l maggior caccia sempre il minor duolo,
di penne l'alma ho ben tarpata e rasa.
Io tengo un calabron in un orciuolo,
in un sacco di cuoio ossa e capresti,
tre pilole di pece in un bocciuolo.
Gli occhi di biffa macinati e pesti,
i denti come tasti di stormento
c'al moto lor la voce suoni e resti.
La faccia mia ha forma di spavento;
i panni da cacciar, senz'altro telo,
dal seme senza pioggia i corbi al vento.
Mi cova in un orecchio un ragnatelo,
ne l'altro canta un grillo tutta notte;
né dormo e russ' al catarroso anelo.

Amor, le muse e le fiorite grotte,
mie scombiccheri, a' cemboli, a' cartocci,
agli osti, a' cessi, a' chiassi son condotte.
Che giova voler far tanti bambocci,
se m'han condotto al fin, come colui
che passò 'l mar e poi affogò ne' mocci?
L'arte pregiata, ov'alcun tempo fui
di tant'opinïon, mi rec'a questo,
povero, vecchio e servo in forz'altrui,
ch'i' son disfatto, s'i' non muoio presto.

I'm packaged in here like the pulp in fruit
compacted by its peel. In lonely gloom,
a genii in a jar. Dumped destitute.
No room for flying high. I'm in a tomb
where mad Arachne and her creepy crew
keep jittering up and down, a spooky loom.
My entryway's a jakes for giants, who
gorge on gut-loosening grapes or suffer flux.
No other comfort station seems to do.
Urine! How well I know it —drippy duct
compelling me awake too early, when
dawn plays at peekaboo, then yonder—yuck!—
dead cats, cesspool and privy slosh, pigpen
guck—gifts for me, flung hit-or-miss?
Can't trudge to a proper dunghill, gentlemen?
Soul gets some help from body though in this:
if guts, unclogged, could ventilate their smell
no bread and cheese would keep it in duress,
while round it now catarrh and mucus jell.
Congestion blocks the postern down in back.
With all the phlegm, top exit's blocked as well.
Gut-sprung and graveled, spavined, out of whack,
done in by drudgery's what I am. I pay
innkeeper Death for a fleabag, grub and sack.
My pleasure: gloomy moping. Old and gray,
discomfort's my repose. Who'd choose it so,
God keep him in the dumps day after day.
The bogeyman, that's me, at a twelfth-night show.
The setting's right, a stable. Disrepair's
conspicuous near fine mansions in a row.
No flames of love within my heart, a bare
cold hearthstone deep in ash. Chill drafts prevail.
Clipped are the wings that rode celestial air.

> Skull hums like a hornet in a wooden pail;
> gunnysack skin totes bones and jute around;
> bladder's a pouch of gravel, edged like shale.
> My eyes: mauve pigment pestled till it's ground;
> teeth: oboe-keys that, when I puff out air,
> whistle it through or else begrudge the sound.
> My face says, "Boo!" It's scary. Rags I wear
> rout-without bow and arrow-flocks of crows
> from fresh-sown furrows even when weather's fair.
> One ear's all spider fuzz. I've tremolos
> in the one an all-night vocal cricket chooses.
> Can't sleep for my raucous snuffling, mouth and nose.
> Amor, flower-quilted grottos, all the Muses,
> for these I scribbled reams—now scraps to tot
> up tabs, wrap fish, scrub toilets, or worse uses.
> The puppets once I postured, cocky lot,
> size up my here and now: I'm like the one
> who, having swum wide ocean, drowned in snot.
> My cherished art, my season in the sun,
> name, fame, acclaim—that cant I made a run for,
> left me in servitude, poor, old, alone.
> O death, relieve me soon. Or soon I'm done for.
> (translation by John Frederick Nims).[15]

These verses reveal a more purely realistic-autobiographical expressive level, characterized by a severe tone, which oscillates between resentment and sore sarcasm. The writing becomes more tormented and punctuated by grave cadences, in particular, where he describes his inner experience, in parallel with a detailed representation of his miserable physical condition: that of an old man with deformed body and face (e.g. eyes, teeth). The image of a tormented and harsh old age, accompanied by a deep *melancholy* (v. 25) is aggravated by the disqualification of his own art. He accuses the art of having reduced him to these conditions. A dramatic concern and a profound pessimism emerge, slightly lightened by the little comfort that he derives from writing. A writing still intended as a personal (private) instrument of investigation of reality (therefore devoid of embellishments, virtuosities or

15 Michelangelo Buonarroti, *Complete Poems of Michelangelo*, trans. by John Frederick Nims (Chicago: The University of Chicago Press, 1998), p. 143.

artifices) but which is losing that inventive-imaginative character despite the moral tension and that originality of the plot, to assume instead a more spiritual and dark form.

Then, in the sonnet entitled *Giunto è già 'l corso della vita mia* (*On the Brink of Death*) composed between 1552 and 1554, it is possible to feel the *voice* and *emotions* of an old Michelangelo, disillusioned and tired, because he cannot find a sort of consolation in his works. These verses reveal the original close link between thoughts and experiences linked to the inner life and the desire to express them with an intense, inspired mystical language. The *anxiety* and, at the same time, the *desire* of approaching *death*, clearly emerge from words. In fact, death represents (in the *Rhymes*), on the one hand, a relief because it frees the body from pains and physical illnesses, also decreeing the end of earthly passions (and, with them, the possibility of committing sin).[16] But on the other hand it sets the human being with all his finiteness, frailty and weakness (or his sins) by the presence of divine judgement: a merciful, but also judgmental God. Indeed, he writes:

> Giunto è già 'l corso della vita mia,
> con tempestoso mar, per fragil barca,
> al comun porto, ov'a render si varca
> conto e ragion d'ogni opra trista e pia.
>
> Onde l'affettüosa fantasia
> che l'arte mi fece idol e monarca
> conosco or ben com'era d'error carca
> e quel c'a mal suo grado ogn'uom desia.
> Gli amorosi pensier, già vani e lieti,
> che fien or, s'a duo morte m'avvicino?
> D'una so 'l certo, e l'altra mi minaccia.
> Né pinger né scolpir fie più che quieti
> l'anima, volta a quell'amor divino
> c'aperse, a prender noi, 'n croce le braccia.[17]

16 Donato Giannotti, *Dialoghi di Donato Giannotti, de' giorni che Dante consumò nel cercare l'Inferno e 'l Purgatorio*, ed. by Deoclecio Redig de Campos (Florence: Sansoni, 1939), pp. 67-69.

17 Michelangelo Buonarroti, *Rime*, cit., 285, pp. 134-135; see also 288, p. 135; 290, pp. 136-137; 295, pp. 138-139.

> 'Now hath my life across a stormy sea
> Like a frail bark reached that wide port where all
> Are bidden, ere the final reckoning fall
> Of good and evil for eternity.
> Now know I well how that fond phantasy
> Which made my soul the worshiper and thrall
> Of earthly art, is vain; how criminal
> Is that which all men seek unwillingly.
> Those amorous thoughts which were so lightly dressed,
> What are they when the double death is nigh?
> The one I know for sure, the other dread.
> Painting nor sculpture now can lull to rest
> My soul that turns to His great love on high,
> Whose arms to clasp us on the cross were spread'
> (*Rhymes*, 285, translation by Christopher Ryan).

Concerning his real illnesses, it has been demonstrated that to paint the Sistine Chapel frescoes (between 1508 and 1512), Michelangelo, according to his biographer Ascanio Condivi, worked in an anomalous position, in a dim and cold space, with toxic dyes and solvents dripping on his body. As a likely consequence he began suffering, in 1510, from eye disease and probably episodic positional vertigo, as evidenced by intermittent nystagmus likely induced by maintaining his head in a prolonged anomalous position: horizontal and looking upwards.[18] Probably, he was also suffering from Osteoarthritis.[19]

In addition, Michelangelo complained of renal and urinary calculi and in a letter to Giorgio Vasari (May, 1557) he writes: '[...] I'm physically enfeebled like all old men, by kidney trouble, the stone and the colic, and Messer Eraldo can bear witness to this, because I owe my life to him'.[20]

18 Pier Enrico Gallenga, Giampiero Neri, Ruggero D'Anastasio, Vito Enrico Pettorrossi, Emilio Alfieri, Luigi Capasso, 'Michelangelo's Eye Disease', in *Medical Hypotheses* 78, 6 (2012), pp. 757-759.

19 Davide Lazzeri, Manuel Francisco Castello, Marco Matucci-Cerinic, Donatella Lippi and George M. Weisz, 'Osteoarthritis in the Hands of Michelangelo Buonarroti', in *Journal of the Royal Society of Medicine* 109 (2016), pp. 180-183.

20 'Messer Eraldo' is Realdo Colombo (a pupil of Andrea Vesalio), the physician who had attended Michelangelo since his first attack of the stone in 1549, cf. Letter No. 434 from Michelangelo in Rome (May 22, 1557, unsigned)

2. *The Representation of the Invisible*

There is no doubt that Michelangelo's creative genius was instrumental in allowing him to recreate the stirrings of the soul (and emotions) with striking immediacy and originality, expressed through the language of the body, its movement and gestures, but at the basis of this skill there was also a desire to work independently and free himself from the iconographic and stylistic models[21] of preceding classical traditions. He was proposing an unconventional and innovative interpretation of the *values* and *principles* of art and, more broadly, of culture itself.

On these aspects it is worth mentioning that the word *genius* derives from Latin and, for the Latins, Genius was the patron god to whom each person was entrusted at birth. In Roman art, the duality and ambivalence of Genius is represented by two Genii: one with a lit torch held upright (to illuminate life) and another with one spent and overturned (as a messenger of death).

In the iconology of the Christian tradition, Genius is represented by two angels: that of good and that of evil. The *guardian angel* protects and guides the individual to seek good, but must be in constant dialogue with his opposite, pushing him/her to do evil. Etymologically, the root of the word *genius* is very close to that of the verb *generate*, which describes the act of creating and giving life (interesting are also the meanings of *ingenium*/temper/talent and of *genialis*/genial or ingenious). But, life does not depend on the person, in the sense that it did not originate from him/her, but gave him/her origin (at birth). Genius, in other words, represents not only existence itself and a vital principle (internal drive), but also the expression of the unique, subjective character

---

to Giorgio Vasari in Florence. See Eileen Hartley Ramsden, *The Letters of Michelangelo*, cit., vol. 2 (1537-1563), p. 176 and footnote n. 4. See also pp. 69-211.

21 Luigi Baldacci, 'Lineamenti della poesia di Michelangiolo' in *Il petrarchismo italiano nel Cinquecento* (Padova: Liviana, 1974), pp. 249-279; Gregory L. Lucente, 'Lyric Tradition and the Desires of Absence: Rudel, Dante and Michelangelo ('Vorrei uoler')' in *Canadian Review of Comparative Literature* 10, 3 (Sept. 1983), pp. 305-332; Glauco Cambon, *La poesia di Michelangelo furia della figura* (Turin: Einaudi, 1991).

of each person: of his/her intrinsic individual vitality and of his/her ambivalence or duality. Essentially then, genius represents two inseparable parts (or sides) of an individual's existence: his/her best and exceptional half and his/her darkest and least known half, thus giving rise to the intrinsic ambivalence of life. A duality that is clearly present in Michelangelo's life (and in his writings).[22]

The individual's 'unknown side' results from those urges and tensions that cannot be controlled and is called the unconscious. As such, each person is unique and original, precisely because he/she is not only made up of conscience (rational thoughts), but also by elusive, ungovernable (irrational) emotions and experiences that coexist with rational life. For this reason, the Latins advised to *indulgere Genio*,[23] that is to abandon oneself to one's genius, to honor and follow it without resistance, without opposing its will. This means that genius embodies the deepest, inner needs, emotions, and desires that drive people to live intensely and have new positive or negative experiences every day.

According to the French philosopher Gilbert Simondon (1924-1989)[24] emotions[25] allow people to make contact with their irrational and unknown side. In other words, they allow them to experience genius that, as noted, expresses itself in ambivalent ways: revealing itself through positive emotions such as joy (or feeling like a sense of security) and through negative ones

---

22 Isabel Violante, 'Le contraddizioni dell' 'io' nelle 'Rime' di Michelangelo', in *Letteratura e arte*, 3 (2005), pp. 35-42.

23 Giorgio Agamben, *Genius* (Rome: nottetempo, 2004), p. 7.

24 Gilbert Simondon, *L'individuazione alla luce delle nozioni di forma e di informazione* (Milan: Mimesis, 2011; original in Gilbert Simondon, *L'individuation à la lumière des notions de formes et d'information*, Grenoble: J. Millon, 2005). See also: Pascal Chabot, *La philosophie de Simondon* (Paris: Vrin, 2003); Jean-Hugues Barthélémy, *Penser la connaissance et la technique après Simondon* (Paris: L'Harmattan, 2005).

25 On these aspects see: Jacqueline Nadel, Luigia Camaioni (ed. by), *New Perspectives in Early Communicative Development* (London: Routledge, 1993); Paul Ekman and Wallace V. Friesen, *Pictures of facial affect* (Palo Alto, CA: Consulting Psychologists Press, 1976); Paul Ekman, *Handbook of Cognition and Emotion* (Sussex, UK: John Wiley & Sons, 1999); Jaak *Panksepp, Affective Neuroscience: The foundations of human and animal emotions* (New York: Oxford University Press, 1998).

such as anguish and uncertainty. The passions reveal genius's intimate desire to know, understand, and experience life; for this reason it induces people to look for others upon whom they can find a reflection of themselves and their own lives (thoughts, emotion, experiences and much more). This mutual mirroring may allow us to better understand ourselves, whenever it helps us to recognize emotions (thanks to the points of view of others and their *gaze* upon us) that we cannot understand by ourselves. These are, above all, those emotions and experiences that make sense and gain meaning when they are shared with others.[26]

Indeed, Michelangelo was called the *divine one* (by his contemporaries) because of his intense spirituality and its impetuous character. On this point, it is possible to affirm that Michelangelo in his sculptures is not seeking to be realistic, or even to achieve a perfect beauty of form, but rather to create a scene full of symbolic and potential gestures (or images) and actions, with the main purpose of bringing to light a higher *idea* or *concept* that rises above our immediate perception. In the case of his *Vatican Pietà,*[27] for example, the concept expressed is the *gift* of a grieving mother who is offering her dead son to all humanity. This profound thought is passed back to the viewer (who is admiring the statue), underlined by Mary's precise and formal hand gesture, below a face so young for the mother of an adult son.

In his search for *harmony* in the composition, Michelangelo, by successfully conveying movement and passion, injected

26 On the problem of identity and how does a mind build itself, see: Walter J. Freeman, *How Brains Make Up Their Minds* (New York: Columbia University Press, 2000); Giacomo Rizzolatti, Corrado Sinigaglia, *So quel che fai. Il cervello che agisce e i neuroni specchio* (Milan: Raffaello Cortina, 2006); Massimo Ammaniti, Vittorio Gallese, *The Birth of Intersubjectivity. Psychodynamics, Neurobiology, and the Self* (New York: W.W. Norton & Company, 2014); Giacomo Rizzolatti, Antonio Gnoli, *In te mi specchio. Per una scienza dell'empatia* (Milan: Rizzoli, 2016); Giacomo Rizzolatti, Corrado Sinigaglia, *Specchi nel cervello. Come comprendiamo gli altri dall'interno* (Milan: Raffaello Cortina, 2019); Georg Northoff, *La neurofilosofia e la mente sana. Imparare dal cervello malato* (Milan: Raffaello Cortina, 2019).

27 Cf. Michelangelo Buonarroti, Vatican Pietà (1497–1499), Vatican, St Peter's Basilica.

absolute humanity into his marble statues and paintings (see the many iconic elements that adorn the vaulted ceiling of the Sistine Chapel and the *Last Judgement*). According to Wittkower,[28] this genial and melancholic[29] artist who isolated himself and cared little for his health or looks, was seen as surly and easily prey to violent passion and often for the totally wrong person,[30] but he was also *vulnerable* (cf. some of Michelangelo's verses on love and death dedicated to a young friend, Tommaso de' Cavalieri, *Rhymes*, 83).[31]

Obsessed by art, throwing all his tremendous outpouring of energy (which he called *fire*) into his work, Michelangelo knew how to give *form* to his highly tuned sensitivity, sculpturing emotions, gestures, and expressions that have become the unique and elusive blueprint of Michelangesque art. His desire to express an idea under the mantle of a symbol is clearly on view in the *Rondanini Pietà*,[32] the statue Michelangelo was working on in his final days and never completed. In this sculpture, the Mother-Son duo is fused into a single block, still not clearly defined (the only polished surfaces are Jesus's legs) and seems to hold within itself the pure essence of the *unfinished*. This is both a concept and a trailblazing *gesture*, precursor to the modern taste.

In line with the principle of *equilibrium* of the whole and search for the elusory, Michelangelo in his work adhered to the principle of *uncovering* the statue imprisoned within a block of marble, where it is up to the artist to extract it, freeing the forms that are in the sculptor's mind: '*Non ha l'ottimo artista alcun concetto / c'un marmo solo in sé non circoscriva / col*

28 Rudolf Wittkower and Margot Wittkower, *Nati sotto Saturno. La figura dell'artista dall'antichità alla Rivoluzione francese* (Turin: Einaudi, 1996), pp. 84-88.

29 Michelangelo Buonarroti, *Rime*, cit., 267, v. 25, vv. 49-51, vv. 52-55, pp. 127-128; Michelangelo Buonarroti, *Rime*, cit., 57, p. 30 and 293, pp. 137-138.

30 Donato Giannotti, *Dialoghi di Donato Giannotti, de' giorni che Dante consumò nel cercare l'Inferno e 'l Purgatorio*, ed. by Deoclecio Redig de Campos (Florence: Sansoni, 1939), p. 68.

31 Michelangelo Buonarroti, *Rime*, cit., 83, p. 46.

32 Cf. Michelangelo Buonarroti, *Rondanini Pietà* (1552-1564), The Pietà Rondanini Museum, Sforzesco Castle, Milan.

suo soperchio, e solo a quello arriva / la man che ubbidisce all'intelletto' ('The greatest artist does not have any concept / Which a single piece of marble does not itself contain / Within its excess, though only / A hand that obeys the intellect can discover it'[33] *Rhymes*, 151, translation by Christopher Ryan).

3. *Conclusions*

The thesis herein presented is that some great artists, such as Michelangelo, were also great *mentors*, not only for future generations of artists, but also for the beholders of their works. Thus, having tested the limits of their own nature, their depiction of the human condition was exemplary, enabling them to interpret both *illness* and *care* for life and death. Michelangelo was a man who, in spite of being afflicted by diseases and life adversities, understood and lived his *suffering* (his real diseases, or illness) to the full, as described in the *Letters* and in the *Rhymes*. Not only this, he was in fact considered misogynistic and melancholic and was also suspected of being homosexual, then considered a crime to be severely punished. Therefore, suffering was a personal experience and a key to interpreting and better understanding himself, others and natural phenomena, such as life, care, illness, disease, and death.

He thus faced, understood, and integrated his suffering into his life, and from his afflictions found a way to relate to the wounds or vulnerabilities of others (as can be seen in his works). All this, in a historical period when *death* and *illness* formed a large part of everyone's life, never far removed from everyday discourse, since these did not represent the sort of a 'social stigma' (*à la* Goffman, or *à la* Sontag) that they do currently.

To conclude, on the one hand, in accordance with a phenomenological perspective, *health* is not 'to feel' but 'to be', understood as an expression of one's 'being-in-the-world' (or *in-der-Welt-sein*, according to Heidegger's meaning). On the

33 Michelangelo Buonarroti, *Rime*, cit., 151, vv. 1-4, p. 82.

other hand, there emerges the ambiguous difference between the biological body (*Körper*) and the living body (*Leib*), but again, as the German philosopher Ludwig Binswanger reminds us, we do not *have* a body, we *are* a body.[34]

Bibliography

Arnheim, Rudolf, *Il pensiero visivo. La percezione visiva come attività conoscitiva* (Turin: Einaudi, 1974).

Bardeschi Ciulich, Lucilla, Barocchi, Paola (ed. by), *I Ricordi di Michelangelo* (Florence: Sansoni, 1970).

Barocchi, Paola (ed. by), *Scritti d'arte del Cinquecento*, 3 vols (Milan-Naples: Ricciardi 1971–1977).

Barolsky, Paul, *Michelangelo's Nose. A Myth and Its Maker* (Pennsylvania: The Pennsylvania State University Press, University Park, 1990).

Bull, George, *Michelangelo. A Biography* (London: Viking, 1995).

Buonarroti, Michelangelo, *Rime e lettere*, ed. by Antonio Corsaro, Giorgio Masi (Milan: Bompiani, 2016).

Buonarroti, Michelangelo, *Rime*, ed. by Paolo Zaja (Milan: BUR, 2010).

Buonarroti, Michelangelo, *Life, Letters and Poetry*, ed. and trans. by George Bull (Oxford: Oxford University Press, 1987).

Classici dell'Arte Rizzoli, *L'opera completa di Michelangelo pittore*, Introduction by Salvatore Quasimodo, Critical and philological research by Ettore Camesasca (Milan: Rizzoli, 1977).

Cometa, Michele, *La scrittura delle immagini. Letteratura e cultura visuale* (Milan: Raffaello Cortina Editore, 2012).

Condivi, Ascanio, *Vita di Michelagnolo Buonarroti scritta da Ascanio Condivi suo discepolo* (Pisa: Niccolò Capurro, MDCCCXXIII).

Condivi, Ascanio, *The Life of Michelangelo* (Louisiana State University Press: Baton Rouge, 1976).

Cosmacini, Giorgio, *L'arte lunga. Storia della medicina dall'antichità a oggi* (Bari: Laterza, 2011).

Costa, Giorgio, *Michelangelo e la stampa: la mancata pubblicazione delle 'Rime'* in ACME - Annali della Facoltà di Lettere e Filosofia dell'Università degli Studi di Milano, Vol. LX, III, (Sept.-Dec. 2007), pp. 211-244.

Dufrenne, Mikel, *Phénoménologie de l'expérience esthétique* (1953), t. II, (Paris: PUF, 1992).

Dussler, Luitpold, *Michelangelo-Bibliographie 1927-1970* (Wiesbaden: Otto

34 Ludwig Binswanger, *Per un'antropologia fenomenologica. Saggi e conferenze psichiatriche* (Milan: Feltrinelli 1970); Alessandro Costa, *Binswanger. Il mondo come progetto* (Rome: Studium, 1987).

Harrassowitz, 1974).

Elsner, Jaś, *Art and the Roman Viewer. The Transformation of Art from the Pagan World to Christianity* (Cambridge: Cambridge University Press, 1995).

Gallerani, Manuela, *L'impegno lieve. Il razionalismo critico e l'ideale estetico* (Naples: Loffredo, 2012).

Gallerani, Manuela, *Prossimità inattuale. Un contributo alla filosofia dell'educazione problematicista* (Milan: Franco Angeli, 2012).

Gallerani, Manuela, 'Narrative Medicine and Stories of Illness: Caring for the Sick requires active Listening', in Laura Formenti & Linden West (ed. by), *Stories that make a difference. Exploring the collective, social and political potential of narratives in adult education research* (Lecce: Pensa MultiMedia, 2016), pp. 341-347.

Goffman, Erving, *Stigma. L'identità negata* (Verona: Ombre Corte, 2003).

Gombrich, Ernst H. J., *Riflessioni sulla storia dell'arte* (Turin: Einaudi, 1991).

Kris, Ernst, Kurz, Otto, *La leggenda dell'artista* (1934) (Turin: Boringhieri, 1980).

Milanesi, Gaetano (ed. by), *Le Lettere di Michelangelo Buonarroti, edite e inedite, pubblicate coi ricordi ed i contratti artistici* (Florence: Le Monnier, 1875).

Nancy, Jean-Luc, *Il ritratto e il suo sguardo* (Milan: Raffaello Cortina, 2002).

Ricœur, Paul, 'Spiegare e comprendere', in *Dal testo all'azione. Saggi di ermeneutica* (Milan: Jaca Book, 1989).

Sontag, Susan, *AIDS and Its Metaphors* (New York: Farrar, Straus and Giroux, 1989).

Zanker, Graham, 'Enargeia in the Ancient Criticism of Poetry', in *Rheinisches Museum für Philologie*, 124 (1981), pp. 297-311.

Nakama Aya 仲間絢[1]

SANDRO BOTTICELLI'S *PRIMAVERA* AND THE BRIDAL MYSTICISM OF THE SONG OF SONGS

The Flower Symbolism of the Bride and the Gaze of Love's Arrow

Sandro Botticelli's *Primavera* (fig. 1), created around the late 1470s and early 1480s, is a large-scale masterpiece of the Italian Renaissance depicting classic mythological gods and goddesses frolicking in a forest of blossoming spring flowers. The history and motivation of the work is still unclear, and it could have been commissioned by a member of the Medici family, such as by Lorenzo di Pierfrancesco de' Medici to celebrate a wedding.

Previous studies have offered a variety of interpretations of the complex meaning of the *Primavera*. For example, it has been read in terms of the earthly paradise following Dante's *Divine Comedy*, an ornament of the bridal chamber, the blooming of the Florentine Republic of the Medicis, the resurgence of painting in competition with poetry and music, or as a medium of inspiration for fertility and beauty.[2]

Although it is still rife with mysteries, one point of general consensus is that the celebration of spring contains very many allegories of love and marriage. One of the interpretations in terms of love and marriage in previous studies relates it to the medieval Christian tradition of bridal mysticism of the Song of Songs in the Old Testament. Recent studies have demonstrated its influence on the visualization of heavenly paradise, the theme of the lovers' rendezvous in garden, and the connection between the beginning of love and spring.

---

1 Tokyo University of the Arts

2 For the recent studies of *Primavera* see e.g., Luigi Capitano, 'Marsilio Ficino e il segreto della Primavera di Botticelli', in *Studi medievali e moderni*, 23-2 (2019), pp. 53-72; Ana Debenedetti, Caroline Elam (ed. by), *Botticelli past and present* (London: UCL Press, 2019).

The Song of Songs of King Solomon in the Old Testament is the primal source of Jewish and Christian bridal mysticism.[3] It is a song in praise of the love of the bridal couple and the beauty of their bodies. In theological commentaries since the Patristics, the woman in the Song of Songs has been understood to be the bride of Christ or of God, which is the Church in general and the Virgin Mary in particular. As Mariology flourished in the twelfth and thirteenth centuries, the flowers mentioned in the Song of Songs and its commentaries began to be popular motives to symbolize the Virgin Mary in various scenes of her life.[4]

Bridal allegories relating to the Virgin Mary have been practiced since the earliest times of Christianity, and because of the diverse and descriptive references to plants in the Song of Songs, these plants came to embody the virtues of the Virgin Mary. The symbolic expressions of these plants in the Song of Songs have been developed in a wide range of domains, including the commentaries on the Song, hymns and lyric poems about the Virgin Mary, and prayers such as in liturgical books, sermons, and books of hours.[5]

According to Rosemarie Bergman's analysis, more than 20 kinds of flowers and fruits are mentioned in the Song of Songs,[6] including lilies, lily-of-the-valleys, roses, grapes, apples, pomegranates, and peonies. At the beginning, the bride declares "I am the rose of Sharon, the lily of the field" (2: 1), to which the bridegroom responds, "My lover among the virgins is like a lily among thorns" (2: 2). Lilies are often referred to as white lilies (Lilium candidum) and are a particularly important bridal

3 For the medieval bridal mysticism of the Song of Songs, see E. Ann Matter, *The Voice of My Beloved: the Song of Songs in Western Medieval Christianity* (Philadelphia: University of Pennsylvania Press, 1990); Friedrich Ohly, *Hohelied-Studien: Grundzüge einer Geschichte der Hoheliedauslegung des Abendlandes bis um 1200* (Wiesbaden: Franz Steiner, 1958).

4 Cf. Rosemarie Bergmann, 'Sicut lilium inter spinas: Pflanzen als Symbolträger', in Peter Wapnewski (ed. by), *Mittelalter-Rezeption* (Stuttgart: Metzler, 1986), pp. 450-472.

5 Rosemarie Bergmann, 'Sicut lilium inter spinas: Pflanzen als Symbolträger', cit., p. 452.

6 Rosemarie Bergmann, 'Sicut lilium inter spinas: Pflanzen als Symbolträger', cit., p. 451.

symbol of the Virgin Mary's virginity. The above-mentioned passage (2:1) has also been interpreted in the Vulgate Bible as "Ego flos campi, et lilium convallium", or lily-of-the-valley. In particular, "lily among thorns" (2:2) was changed to a "rose without thorns", and roses then also became preferentially associated with the Virgin Mary.[7]

As a collective image, the Virgin Mary as the garden of heaven became particularly significant; the source for this in the Song of Songs reads: "My sister, my bride is an enclosed garden, a closed garden, a sealed fountain" (4:12).[8] The text is suggestive of the Virgin Mary's womb and her realizing the birth of Christ while remaining a virgin. Furthermore, the iconography of "the enclosed garden" has given rise to a variety of images of the plants of heavenly paradise described by the Song of Songs (fig. 2).[9]

According to Ulrich Rehm, the *Primavera* could refer to the Song of Songs for the following reasons: the garden as a place of lovers where the bride and bridegroom meet each other is a highly popular motif from the biblical scriptures, the Song of Songs. It describes the beginning of love as spring, filled imaginatively with flowers and plants.[10] Not only Rehm, but also Tobias Leuker agrees that the imagination of the Florentine Paradise made it possible to illustrate in the *Primavera* a verse of the Song of Songs (2, 11): "Winter has already passed and

---

7 Simone Widauer, *Marienpflanzen: Der geheimnisvolle Garten Marias in Symbolik, Heilkunde und Kunst* (Baden und München: AT Verlag, 2009); Margarethe Schmidt, *Warum ein Apfel, Eva?: die Bildsprache von Baum, Frucht und Blume* (Regensburg: Schnell + Steiner, 2000), p. 101f.

8 Brian E. Daley, 'The "closed garden" and the "sealed fountain": song of songs 4:12 in the late medieval iconography of Mary', in Elisabeth B. Macdougall (ed. by), *Medieval Gardens* (Washington, D.C.: Dumbarton Oaks Research Library and Collection, 1986), pp. 253-278.

9 Cf. Esther Gallwitz, *Kleiner Kräutergarten: Kräuter und Blumen bei den Alten Meistern im Staedel* (Frankfurt am Main: Insel, 1992).

10 Ulrich Relm, '„La Primavera" von Sandro Botticelli: Annäherung an ein Bildkonzept im historischen Kontext', in: Kristin Marek, Martin Schulz (ed. by), *Kanon Kunstgeschichte: Einführung in Werke, Methoden und Epochen*, Bd. II Neuzeit (Paderborn: Wilhelm-Fink-Verlag, 2015), pp. 149-169.

the rain has gone. Flowers have appeared in our land" — which had always been referred to the heavenly Paradise in the various branches of medieval exegesis of the Song of Songs.[11]

From here I will explore the tradition of the bridal mysticism of the Song of Songs from other points of view. However, I would like to first note as a premise that I interpret the Song of Songs as one source of this picture, as only one layer of multi-layered meanings embodied in the *Primavera*. Therefore, this is not meant as a denial of other interpretations. Rather they coexist with my interpretation. There is a Christian tradition of appreciating the multiple layers of images dating back at least to St. Augustine, the early Christian theologian and neo-Platonic philosopher of the 5th century B.C.[12]

There are two primary reasons why the Song of Songs could be one of the main themes of the *Primavera*: Firstly, Botticelli referred to the Song of Songs as a source of flower symbolism in other paintings as well, and secondly, Dante's *Divine Comedy*, which was influential in the Medici circle, impressively reflected the Song of Songs.

Previous studies have demonstrated that Botticelli made reference to the Song of Songs in for example the *Bardi Altarpiece* (fig. 3), the *Madonna of the Pomegranate*, the *Virgin Adoring the Sleeping Christ Child* (fig. 4), and *Madonna and Child with Eight Angels*, along with the images of the Virgin with child and the infant St. John or with angels. As mentioned above, the visualization of earthly paradise of Dante's *Divine Comedy* is one of the main streams of interpretations in previous studies. Additionally, I would like to mention the connection with the *Divine Comedy* and the Song of Songs in the scene where the poet and his ideal lady Beatrice are welcomed into the

---

11 Tobias Leuker, *Bausteine eines Mythos: die Medici in Dichtung und Kunst des 15. Jahrhunderts* (Köln: Böhlau, 2007).

12 Cf. Gerald P. Boersma, *Augustine's Early Theology of Image: A Study in the Development of Pro-Nicene Theology* (New York: Oxford University Press, 2016).

paradise by music quoting three times from the Song of Songs.[13] Moreover, it is very interesting that, according to Margherita Pelaja and Lucetta Scaraffia, Dante's ideal woman Beatrice is depicted as a figure in which the bride of the Song of Songs and the Venus are superimposed.[14] Therefore, the Venus in the *Primavera* could reflect the idealized woman in Dante's Divine Comedy mixed with the bride of the Song of Songs.

The Venus is occasionally interpreted as the Virgin Mary by her belly showing sign of pregnancy and also by the background plants forming something resembling a niche in church (fig. 5). Moreover, Rehm pointed out that it is anything but a coincidence that the Venus appears as exceptionally chaste, comparably to the Virgin Mary.[15] The Venus wears the red stole only at her right side and it goes on to cover her belly. It could be suggested that her belly implying pregnancy contains Christ and she shows that this baby appears noticeably on her right side. Also, her head is noticeably declined to her right side. The Virgin Mary could be indicating the direction of the bridegroom Christ, that is, Mercury. Moreover, her hand could be also interpreted as a sign of mystical marriage, with the right hand raised and the palm turned toward the bridegroom in *unio mystica*, mystical union with God (e. g. fig. 6). The triangle formed by the hands of three dancing goddesses (fig. 7) looks as if they are implying the ecstatic rapture of this mystical union between the bride Venus and bridegroom Mercury at both of their sides.

In a second step the symbolism of flowers and fruits will be analyzed. Botticelli is said to have had a great interest in the symbolism of plants, which can be seen in the above-mentioned *Bardi Altarpiece* (fig. 3), the closest work to the *Primavera*. Here

13 Cf. Robert M. Durling, *The Divine Comedy of Dante Alighieri: Volume 2: Purgatorio* (Oxford University Press, 2003), p. 518ff.

14 Margherita Pelaja, Lucetta Scaraffia, *Due in una carne: Chiesa e sessualità nella storia* (Roma-Bari: Laterza, 2014).

15 Ulrich Relm, '„La Primavera" von Sandro Botticelli: Annäherung an ein Bildkonzept im historischen Kontext', cit., p. 167.

a Latin quotation from the Song of Songs (2:2) is inscribed on the banderole, "as a lily among thorns" in Latin, and together with the symbolism of other plants like a palm tree beside her, Antonia Fondaras interprets this Mary as the bride of the Song of Songs.[16] Rehm also argued that the tradition of bridal mysticism of the Song of Songs plays a decisive role in *Primavera*, not least because of the Madonna in the rose bush, which is a type of image of which the Botticelli workshop made many variations. The fantastic ornaments of the garden of the marriage in this painting include 500 acknowledged plant species, of which 190 are flowers,[17] and 40 types of flowers that are easy recognizable have been analyzed in detail, for example by Mirella Levi D'Ancona, as a symbol of love and marriage that was particularly vivid in Florence.[18] However, it has not sufficiently pointed out in previous studies that most of them are also the symbolic flowers of the Virgin Mary and also of the bride of the Song of Songs.

Among these forty flowers the primary symbolic flowers from the Song of Songs could be identified, which are, for example, the lily, lily-of-the-valley, pomegranate, rose, iris, and daisy. The other flowers symbolizing the Virgin Mary include anemone, strawberry, violet, poppy, crocus, chrysanthemum, jasmine, chamomile, borage, bachelor's buttons, cornflower, cress, dandelion, carnation, hyacinth, myosotis, myrtle, orange, periwinkle and ranunculus. Almost all flowers from the Song of Songs are present in this painting and are also depicted prominently in the picture, such as the large iris in the very right corner below (fig. 8).

Finally, and most importantly, the orange trees covering the painting not only symbolize the crest of the Medici family, as previous research has demonstrated, but were also one of favored motifs of the Renaissance for purity, spotlessness, and fertility. We should note that they are depicted with many blossoms; the

16 Antonia K. Fondaras,'Our Mother in the Holy Wisdom of God: Nursing in Botticelli's Bardi Altarpiece', in *Storia dell'arte*, (2005), pp. 7-34.

17 Elena Capretti, *Botticelli* (Firenze: Giunti, 1997), p. 49.

18 Mirella Levi D'Ancona, *Botticelli's Primavera: A Botanical Interpretation Including Astrology, Alchemy and the Medici* (Firenze: Olschki, 1983).

orange blossom was the flower of the Virgin Mary as the bride of the Song of Songs. For example, this was the meaning given to it by Armando de Bellovisu from Bologna who lived from 1296 to 1323.[19] The orange tree was also depicted in many Renaissance altar images of the Virgin Mary.

The ornament of Venus is a brooch of ruby surrounded by a gold crescent moon hung on a necklace of pearls (fig. 9). The ruby is the symbol of passionate love and is used to praise the bride's beauty in the Song of Songs: "Red like ruby" (5:10). The bride of the Song of Songs in Van Eyck's Ghent altar also wore a pearl and ruby brooch. At that time the pairing of pearl and ruby was the favored motif of ornaments such as brooches or headdresses worn by Mary in many Renaissance paintings. In the iconography of the immaculate conception, one of the sources of which is the Song of Songs, a downwardly opened crescent moon is in many cases an attribute of Mary as the Queen of Heaven.[20] Moreover, in the Song of Songs (6:10), the bride is praised as "fair as the moon", the beauty of Mary as the Bride of Christ.

The lily ornament of Mercury's sword could indicate him to be the sacred bridegroom of the Song of Songs. The most influential commentator of the Song of Songs, Origen of Alexandria of the 3rd century, interprets the bridegroom as a lily. As if to prove this, lilies are impressively blooming just next to him (fig. 10).

The Cupid above her head at the top center of the picture reminds the viewer of the infant Jesus. Erwin Panofsky interprets the blindness of Cupid as a medieval addition growing out of the belief that "love is blind."[21]

The Cupid is at the top center, the most prominent position in the picture. He is the child of Venus and is shooting Love's

---

19 Mirella Levi D'Ancona, *The Garden of the Renaissance: Botanical Symbolism in Italian Painting* (Firenze: Olschki, 1977), p. 273.

20 Cf. Gertrud Schiller, *Ikonographie der christlichen Kunst,* Band 4, 2: "Maria" (Gütersloh: Gerd Mohn, 1980).

21 Erwin Panofsky, *Studies in Iconology: Humanistic Themes in the Art of the Renaissance* (New York: Harper Torchbooks, 1962), p. 121.

Arrow (fig. 5). The metaphor of Love's Arrow comes not only from Ovid, but also from the Song of Songs (4:9): "You have stolen my heart, my sister, my bride; you have stolen my heart with one glance of your eyes".[22] Joanne Snow-Smith, drawing on the neo-Platonic view, has interpreted Cupid as Christ by way of the Holy Spirit and the soul of Mary uniting in Christ as an ascending soul, which is realized here not only from the neo-Platonic view but also in terms of the Christian tradition, as the Cupid was interpreted to be Christ shooting Love's Arrow as the God of Love.[23] The *Primavera* is also known as a strong reflection of the ideas of Neoplatonism. According to F. B. A. Asiedu, the neo-Platonic conception of transcendent love is similar to that of the Song of Songs.[24]

The background of the painting, the spreading stems of orange trees, forms a low triangular shape culminating in the figure of Venus. This structure in particular seems to be intended to make the viewer's gaze focus on the face of the Venus. Above all, Venus's eyes (fig. 11) are very mysterious and have been thought in previous studies to be expressing love or grief, to be prophetic or sympathetic. Horst Bredekamp notes the very different impression of the left and right eyes stemming from their different expressions and the differing eyelids and size and height of the eyes, and describes the two different eyes as producing values of their own without any unity of the physiognomy.[25] Moreover, the Song of Songs emphasizes "one of the eyes." In the medieval tradition, the commentaries of the relevant verse of the Song of

22 Barbara Newman, 'Love's arrows: Christ as Cupid in late medieval art and devotion', in Jeffrey F. Hamburger, Anne-Marie Bouché (ed.by), *The Mind's Eye: Art and Theological Argument in the Middle Ages* (Princeton, NJ: Princeton University Press, 2006), p. 264.

23 Joanne Snow-Smith, *The Primavera of Sandro Botticelli: A Neoplatonic Interpretation* (New York: P. Lang, 1993), p. 211.

24 F. B. A. Asiedu, 'The Song of Songs and the Ascent of the Soul: Ambrose, Augustine, and the Language of Mysticism', in *Vigiliae Christianae*, 55-3 (2001), pp. 299-317.

25 Horst Bredekamp, *Botticelli, Primavera: Florenz als Garten der Venus* (Frankfurt am Main: Fischer, 1988), pp. 13-15.

Songs (4:9) completely distinguish the meaning of the right eye and the left eye with the right eye generally seeing the eternal love of the God and Christ the bridegroom while the left eye sees earthly and transient things.[26] This meaning of different eyes was widely known in the medieval tradition. I would also like to point out here that the bride as the shooter and receiver of the Love's Arrow was a trope of courtly love poems. The "wounded heart" indicating lovesickness came to be depicted as a heart symbol pierced with an arrow. Cupid flying just above her implies this theme of the gaze of Love's Arrow. For another example, the miniature of the *Divine Comedy* (fig. 12) shows the enormous power of Beatrice's radiant gaze as Love's Arrow staring down at Dante.

These analyses reveal one of the multi-layered meanings of images: Mercury as Christ/bridegroom and Venus as Mary/Ecclesia/bride of the bridal mysticism of the Song of Songs. The concept of love of the Song of Songs also helped to realize a harmony of pagan and Christian images, providing the poetic imagery of the soul's cosmic and mystical love for God in the *Primavera*.

Finally, I would like to focus on the most impressive and largest flower in the picture, which is depicted in a conspicuous position at the right bottom corner (fig. 8). It might be the key to reveal the hidden central theme of this picture. I would like to offer one suggestion for why it is a "black" iris. As I mentioned before, the iris is a symbol of the Virgin Mary as the bride of the Song of Songs, and moreover in the passage in which bride is declaring "I am black and beautiful" (1:5); this verse was interpreted as meaning that the Virgin Mary is black,[27] and this flower is called the "Black Madonna." There was a popular cult of the black Madonna in Italy. According to Luica Chiavola Birnbaum, the cult of the Black Madonna was popular since the 4th century as well as in Renaissance Italy as the pregnant

26 Gudrun Schleusener-Eichholz, *Das Auge im Mittelalter* (München: Fink, 1985), pp. 787-796.

27 Cf. Paul J. Griffiths, *Song of Songs* (Ada, MI; Brazos Press, 2011), pp. 23f.

earth-mother divinity was also connected to the cult of Venus.[28] We can see also a good example in the impressive icon of the Black Madonna in the Sanctuary of the Madonna of San Luca in Bologna.

In conclusion, based on the *Primavera* as well as the reference to the Song of Songs in Botticelli's other paintings, it could be said that the Song of Songs was one of Botticelli's favorite resources for his rich imagery of love and nature.

Figure 1 Sandro Botticelli, *Primavera*, Uffizi Gallery, Florence, Tempera on panel, 2.03m x 3.14m, late 1470s or early 1480s

Figure 2 Master of upper Rhein, *The Garden of Heaven*, Frankfurt städel museum, ca. 1410

28 Lucia Chiavola Birnbaum, *Black Madonnas: Feminism, Religion, and Politics in Italy* (Boston: Northeastern University Press, 1993).

Figure 3 Sandro Botticelli, *The Virgin and Child Enthroned* (Bardi Altarpiece), 1484, Tempera on panel, 185 x 180 cm, Staatliche Museen, Berlin
Figure 4 *The Virgin Adoring the Sleeping Christ Child*, ca.1490, National Gallery of Scotland, Edinburgh

Figure 5, 7 *Primavera*, Detail

Figure 6 Giovanni dal Ponte, *The Mystic Marriage of St Catherine of Alexandria*, Florence, 1421, Museum of Fine Arts, Budapest

Figure 8, 9, 10 *Primavera*, Detail

Figure 11 *Primavera*, Detail

Figure 12 Dante Divine Comedy Paradiso IV, Padua Seminario, MS. 67 fol. 208r Early fifteenth century (from Barbara Newman, 'Love's arrows: Christ as Cupid in late medieval art and devotion', cit., p. 282)

IMAGES AS BRIDGE

Marcello Ghilardi[1]

TOWARD INTERCULTURAL THOUGHT

Steps between European and Japanese Aesthetics

In the general frame that binds "Images, Philosophy, and Communication", I would like to focus on the possible pathway that allows to move on the way to an intercultural thought and experience. In these pages I will thus discuss some notions, experiences and arguments, crossing philosophical concepts and artistic insights, in order to provide a possible mutual understanding and self-reflection among different cultures. Going beyond personal interest and involvement, the effort to decode some Japanese categories and put them in dialogue with European patterns reveals itself not only as a sort of methodological lever for questioning the general framework of the so-called "Western rationality"; it is also an opportunity to create a space of cross-cultural inquiry "that maintains the integrity and the richness of both Eastern and Western schools of thought".[2] It should be clear enough that this method does not imply at all that Europe should follow Japan, or vice versa. Reflecting each other on the grounds of different languages, images, and aesthetic experience means rather to strengthen "the sensitivity of 'being affected' […] as an aspect of 'being in phase' […] with the environment. Reflexivity as self-reflection of what it means to be humans in nature and in culture could favor a sustainable hygiene".[3]

---

1 University of Padova

2 Sybille Persson, Paul Shrivastava, 'Sustainable Development of Human Resources Inspired by Chinese Philosophies: A Repositioning Based on François Jullien's Works', in *Management and Organization Review*, 12-3 (2016), pp. 503-524 (quotation p. 520).

3 Sybille Persson, Paul Shrivastava, 'Sustainable Development of Human Resources Inspired by Chinese Philosophies: A Repositioning Based on François Jullien's Works', cit., p. 520. On this topic, see also François Jullien,

In this perspective, aesthetics and the role of images are particularly important. Through their "practice" we can recognize our embodied dimension, the implication of intellect and thought with sensitivity, and the role of the imagination and emotions. Exceeding the intellectual frame, images possess a specific performativity and summon us to a deeper awareness of the exchanges, translations, or intercourses that we are always involved in. Such reflexivity may help us to avoid a narrow-minded ethnocentrism, a deluded universalism, and post-colonial attitudes. Therefore, a passageway could be opened, in order to shift from an exclusive (i.e. meaning exclusion and seclusion) notion of identity to a thought of an inclusive and open identity, setting forth the centrality of sensation and images for intercultural communication. In other words, the relation between art and existence can enhance and foster the awareness of the situatedness of subjectivity, involving us in an ethical transformation.

To do so, I would exploit two main philosophical traditions' resources. In fact, I am trying to intertwine 1) a *phenomenological exercise*, focused on theoretical notions, works of art, and patterns of recognition (here philosophy meets art criticism, history of art, history of religion, or anthropology), and 2) a *hermeneutical understanding*, taking into account the overall architecture of textuality, that is always at work when concepts are produced or interpreted. The general frame of this methodology has been provided years ago by the research of Giangiorgio Pasqualotto, who elaborated a "three interdependent dimensions" scheme[4]: "The 'field', that makes possible the existence of the two poles and their mutual interaction, coincides with the space that cannot be closed due to the force of problems. […] In this perspective […] a dynamic with three variables which condition each other is produced". The comparison or the *vis-à-vis* of theoretical objects (notions, concepts, images) is constantly in relation with

---

Vital nourishment. Departing from happiness (New York: Zone Books, 2007).

4 See Giangiorgio Pasqualotto, *East and West. Identità e dialogo interculturale* (Venezia: Marsilio, 2003), pp. 47-48.

the comparing subject, and vice versa. None of them can stand isolated and autonomous, but interact with all the others. Of course, "comparison" is to be understood here not as a positivistic exercise of a neutral observation, but the existential engagement in a vital movement of experience and thought.

So, *aesthetics* in a wide sense (i.e. not only as a philosophical discipline that deals with beauty or art, but as a philosophical enterprise that takes into account sensation, perception, and the embodied dimension of human thought) can be a valid pathway, in order to make different cultures and patterns of meaning communicate. The respect of difference and distance, and the acceptance of some unavoidable gaps, is mandatory – but this does not imply to give up the effort of a mutual, strenuous clarification and the task of translating one's categories into each other's language.

I will deal here with a couple of examples, trying to show how challenging can be putting *vis-à-vis* some philosophical concepts – communicating and enriching each other is not at all a lazy or pacifying activity, it is indeed a demanding task.

Firstly, we could stress the specificity of the Sino-Japanese notion of "image", focusing on the character *zō* 像 (also *shō* 象). My approach will depend mostly on the notion of image as it is elaborated in the texts and teachings of traditional ink painting, and by the observation of classical ink landscapes and calligraphy. For this reason, I would translate *zō* 像 or *shō* 象 by coupling two terms, "image-phenomenon": two terms that in Western tradition – at least since Plato[5] – have been normally separated, or well differentiated. The image is as "valid" (ontologically) as the phenomenon it depicts. Every image is alive, and contributes to the global flowing of the vital energy (*ki* 気) that permeates every single aspects of reality. An image that does not express that breathing character is far from the vitality of the phenomenon, but this fact does not depend on its ontological dimension: it depends only on the painter's low skills. If the painter is not able to convey in his picture the life of phenomena,

5 See Plato, *Crat.*, 432b; *Soph.*, 236e-237a, 240a-240c; *Parm.*, 132d-133a.

so the painting will be "dead", detached from the general process of reality. What really counts is not the perfect, "photographic" representation. Figuration is rather the attuning to the movement of *ki*, to the dynamic character of life, expressed in this case as ink traces on the white page.

Chinese and Japanese traditions make us think of another possible relationship between the "thing" and the "image", apart from any metaphysics or transcendence of the phenomenon to the sign that stands in its place. Every dualism between the event and its representation is useless and "out of order". The Western classical notion of *mimesis* (μίμησις: "imitation, representation") falls and comes out of order in this context. Painting does not mean imitating objects, persons, landscapes, giving the illusion of a new reality; image itself is already admitted to the realm of natural entities, it belongs to the same reality. Here we cannot find any dichotomy or tension opposing the physical to the intelligible world, the domain of appearance to that of essence. *Zō* is considered an emergent formation, it is the process of "emerging" in the realm of visibility, guided and fostered by brush strokes. It conveys the idea of a dynamic process that brings on the movements of a new developing situation, of a relational system.

In this context, the notion of "representation" loses its importance in the debates or researches about art. In Western history of art we can say that the image struggles with the phenomenon to attain true presence, showing to what extent the thing really "is" and placing the thing itself in its presence; but in ink paintings the logic is different. Here, every single brush stroke expresses a relational system. There is not an "inside" and an "outside", two detached domains, but an energetic process, flowing by the means of the painter's hand and brush in the work. When we speak about representation we think implicitly to the notion of presence (from the Latin word *praesentia*: *prae(s)ens*, the being that is up there, in front of us). It is the presence that we must *re*-present to the eye and to the mind. In the Japanese tradition, true painting means rather going beyond the images' exteriority and being able to generate them as living forms. The painter's action brings to a new birth, and at the same time is a regeneration of the landscape in the artist's interior, and a regeneration of the artist in the landscape's dimension, in its rhythm and vital flux.

This frame brings us to a second crucial issue: the *body* as something distinct, but not separated, from the inner or invisible dimension (be it called soul, spirit, heart, or mind). So, the somatic (or "soma-aesthetic") domain is another important field of comparison and research, to cross different aspects, perspectives, and insights, from the Eastern and the Western extremes. The binomial word *shinjin* 身心 – its striking originality occurs in Eihei Dōgen's *Genjōkōan* 現成公案 – is very interesting and almost shocking, for a Western reader. In fact, it reveals the non-separation of the two realms, or substances, as they are usually conceived in the West after the vulgarization of Descartes' philosophy and his classical distinction of *res cogitans* and *res extensa*. Nonetheless, due to the twentieth-century phenomenological attitude, some passages or doorways have been enhanced. The follwing quotation, by Merleau-Ponty, testifies to a possibility of dialogue:

> Whether we are concerned with my body, the natural world, the past, birth or death, the question is always how I can be open to phenomena which transcend me, and which nevertheless exist only to the extent that I take them up and live them; *how the presence to myself (*Urpräsenz*) which establishes my own limits and conditions every alien presence is at the same time depresentation (*Entgegenwärtigung*) and throws me outside myself.*[6]

It is not by chance that one of the chapters in the book written by Yuasa Yasuo on *The Body* deals precisely with phenomenology, and with Merleau-Ponty's fruitful insights:

> For Merleau-Ponty the important issue was not finding some compromise for mind-matter dualism, but clarifying the condition in which the for-itself (*pour soi*) is incarnated in the bodily in-itself (*en soi*),

6 Maurice Merleau-Ponty, *Phenomenology of Perception* (London: Routledge & Kegan Paul, 1962), p. 381.

> that is, clarifying the concrete mechanism of a human subject's existence as a being-in-the-world.[7]

A couple of pages before, Yuasa had stated that "in the Japanese language, such expressions as 'learning with the body' and 'the body learns' are often used with regard to the skills and techniques acquired through repetitious training".[8] So, a Japanese attitude that comes up and reveals itself through language and idiomatic expressions finds a counterpart in a French philosopher's thought, and that convergence conveys new meanings and a mutual clarification or fecundation. In the field of art practice, we could also summon an excerpt by the calligrapher Morita Shiryū (1912-1998), a perfect example of communication and dialogue among art, philosophy, and poetic prose, in which different concepts resound – from the classical aesthetic notions of ink and brush to the Nishidian concept of *basho* 場所, to the typically Western term "I":

> Because there is no self by itself and no brush by itself, no relationship comes about between some prior "me" and some prior "brush". Rather, we must say that what exists is a whole we may call "me and my brush". The one, inseparable whole lives here and now, and that is the very substance of my being a calligrapher here and now. Let us call this single totality *place*. [...] In the sense that I and my brush are born in a place and that a place gives birth to us. [...] In the unity of the place, I and the brush are one. As a calligrapher I transcend myself and am released from myself.[9]

Not only an intellectual knowledge is necessary, but a sort of bodily understanding. Again, the Japanese language gives to us a perfect hint with the word *taitoku* 体得, "to get (*toku*) by the

---

7 Yasuo Yuasa, *The Body. Toward an Eastern Mind-Body Theory* (Albany: State University of New York Press, 1987), p. 169. See also Gereon Kopf, 'Merleau-pontean body and the buddhist theory of five *skandhas*: Yasuo Yuasa's philosophy of the body', in Jin Y. Park & Gereon Kopf (ed. by), *Merleau-Ponty and Buddhism* (Lanham: Lexington Books, 2009), pp. 59-64.

8 Yasuo Yuasa, *The Body*, cit., p. 166.

9 Morita Shiryū 森田子龍, 'Sho to chūshōkaiga' [Calligraphy and Abstract Painting] 「書と抽象絵画」, in James W. Heisig, Thomas P. Kasulis, John C. Maraldo, *Japanese Philosophy. A Sourcebook* (Honolulu: University of Hawai'i Press, 2011), pp. 1200-1202.

body (*tai*)". This binomial term is close to other words, like *rikai* 理解, or *etoku* 会得: they all generally mean "understanding", but *taitoku* emphasizes the presence and role of our body in our uptake of the world.[10] It is like when you are surrounded by water, while you are swimming: you get used to a different gravity and to unusual movements, and at the same time you learn to be in the world in a different way, you learn a new posture or attitude, and unprecedented gestures. You get accustomed to your own body, and you re-discover yourself. In this sense, artworks are a sort of "diving sites", by which we experience an enterprise of de-coincidence, in the way François Jullien explains this notion.[11] De-coinciding means to open a "gap" (but the French term *écart* is more effectve, in this context) with respect to a congruity that does not concede any further initiative; it means to get out of a fulfilled perspective, out of an order that inhibits any new solution and, finally, sterilizes by an excess of coincidence, adequation, or adaptation.

We could go further, claiming that a core issue at the basis of this enterprise of a cultural translation goes around the experience of visibility, or the relation between the visible, invisible, and visibility itself. In the West, *theory* (from the Greek verb *theorò*, "I see") is indeed a crucial form of practice since ancient philosophy. The original move by Plato, who distinguished the sensible vision of the eye and the body from the metaphysical vision of the mind or soul, is still at work in the modern scientific revolution.[12] In the Chinese and Japanese languages, the verb *jian*/*miru* 見 ("to see") and also the term *guan*/*kan* 観 ("to see deeply, to contemplate") have often been used to grasp – or to get in touch with – what lies beyond the visible forms, but with

10 See also the important work by Kitarō Nishida, *Shisaku to taiken*: not only "Thought and experience", but more insightfully "thought and *embodied* experience". See Kitarō Nishida 西田幾多郎, *Shisaku to taiken* [Thought and Embodied Experience] 『思索と体験』, in *Nishida Kitarō Zenshū* 西田幾多郎全集 (Tokyo: Iwanami shoten, 2002-2009), vol. I, pp. 161-337.

11 See François Jullien, *Dé-coïncidence: D'où viennent l'art et l'existence* (Paris: Grasset, 2017).

12 On this crucial topic, see Carlo Sini, *Filosofia teoretica* (Milano: Jaca Book, 2018), pp. 10-17.

no ontological separation between the so-called (in the West) physical and metaphysical worlds. Anyway, the three dimensions of the visible, invisible, and visibility cannot be thought or inquired as three different "things", substances, or objects that stand in front of us. As Merleau-Ponty underlined in his analysis, an "absolute vision" takes place when the roles between the artist and the visible are reversed[13], and the represented objects appear as iridescent processes. When an image can give the impression of coming "from me, and yet from beyond me and over me",[14] thus a work of art can reveal itself as an *intensification of a space-time*, of a gesture, and a vision. A work of art is not only a form, not only an event: a form and an event take place at the same time.

In attempting to give way to the source of visibility, by the means of a visible form/event, we can also experience a sort of "conversion" of the gaze. In ink painting (*sumie* 墨絵), we are not simply standing in front of an image, we find ourselves *in* the painting, plunged into it, integrated with it. This is the great insight of traditional landscape painting, where the invisible becomes "sensible", and you feel a respirational reversibility by the diffused luminescence and the transition from the physical dimension to the spiritual one, back and forth. In calligraphy and painting, brush strokes clearly exhibit the character of gesture, carrying the trace of the original movement that generated it, bearing its memory. The calligrapher or painter abandons (a part of) his or her psychological self in order to give space to a play between background and figures. The drawn image is the tentative result of a single touch, which weaves into the visible the intention and the senses of sight and touch.

The picture, however, is not simply a "thing", it is rather the name we give to a meeting that happens, to a mode of relation to the world. That particular image that you objectify on a surface is for us a sort of *metaxy* (μεταξύ: "in-between", "middle",

13 See Maurice Merleau-Ponty, *The Primacy of Perception* (Evanston: Northwestern University Press, 1964), pp. 167-169.

14 See Martin Heidegger, *Being and Time* (New York: Harper and Row, 1962), p. 320.

"mediation") an intermediary or mediating dimension that stretches out toward the subject and the world at the same time. It keeps them connected and it belongs to both of them; it shows that they are never disjointed, even if they are distinguished. The creation of the work is the upcoming of this reflection, its turning into experience; it is the movement – that coagulates in an object – that the world makes in itself, a sort of self-drawing. Subject and image are not external to the world, they are peculiar modes of it.

Every stroke implies what escapes the gaze, what has been removed. It is the result of an attentive moment that once took place, it is the record of an event you can reactivate if your eye turns on it. It wakes up again and repeats itself, but always differently – there is never an identical repetition, there is rather a continuous twisting of the same. From this sameness, the renewal of perception and its senses are fostered. We could say that there is a form of *askesis* (ἄσκησις, that could be translated into *shūgyō* 修行) that is, discipline, effort, training: a continuous renewal, a never exhausting exercise of the line.

A thread can be followed between European mysticism and Japanese philosophical and religious insights, assuming that what gives rise to the visible is not visible in itself. On this basis, Plato can be put in dialogue with Zhuangzi, or Heidegger with Nishida.[15] It is no-*thing*, it is *not a thing* – or a ground, an ontological substance; it goes beyond, or stays below, the opposition between transcendence and immanence.

> The Nothing on which even blandness pivots does have something transcendent about it, though not to the exclusion of immanence, especially not of total immanence. Yet such *total* immanence transcends itself and can no longer be adequately conceptualized as only or exclusively 'immanence'. The idea of absolute transcendence cannot be excluded from it either. Immanence as such absolutely transcends every possible

15 See for instance Plato, *Republic*, 507d-508d; Zhuangzi, § 2; Martin Heidegger, *The Essence of Truth: On Plato's Cave Allegory and Theaetetus* (London: Bloomsbury, 2013); Kitarō Nishida, *Hataraku mono kara miru mono e* [From the Actor to the Seer] 『働くものから見るものへ』, in *Nishida Kitarō Zenshū*, cit., vol. IV.

> conception of it. *Total* immanence is without confines and involves or contaminates everything, transcending all limits.[16]

As we have already seen, we can thus learn to loosen the fixation about "representation". In the Western history of art, generally speaking, the image struggles with the phenomenon to attain true presence, but in Japanese ink paintings every single brush stroke expresses a relational system. There is not an "inside" and an "outside", two detached domains, but an energetic process, flowing by the means of the painter's hand and brush in the work. When we speak about representation, it is the presence that we must *re*-present to the eye and to the mind. "Representing" means also bringing to a new presence what was concealed, hidden, or forgotten. The substance (*ousia* οὐσία) should be taken in presence (*parousia* πᾰρουσίᾱ) in order to feel and live the actual living dimension of Being. We cannot understand the most part of Western art without these links between ontology, theology and aesthetics. But if we read some lines by one of the most important texts in the Chinese pictorial tradition, the *Huayulu* 画語録 (*Treatise on Painting*) by Shitao (1642-1708), we can find precious hints to get closer to the theory of image and art that belongs to East-Asian culture:

> The inner nature of landscape is caught by getting the universe's intimate structure. Possessing the techniques of brush and ink, one realizes the external aspects of landscape. […] The landscape expresses the form and tensions of the whole universe. […] Before I was fifty, I was not generated in the landscape. It is not to say that I treated landscape as a meaningless thing, but I let it as an independent thing, on its own. Now the landscape speaks by myself, it is expressed by me. It is generated by me, just like I am generated by the landscape.[17]

The symbolic aspect of every artistic endeavour consists in the dissolution of the imaginary identity of the subject and the object as well. This uncovers, properly, a transformation or passage

16 William Franke, 'All or Nothing? Nature in Chinese Thought and the Apophatic Occident', in *Comparative Philosophy*, 5-2 (2014), pp. 16-17.

17 Han Linde, *Shitao yu 'Huayulu' yanjiu* 石濤畫語錄研究 (Nanjing: Meishu Chubanshe, 2000), § 8, p. 200 (my translation).

from an aesthetical concern to an ethical one. Each ink stroke can also be figured out as a "threshold"; each painting can be a shadow line that allows you to know in an unexpected way a fragment of the world, a fragment of yourself; each time it can produce a metamorphosis of the gaze. During an artistic and aesthetic experience, you undergo the experience of a shattering of all objectifications and reifications of the self, something that comes from beyond my own subjectivity.

It is the internal vibration of the picture that makes it unavailable to any determination of possession or knowledge. In ink painting, an attempt at a progressive purification and decantation is fostered – it is a sort of liberation from stereotypes, means and techniques that are taken for granted. The result is a new attention to the vital breath that animates the act of painting, in order to get in touch with what emerges from the paper. One tries to be a receptive place for the *sign* of that event, of that apparition. In fact, you can contemplate a poetic landscape, but you cannot stare at it. You must learn to move in it, along with it, and feel it with all your senses, in order to capture a "figuration over the figuration" (in a classical Chinese expression: *xiangwai zhi xiang* 象外之象). The nature of landscape is as elusive as that of the vapor rising from the fields in the summer heat; you can contemplate the vapor, and the impalpable atmosphere, but you cannot fix it, because it is not an object you can catch.

As an empty, or nearly-empty image, it can be the occasion of the gaze's movement – being kept in suspension, the gaze stays alive. Beyond figuration lies the origin of every figure. As its origin or source, it never becomes a figure in itself. It is as the pure light that the eye cannot see, that the hand does not grasp; the light which allows all the other things to be seen and held. It is necessary that eye and hand try to shape the background and figures stemming out of it, so that they are traces leading to the source of visibility. In this perspective, the visible – what is offered to the gaze: the picture, the canvas, the paper and the traces that appear there – works as a screen. It is the screen on which the eye can notice that it cannot see directly the source of the visible, because as soon as it grasps some-*thing* to see, it turns this "some*thing*" into an object, and loses what it was looking for. *The visible is a screen, that reveals by hiding what lies beyond the visible itself.*

At the same time, the exercise of seeing manifests the fact that every entity is "empty", both spatially – it has no autonomous, substantial nature but always exists in relation to something other than it; it is always penetrated and permeated by that which surrounds it – and temporally – every physical or mental entity is impermanent, transitory. The world is structured as an infinite network of interdependent, non-self-sufficient elements. And this "vacuity of essence" is not a matter of theory, but a question of experience. Breathing, in its alternation between fullness and emptiness, is the prime instrument of meditation in bringing the practitioner closer to the substanceless and impermanent dimension of being. Voidness is an infinite condition of possibility for the occurrence of any phenomenon, any physical, psychological, or metaphysical manifestation which, like a wave, rises from the great ocean and returns to it.

Art can be one of the different ways of coming into contact with the experience of the void, of making it an operating principle. There is no longer a subject who performs the work; the work occurs, gratuitously, giving a "sensible body" to the circulation of energy and interrelations. It is precisely the void that allows the circulation of the vital breath, the energetic exchange between subject and object, which are discovered to be one – not separate – in the process of generation and dissolution, inspiration-exhalation emersion-immersion against the backdrop that animates and accommodates them. At the same time, however, the backdrop exists only in virtue of the phenomena played out against it. The backdrop is not a metaphysical foundation that exists *before* and *beyond* things, bodies, or events: backdrop and phenomena are one. The void is a phenomenological *here-and-now*, and can be made distinct from phenomena only by the intellect's need to discern; in terms of processes it can never be separated or detached from them. Art is a function of the void: the power and efficacy of the void are brought back via figuration. The fullness emerges from the void while revealing it by contrast. It shows the efficacy of the void the same way that the void contains the potentials for fullness, without there being a splitting of planes – here the visible, the manifest, the tangible; there the latent, the extrasensory. The variation of fullness and emptiness confers dynamism and preserves the invisible within the visible; it is the only thing that can render the figuration in its totality.

The unproductive nature of art and its untimeliness make it so necessary. Today's art market integrates it by inscribing it into the orbit of economic value, while the repeated gesture that realizes it extracts art from any monetary evaluation. The more a work of art is rooted in an age, or in an existence, and influences it, the more it is eccentric to the dynamics of production and fruition; it shows that there is something exceeding, something that does not fit into the logic of production, exchange, or usability. In this sense, the work of art goes beyond the idea of a linear progression of time, with an absolute beginning and a final destination, and with a necessary journey. A work of art is carried out in time and it translates it into space, but it is not limited to it. It is a way to resist and cope with the days, with the hours, without being inscribed in a chronological succession of moments.

A work of art, at every latitude on the Earth, is like a promise that constantly delays its fulfillment. The promise "is kept" because it continues to be pronounced and repeated in every brushstroke – as a fishing hook repeatedly is thrown into water: what really matters is throwing the hook, more than the likelihood of catching the fish. That is the reason why art requires extreme fidelity, the simple trust in its gesture. Unlike the psychological ego, art and the self that plunge in it do not ask for any compensation – hence the tension that one often feels. You feel it, however, when you are not deeply immersed in the work. In the particular act that tradition generally defines as "artistic activity" you find a unique kind of knowledge, and a particular type of practice – such as a form of ethics. Through the work of art, the world is not revealed as a set of things to be manipulated; it appears as a pure befalling. Through the experience of the figure emerging from the paper or canvas, we experience the world as pure befalling, where new forms continuously interweave with each other.

The figure emerges from the sheet of paper, from the canvas, and at the same time it emerges from the world. Vice versa, the world appears and is configured in each figure and single gesture. It is a circular movement: the world and the sign spring up together. Observing the world, and translating this observation in drawing or painting, you detach and approach the existing things, which are regained and re-discovered in an unexpected way. So, the relationship with the world is changed, the boundaries of disciplines such as aesthetics and ethics are left apart and exceeded. The line, the stroke that is traced by the pencil, by the brush, by one's fingers, or the whole body witnesses a form of stubbornness, or obstinacy. It is not only a form of resistance to the virtual or digital image, to the lines that avoid dependency from the hand. It is a more hidden resistance to the kaleidoscope of colours and shapes that cross the visual field without carving and influencing it; it is a setback that diffracts time: on the one hand it imposes a slowing down, a disposition to patience, in order to observe and follow the line on the surface; on the other hand it ushers the imminence of a possible discovery, it prepares to waiting without any immediate visible solution.

It is as if art was nothing but a way to enhance the quality of our own time, not wasting it, but without the claim of retaining it. Starting to work on a new painting does not depend on a calculation, or on an intellectual choice. Immersing in the background shows the concurrence of two opposite movements: a proximity and a distancing, a contact and a separation. A work of art is a form of self-education to keep your feeling alive, otherwise it could become dull and then extinguished – along with the question that once gave rise to the work of art, to your path in life, starting from a gaze that was not initiated by your eyes, but it came to meet them. It is not by balancing forms that you can abolish the distance, or you can find a final answer. The work of art is a continuous reactivation of a basic, original question. It is a slow and silent learning to stay in that question, proposing it again and again, creating in this way a possible access to life.

So, the painter's task is not a representation of forms. The task is enhancing the image's energy, making the observer feel the *ki* in the image. Shitao underlines this issue many times: the inner accord is the most important, far beyond the imitation of the external shape. True "similarity" with the living character of nature can be attained only by letting go of the worry for the external figuration. The true, the great, the wonderful image must be an effective image, carrying on the spiritual dimension, vibrating with nature itself. It is involved in a different modality of seeing. What really counts is a participating look, that embraces and is embraced at the same time by what lies beyond the onlooker, detaching him from the usual subject-object distinction. The onlooker and the looked, subjectivity and environment, are elements inscribed one in each other; their abstract division and separation is only formal, it comes from the analytical necessity of the language. But the deeper seeing also becomes a hearing, a touching, a form of contemplation, in resonance with the environment; and the onlooker is in his turn looked at, and heard, and touched, embraced in the same environment in which his gaze wanders, moves, circulates – just like the *ki*. The gaze itself won't be no more a straightforward optical ray, but changes and transforms into a breathing, energetic circulation. The true act of seeing means to recognize themselves *one* with what we see, parts of the whole, and not external elements, apart from the scene. The image should foster an experience of exploration and familiarization, or setting: by the means of the image we can enter the landscape, becoming one with it and with all that encompasses us, finding our place. Landscape and painter, subject and object, I and thou penetrate each other, complete each other. This modality of experience of the world shows that looking at images, in particular through artistic expression and the creative movement it conveys, shows that the landscape is not something to represent, but rather a way to see.

The neutral, detached, scientific gaze will be replaced by a form of meditation, an inner disposition, or a sort of contemplation. We do not have to stare, exhausting our eyes, in order to capture the forms that nature offers to perception; but we have to "listen" to the landscape, feeling with our *kokoro* 心 (heart/mind/soul/

emotion) vibrating with it. By this faculty, man can place himself in a resonating disposition, in which perception happens not only by the physical senses but also through a work of introspection. A great painter is thus able to paint an accomplished landscape even without seeing it. Expressing on paper the image of a stone, of a mountain, of a pond is important as far as re-creating the vital character, after having absorbed and transformed its qualities in his own inner dimension. Through the attention and accord with the inner structure (*ri* 理) of what is seen, the painter can meet and give a figuration to the "formless form" full of energy and breath. Pure attention is impersonal: only by this kind of attention and care for the world will the onlooker be able to go beyond the attachment to the form, to find in images the doorstep to link visible and invisible, art and morality, nature and ethics.

Alberto Giacomelli[1]

KIRE-TSUZUKI AND *SHŌJI*

A Pictorial Analysis of the "Flower" as Image of Dis/Continuity between Life and Death

1. Kire-tsuzuki, geidō *and* dao

The following essay will focus on the meeting points between image and philosophy in Japanese thought starting from the work of Ōhashi Ryōsuke *Kire. The beauty in Japan.*[2] In particular we will try and propose a reflection on the subject *kire-tsuzuki* (切れ・つづき) through an iconographic and symbolical journey based on the image of Japanese flowers. We will also attempt to put the notion of *kire-tsuzuki* in connection with some western pictorial experiences (van Gogh and Rembrandt), starting from the remarks of Martin Heidegger and Georg Simmel.

The Japanese word *kire* as a verb means "to cut" or "to separate". As a noun *kire* means "cutting" or a "cut", a "piece cut off", a "slice", a "section" or a "segment". As an adjective, *kire* can today be used in the sense of "racy", "sleek", "dashing", "edged" or "elegant" to characterise, for example, a car, a wine or a person.[3] The term *kire*, however, does not only refer to a static quality but also to a dynamic artistic action and an aesthetic *practice*: the "concept" or "aesthetic category" of *kire*

---

1 University of Padova

2 Ōhashi Ryōsuke 大橋良介 *Kire no kōzō: nihonbi to gendai sekai* [*The structure of Kire: Japanese beauty and contemporary world*] 『「切れ」の構造：日本美と現代世界』 (Tōkyō: Chūōkōronsha, 1986). In this paper we will refer to the recent Italian version of the text (Ōhashi Ryōsuke, *Kire: il bello in Giappone*. [Milano: Mimesis, 2017], from now on: K). The Italian translation was based on the German version of the Japanese original text (Ōhashi Ryōsuke, *Kire. Das Schöne in Japan*. [Paderborn: Wilhelm Fink, 2014]. The English translations are mine.

3 See Simon Frisch, 'The Aesthetics of Flow and Cut in the Way of Film: Towards Transnational Transfers of East Asian Concepts to Western Film Theory', in *Arts*, 8 (2019), p. 3.

is in fact primarily a procedure expressed in the peculiar action of cutting away and severing. This practice is contained in the expression *kire-tsuzuki* literally: "to cut and continue", but also "cut-continuum" or "dis/continuity". This expression describes a peculiar dynamic between nature and artistic figuration. As Ōhashi points out, the intervention of *kire* "cuts away" the spontaneous "naturalness" given to the object "in such a way that its original naturalness, that is, interior and intimate naturalness, is made visible and brought to light".[4] "This act of liberating things from their natural ambience", claims Frisch, "is considered to be a process of enlivenment or vivification. A specific way of cutting gives birth to things in a new way of being, which is considered essential. The concept of *kire* literally implies an act or process of 'bringing something to life', which can only be roughly captured by the translations used here".[5]

The most immediate example of *kire*'s action is the image of the flower in *ikebana* compositions. It is not a matter of tearing the flower away from its natural context and destining it to death, but of bringing out the flower's deepest and most essential naturalness.[6] The term *ikebana* (生け花) literally means "bring the flower to life".[7] It is an art (芸道, *geidō*) precisely because natural life is "cut off". As in the case of the compositions of the master Shuhō Sano (佐野珠寳), flowers in *ikebana* are considered a symbol of the moment, also called "appreciation of time".[8]

---

4 K, pp. 16 and 238.

5 Simon Frisch, 'The Aesthetics of Flow and Cut in the Way of Film', cit., p. 3.

6 See K, pp. 87-88; Nishitani Keiji 西谷啓治, 'Ikebana. *Über die reine japanische Kunst*', in *Philosophisches Jahrbuch*, 98-2 (1991), pp. 314-320.

7 K, p. 87.

8 Regarding the collaboration between Ōhashi Ryōsuke and Sano Shuhō see Ōhashi Ryōsuke-Shuhō, *Kashin no kokoro. Hana to Zen* [*The Flower Message. Flower and Zen*] 『花信のこころ一花と禅』(Kyōto: Shōwadō 昭和堂, 2009). "The master Shuhō", writes Ōhashi, looked like a person in whom the flower spirit was hiding to let the artist put the flowers. Her book *Ippon-sō* ("The One Blade of Grass" 『一本草』 [Tōkyō: Tokuma shoten 徳間書店, 2016]) looks like this spirit expressed itself through the mouth of Shuhō". Ōhashi Ryōsuke *Der Philosophenweg in Kyōto. Eine Entdeckungsreise durch die japanische Ästhetik* (Alber: Freiburg-München, 2019), pp. 12, 71-72. See also Stella Coe, *Ikebana : A practical and philosophical guide to Japanese flower arrangement* (London: Century, 1984); Josiah Conder, *The flowers*

With their finite and mutable nature, flowers – as we will see with cherry blossoms – are also a symbol of change, which is described as *mujō* (無常), the Buddhist term for impermanence. In Buddhism, the expression *mujō* indicates the mutable nature of all phenomena and experiences: all things are without substance and subject to change. This awareness, however, is not a reason for nihilistic despair, but rather encourages us to capture a particular beauty in instability and imperfection. For this reason the fragility and delicacy of the flower recalls Buddhist impermanence as an appreciation of the ephemeral. The appreciation of change and of the unavoidable transience of life, expressed, for example, in the contemplation of cherry blossoms, is also linked to the expression *mono no aware* (物の哀れ). This key term in Japanese culture essentially refers to the "pathos" (*aware*) of "things" (*mono*) resulting from their transience, often associated with a poignant feeling of fleetingness. It is a beautiful sadness in the passing of lives and objects, like the evanescence of cherry blossoms or like the red colour of autumn leaves as they are about to fall.

Unlike flowers, trees, especially evergreen trees such as a pine or a cedar, are considered as symbols of eternity. So, if flowers express impermanence, evergreen trees are a symbol of the eternity of *shinnyo* (真如), the eternal-dynamic nature of all things, referring to Buddhism.[9] As a combination of flowers and tree elements, *ikebana* can be considered as a scenic description and a symbol of the dis/continuity (*kire-tsuzuki*) between moment and eternity, change and immutability.

The process of *kire-tsuzuki* differs both from the sphere of natural spontaneity and from the sphere of simple manufacture of objects (ποίησις, *póiesis*). It is an aesthetic experience that

---

of Japan and the art of floral arrangement (Tokyo: Kodansha International, 2004 [Original work published 1891]).

9 The expression *shinnyo* refers in particular to the Buddhist Shinnyo-en school (真如苑, Borderless Garden of Truth). For both Zen and Shinnyo-en Buddhism, eternity does not mean perfect, timeless fixity, that is, it does not mean an absolute state removed from the flow of becoming, but it does mean eternal becoming, change without beginning and without end. See Giangiorgio Pasqualotto, *Dieci lezioni sul Buddhismo* (Venezia: Marsilio, 2008), pp. 138-139.

does not manipulate and debase nature, but reveals its deep essence through art.

Kire-tsuzuki means therefore that there is a "transition" (移り渉り, *utsuri watari*) between art and nature, a transition that is neither simply continuity (連続, *renzoku*), nor simply discontinuous "cut off" (*kire*). Japanese beauty is closely linked to this dynamic: the mastery of art consists in "cutting" nature not to exclude or surpass it, but to enhance it in its purest form. Through art, the deepest and most intimate beauty of nature comes to light. The expression "cut-continuum" thus indicates the paradoxical coexistence of transition and break permeating the Japanese concept of beauty in the highest sense of the word.[10]

As well known, one of the crucial concepts of Western aesthetic is *mimesis* (μίμησις), which includes "imitation", "similarity", "illusion" and "representation" among its various meanings.

The philosophical debate on the notion of *mimesis* in the artistic field is based, starting from Aristophanes and Plato, on the ontological difference between sensitive form and supersensitive model.[11] As imitator (*mimetés*, μιμητής), the artist is, for Plato, a liar, a simulator, an actor in the worst sense of *hypocrites* (ὑποκριτής). Art, according to Plato, is what intoxicates souls and distances them from the truth. Even if this radical separation between what appears (the phenomenon, φαινόμενον) and what is essential (the idea, ἰδέα) will be denied by Aristotle,[12] however, the Platonic conception of art as the lowest simulation of a true essence will constitute a leitmotif destined to permeate much of the Christian European aesthetic reflection.

In the Japanese context conventionally enclosed between the

---

10 In his book *Kire. The Beauty in Japan*, Ōhashi never speaks explicitly of *utsuri watari*. On the comparison of this expression with the notion of *kire-tsuzuki* see A. Giacomelli, *Übergänge und Übersetzungen. Kire-tsuzuki als «Schnitt-Kontinuum» zwischen Kunst und Natur*, in *Übergänge – Transitions – 移り渉り: Crossing the Boundaries in Japanese Philosophy*, ed. by Leon Krings, Francesca Greco, Yukiko Kuwayama (Nagoya: Chisokudō 2021), pp. 51-79.

11 See Cfr. Aristophanes, *Thesm.*, vv. 154-156; Plato, *Resp.*, III, 393d-394d, X, 596b-607b.

12 Aristotle, *Poet.*, 1447a 14-18.

Kamakura era (鎌倉時代, 1185-1333) and the Edo era (江戸時代, 1615-1867) there is either an univocal approach to truth, nor an ideal-essential model which art can imitate and falsifie: Art is an exercise of life, and therefore a "way" (道, *dō*) as a way of life.[13]

To understand some important differences between one European conception of art (which has its roots in Greece and in the idea of *mimesis*) and a Japanese one (which has its roots in China in the idea of *dō*), it is important to underline that in the denomination of traditional "artistic practices" (芸道, *geidō*) in Japan, such as *chadō* (茶道, way of tea), *kadō* (華道, way of flowers), *kodō* (香道,way of perfumes) *shodō* (書道, way of calligraphic writing) the suffix *-dō* indicates a relation to Chinese Daoism. The same suffix occurs in "martial arts or practices" (武道, *budō*) such as *jūdō* (柔道, gentle way), *kyudō* (弓道, way of archery), *kendō* (剣道, sword way).

The Chinese cosmic model, unlike the Western metaphysical-platonic conception, is not based on the opposition between original and copy, true and false, over-sensitive and sensitive. The *dao* (道) is the expression of a polar and a-dual dynamic of the cosmos, in which all hierarchy between the *forma-éidos* and the *simulacrum-éidolon* disappears, while what remains active is the exchangeable and fluid relationship of the elements. Concerning Japanese art, Frisch notes: "The expression *geidō* has not to do with lifelike effects. The aspect of vivification in *geidō* must not be understood as an 'as if…'; rather, it is considered a real instance of vivification – a new and different kind of life and reality. The contrast between 'real' and 'aesthetic' or 'real' and 'artificial' is not crucial. Pygmalion's Galatea is the opposite of *geidō*".[14]

The concept of *kire-tsuzuki* developed by Ōhashi is intrinsically linked to the notion of the way (*dō* or *dao*): the sense of *kire*, writes Ōhashi, "is to 'cut out' the daily naturalness, so that it reappears

13 See H.E. Davey, *The Japanese way of the artist* (Berkeley, CA: Stone Bridge Press, 2007).

14 See Simon Frisch, 'The Aesthetics of Flow and Cut in the Way of Film', cit., p. 3. The reference is obviously to the sculptor Pygmalion, who had modelled a naked ivory female statue with which he had madly fallen in love. On the

in a deeper form. This 'cutting out' is the authentic 'mastery'. The so-called 'art way' (芸道, *geidō*) of traditional Japanese art forms is the way in which naturalness gets a new life through *kire*".[15] This link between "cut-continuum" or "dis/continuity" (*kire-tsuzuki*), the "art way" (*geidō*) and the Chinese notion of *dao* allows to conceive art and nature not as rigidly separated and opposed, but as symbolically united and complementary. The polarity between art and nature is not static, contrastive and dualistic, but dynamic, dialectical and circular. Traditional Japanese art, and in particular the practise of *kire-tsuzuki*, therefore evokes the well-known structure of the *dao*, where *yin* (陰) and *yang* (陽) establish a relationship of dis/continuity between them. The black-negative principle (night, darkness, technique) and the white-positive principle (day, light, nature), fit symbiotically into each other. Art and nature maintain their own peculiarities and yet they assert themselves only in their mutual kinetic relationship. In the *dao* we can recognize the "separation" of *kire*, and at the same time the "continuity" of the elements: "the cut is an end and a beginning" at the same time.[16] Each element therefore contains within itself the generating nucleus of its opposite, and the work of art does not betray any "truth", but rather is involved in a dynamic circulation of energy and "vital force" (*qi* 氣) just like any other event.

After having highlighted the deep affinity between the dis/continuous action of *kire-tzuzuki*, the Japanese "way of art" and the polar dynamics of the Chinese *dao*, we aim to show how the practice of *kire* works in the context of pictorial images of flowers.

---

occasion of the ritual feasts in honour of Aphrodite, Pygmalion went to the temple of the goddess and begged her to fill the gap between art and reality and to give him in marriage the sculpture created with his hands making it a human creature (see Ovid, *Metamorph.*, X, vv. 243-297). Compared to the passionate attachment to the single and unrepeatable piece of work symbolized by Pygmalion, the *dō* or *dao* as *flow* is the way that teaches to focus on the process of creation, on the internalization of practice.

15 K, p. 35.

16 See Simon Frisch, 'The Aesthetics of Flow and Cut in the Way of Film', cit., p. 3.

2. *"Cherry blossoms" by Kyūzō and the "genuine flower" of* nō *by Zeami*

As shown by Ōhashi, in the field of pictorial images the notion of *kire* is mostly linked to that of *shōji* (生死).[17] The spiritual disposition of *shōji*, composed of the two characters that stand for "life" (生) and "death" (死), simultaneously expresses the dis/continuity, the polar unity and the incessant circularity of life and death that is peculiar to Daoism and Buddhism. Just as art and nature, so life and death are not understood to be separate from each other. Particularly significant to explain the expression *shōji* as a "cut-continuity" of life and death is the work *Cherry blossoms* (『桜図』) which was initially attributed to Hesegawa Tōhaku (長谷川等伯, 1539-1610, 桃山時代, Momoyama period, 1568-1615) but today is considered a work of his son Hasegawa Kyūzō (長谷川久蔵, 1568-93).[18]

Cherry blossoms by Kyūzō is a painting on a golden background on sliding doors belonging to the category of *shōhekiga* (障壁画, drawings on dividers).[19] In the rich Japanese floral language (花言葉 *Hanakotoba*)[20] the ever-popular *sakura* (桜) symbolize the volatility, transience and ephemeral brevity of life. Japanese interest in cherry blossom as a theme for poetry and painting developed during the Heian period (平安時代, 794-1185). At that time, along with the evolution of a native artistic sensibility heavily influenced by the passing seasons, the flowers gained

17 See K, pp. 107; 254.

18 Doi Tsugiyoshi 土井次義, *Hasegawa Tōhaku kenkyū* [Hasegawa Tōhaku Study] 『長谷川等伯研究』 (Tōkyō: Kōdansha 講談社, 1977); Doi Tsugiyoshi, *Decorative Painting, The Heibonsha Survey of Japanese Art*, Volume 14, (New York-Tokyo: Heibonsha 平凡社, 1977), pp. 18, 90-91,106-107; Takeda Tsuneo 武田恒夫, Kano Hiroyuki 狩野博幸 (ed. by), *Kachōga no sekai* [The World of Bird-and-Flower] 『花鳥画の世界』 (Tokyo: Gakken 学研, 1982), pp. 121-123, 128.

19 In particular the style of the painting is called *kinpekishōhekiga* (金碧障壁画, painting executed on dividing panels or walls on a gold background). See K, p. 111.

20 Gustie Luise Herrigel, *Zen in the art of flower arrangement. An introduction to the spirit of the Japanese art of flower arrangement* (transl. by R.F.C. Hull, London: Souvenir Press, 1999 [Original work published 1958]).

their place as one of the main symbols of spring. Since the Heian period, the cherry blossom has been revered by the Japanese, for its natural beauty and grace, its brief blossoming period and the fragility of its delicate flowers. Precisely the transitory nature of the flower has often been associated with mortality.[21] What Ōhashi emphasizes in the description of Kyūzō's work is the fact that the myriad of flowers that bloom from the cherry tree do not have a uniquely decorative value, linked to the beauty of spring. The beauty of the flowers subtends a gloomy and mournful side: as if in the full bloom of life there was somehow already present the withering of death.

Figure 1 Hasegawa Kyūzō, *Cherry blossoms* (『桜図』)

The huge trunk of the cherry three rises upwards and overflows beyond the sliding door, meaning that it is "sharply separated and cut out" in an abrupt manner. The thin branches on both sides of the trunk hang down, touching it and separating from it. The painter cuts unnecessary parts and represents only the important ones. Each of the magnificent cherry blossoms appears to hover freely in space, yet their extraordinarily beautiful appearance possesses a "shade" (翳り, *kageri*), revealing the co-presence and the dis/continuity of life-death (*shōji*) in bloom.[22]

The *kire-tsuzuki* and the *shōji* appear when the "withering" (枯れ *kare*) of the flower can already be sensed in full blossoming.

21 Lee Khoon Choy, *Japan. Between Myth and Reality* (Singapore: World Scientific, 1995), p. 142.

22 See K, p. 108.

As Ōhashi points out, this dynamic was already present in the reflection on *nō* theatre by Zeami (世阿弥, ?1364-?1443). The titles of Zeami's theoretical works often contain the character indicating "flower" and "bloom" (花, *hana* or *ka*):[23] particularly in *Fūshikaden*, the art and physiognomy of the actor are described according to the metaphor of the flower. The "flower" of 12 and 13-year-old actors, writes Zeami, "is not the genuine flower",[24] since the "genuine flower" – namely the true craftsmanship – can only be achieved through a long refinement of the art-way. The "genuine flower" therefore is not the unripe flower of youth, but the mature flower of old age. The "flower" is not pure nature, but nature stylized in a form (型, *kata*) by means of mastery. The withering flower – which we could compare to *ikebana* – symbolizes the actor's old age. The actor of *nō*, in his relationship with death, or rather in his being essentially mortal, brings to light naturalness in its authentic essence. Again, through the *kire* nature is "cutted" by the "technical" intervention of man to obtain a new and deeper life. The beauty of the flower of old age contains in itself – as in the case of cherry blossoms – the blooming and fading, the dis/continuity of life and death. It is important to underline, in the light of these considerations, that the Chinese character that expresses "flower" (花) contains the sign indicating "transformation" (化). This last sign also means "to go beyond", "to expire", and therefore alludes to the transition and to the perception of the whole as transitory.

In *Cherry blossoms* of Kyūzō it is possible to recognize precisely that quality of withering which also characterizes the flower of Zeami. However, while in Zeami the withered flower (枯れた花, *kareta hana*) appears predominant in the form of

23 Zeami Motokiyo 世阿弥元清, *Kakyō* [A Mirror Held to the Flower] 『花鏡』; *Fūshikaden* [Teachings on Style and the Flower] 『風姿花伝』; *Shikadō* [The True Path to the Flower] 『至花道』; *Shūgyokutokka* [Finding Gems and Gaining the Flower] 『拾玉得花』; *Kashū no uchi nukigaki* [An Extract from Learning the Flower] 『花習内抜書』 (Princeton: Princeton University Press, 1984). See. K, pp. 29, 31-32.

24 Zeami Motokiyo, *Fūshikaden*, cit. in K, p. 31 (transl. by ours).

declined old age, in Kyūzō death is only hinted at and the beauty of the flowers remains in the foreground.

The condition of death is also symbolically reiterated by the fact that the trees are painted on the golden background, which is an unusual colour, in fact it is not really a colour, but rather a concentration of brightness that on one side symbolizes the richness, authority and power of the world; on the other side it is a glow that also adorns the world of gods. While gold expresses the glory of this world, it reflects both the power and shining of a world beyond. This double vision, that is the cut/continuity of real world and beyond, is further justified by the fact that the painting was commissioned by Governor Toyotomi Hideyoshi (豊臣秀吉, 1536-98) for the family temple in which his beloved son is buried.

Although the *Cherry blossom* painting does not explicitly represent Hideyoshi's mourning, the specific emotional tonality that permeates the work is for Ōhashi that of life and death.[25]

3. *The Tōhaku Maple, the grave of Queen Sōjun and the Red and White Plum Blossoms by Kōrin*

The theme of the dis/continuity between life and death is also clearly represented in the tree of the painting *Maple* (『楓図』) by Hesegawa Tōhaku. The trunk of the maple tree is even sturdier and knottier than that of the cherry tree. The foliage of the maple, which in autumn turns dark red and whose single leaves in Japan are particularly minute and delicate, contrasts with the strongness of the trunk. This trunk, however, as Ōhashi points out, is not only an expression of worldly life force.[26] The lespedeza flowers and white chrysanthemums around the trunk are premonitory signs of the sad winter season. If cherry blossoms are the image par excellence of spring, maple and chrysanthemum are typical autumn plants: Behind the thick

25 See K, p. 109.
26 See K, p. 109.

patch of autumn foliage represented in the painting, two further half-hidden trunks can be recognized. They create the effect of shadows (影, *kage*) behind the huge tree in the foreground. The shadows, the chrysanthemums, and the golden background similar to that of *Cherry blossoms* give the impression that an emotional tone of solemn death envelops this mighty tree. Again, in fact, the radiance of gold reflects the splendour and light of a world beyond. In addition, the autumn atmosphere created by the chrysanthemum flowers and maple leaves alludes to a slumbering nature. The mighty maple also seems to show Hideyoshi's power, but, at the same time, the fragility of life, as witnessed by the death of his favourite son.

Figure 2 Hesegawa Tōhaku, *Maple* (『楓図』)

The relationship of dis/continuity between life and death in the painting *Maple* emerges in a concrete way at Kyōto's Way of Philosophy (哲学の道, *tetsugaku-no-michi*). In particular, as Ōhashi observes, sometimes there are miraculous places and moments in which past lives return.[27] A special place on Kyōto's Way of Philosophy that has the power to correlate life and death is the grave of Queen Sōjun.[28] A large maple tree stands there, whose leaves turn a splendid colour in late autumn and whose branches hang down over the white wall. These leaves turn deep red in very late autumn, when the leaves of the other

27 See Ōhashi Ryōsuke, *Der Philosophenweg in Kyōto*, cit., p. 170 (transl. by ours).

28 Queen Sōjun's father was Prince Fushimi no miya Sadayuki 伏見宮貞敬 (1776-1841), while the mother was the daughter of Kanpaku 関白 (the highest

maple trees have almost fallen off. "In Kyōto", writes Ōhashi, "there are several places known for their maple leaves and also at Kyōto's Philosopher's walk there are many maple trees. But the splendour of the maple leaves at the grave of Queen Sōjun, with its contrast to the white wall, is simply incomparable. When I see these maple leaves, I can't help but connect them to the unknown and isolated Queen Sōjun who died in seclusion. It seems to me that the maple leaves express the posthumous luminescence of the Queen's life".[29]

The contrast between the red of the maple leaves and the white of the wall in the background may perhaps refer to that between the maple leaves of Tōhaku and the golden background. In both cases the beauty of natural life activates a peculiar relationship with time. The past is never dead and sharply separated (切れ) from the present, and death is not the opposite of life. *Kire-tsuzuki* expresses thus the interpenetration of the here and now (此岸, *shigan*) and of the beyond (彼岸, *higan*).

Figure 3
The grave of Queen Sōjun

ministerial rank) Ichijō Teruyoshi 一条輝良 (1756-1794). The "queen" (*joō* 女王) Sōjun, emphasizes Ōhashi, was not in fact a queen, but a lady of the highest level. See Ōhashi Ryōsuke, *Der Philosophenweg in Kyōto*, cit., pp. 79-80. "The Queen Sōjun had played an important role in the movement "Imperial Declaration on the Dissemination of the Great Teaching" (*Daikyō-senpu-undō* 大教宣布運動) started by the Meiji government. This was the political-religious measure authorized by the state to make Shintō the state religion". Ōhashi Ryōsuke, *Der Philosophenweg in Kyōto*, cit., p. 81.

29 Ōhashi Ryōsuke, *Der Philosophenweg in Kyōto*, cit., p. 170.

The unity of life and death manifests itself significantly in the painting *Red and White Plum Blossoms* (『紅白梅図』) by Ogata Kōrin (尾形光琳, 1658-1716). Between the two trees is depicted a river that at the same time unites and cuts – in the sense of *kire-tsuzuki* – the two parts of the painting. If we follow the lines of the river waves, we can see that they flow out of one vortex and then vanish into another. It seems as if in a certain way every single wave arises from one abyss and vanishes into another.[30] Every single wave is independent of the others. Each wave seems to "split" from thc othcrs. At the same time, however, the waves converge in a vigorous common flow. There is therefore a dis/continuity between the individual waves and the overall river flow. "Rising from the abyss and vanishing again into it", writes Ōhashi, "to be 'separated' from the others and independent, but not being able to exist without the others, is not only about the way of being of the individual waves in the watercourse. This also corresponds to the way of being of life (命, *inochi*), which arises and dies".[31]

Figure 4 Ogata Kōrin, *Red and White Plum Blossoms* (『紅白梅図』)

30 See K, p. 135.
31 K, p. 135.

The river separates a white plum tree painted on the left side from a red plum tree painted on the right side. According to Ōhashi the two trees are contrasting not only chromatically but also formally. If the river in the middle makes life appear as a fundamental element, the two trees indicate the polarity of sexual gender. The red and white flowers of the plum tree are separated and "cut" from the river as the sexes are differentiated. Yet, like the waves of the river, the flowers belong to a single vital flow. Again, the unity of life and death is shown in the trees that stand out against a golden background. The "life" of the watercourse and the "sexual genders" of the plum blossoms are surrounded by this golden background, which expresses the dis/continuity between what is human (情, *jō*) and what is not (非情, *hijō*), between life and death.

"What emerges here" writes Ōhashi, "is not the oppressive omen of death of Hasegawa Kyūzō's *Cherry Blossoms*, but rather the gaze that recognizes the non-human indifference of death in the midst of life's blossoming".[32]

4. Kire-tsuzuki *and Western art. Van Gogh and Rembrandt according to Heidegger and Simmel*

This polar-circulatory in-difference and dis/continuous relationship characteristic of *kire-tsuzuki* and *shōji* can be compared to the relationship of mutual co-ownership (*Zu-einander-Gehören*) between man and the ontological difference, that is between *Dasein* and Being (*Sein*), according to Heidegger. "Man and Being", claims Heidegger in "Taoist" terms,[33]

---

32 K, p. 136.

33 On Heidegger and "Eastern thought", and in particular his relationship with Taoism and Zen Buddhism, see Fabian Heubel, *Gewundene Wege nach China: Heidegger – Daoismus – Adorno* (Klostermann: Frankfurt a. M., 2020); Katrin Froese, *Nietzsche, Heidegger, and Daoist Thought: Crossing Paths In-Between* (Albany: State University of New York Press, 2006); Steven Heine, 'The Flower Blossoms "Without Why": Beyond the Heidegger-Kuki Dialogue on Contemplative Language', in *The Eastern Buddhist Society* 3-2 (1990), pp. 60-88; Carlo Saviani, *L'oriente di Heidegger* (il melangolo:

"have already reached each other […] since both are mutually appropriated, extended as a gift, one to the other".[34]

What seems to have definitely disappeared in the age of technique is for Heidegger the experience of Being as *Ereignis*. This experience is similar to the one contained in the Chinese expression *dao* and in the Japanese expression *kire/tsuzuki*, as far as a relationship of complementarity, dependence, connection and dis/continuity is expressed with these notions.

In *A Dialogue on Language between a Japanese and an Inquirer* by Heidegger the theme of the difference – namely the dis/continuity – between Being and entity is central and constitutes the point of convergence between the interlocutors. For the "Inquirer"-Heidegger, as well as for the "Japanese" Tezuka Tomio (手塚富雄, 1903-1983), the language itself is nothing but a response to the call of the "difference" (*Zwiefalt*). The "event" of language as "difference" – that is, as dis/continuity and exchangeable belonging of man and Being – is not the expression of an "ethnic" dualism between cultures, rather a place of conjunction between worldviews, a common access to the open (*das Offene*) beyond any grammatical particularism. The Japanese word for this conception of language, as the place of the "difference", is *koto ba* (言葉).

"And what does that say?", asks Heidegger to the Japanese. "*Ba* means leaves", answers Tezuka, "including and especially the leaves of a blossom – petals. Think of cherry blossoms or plum blossoms".[35] *Koto* literally means "to say", but in a deeper sense it expresses "the pure delight of the beckoning stillness […]. But *koto* always also names that which in the event gives delight, itself, that which uniquely in each unrepealable moment comes to radiance in the fullness of its grace". The meaning of

Genova, 1998).

34 Martin Heidegger, *Identity and Difference* (New York, Evaston, London: Harper & Row, 1969, [Original work published 1957]), p. 33.

35 Martin Heidegger, *A Dialogue on Language*, in Id., *On the Way to Language* (New York et al.: Harper & Row, 1971, [Original work published 1957]), p. 45.

koto, which Heidegger and Tezuka share, is therefore that "of the lightening message of grace".[36]

Language can thus be seen as "a flower", since it allows the sprouting of *ba* – leaves and "petals" of words – and expresses the common generating function of Japanese language and German "saying" (*die Sage*). *Koto* and *Sage* therefore represent a common background – or better a dis/continuity – between East and West: From the original language (*die ursprüngliche Sprache*) the particular languages sprout like leaves or blossom like petals.

The in-difference between being and entity evoked in language as event, which expresses the dis/continuity between the original saying and the everyday word, is equally evident in the work of art. For Heidegger the work of art is not a simple representation aimed at the spectator's pleasure, but an event in which being manifests itself and hides itself at the same time. Like language, art is not the subjective product of a painter or a poet, on the contrary: the work "flourishes" from art and secondarily makes the artist possible. Art is the origin of the work, not the creative subject.

So in van Gogh's famous painting *A Pair of Shoes* (1885) what comes to light is not for Heidegger the ready-to-hand (*Zuhandenheit*) function of the shoes, but rather the being of the entity itself: the painting depicts "the thing" (the peasant shoes) letting it be as thing.[37] Van Gogh's work is therefore not the consequence of the action of genius as a sovereign subject, but it is considered a poietic fact in itself. In the apparent insignificance of the peasant shoes the event of the being unfolds itself: "The emergence of createdness from the work does not mean that the work is to give the impression of having been made by a great artist. The point is not that the created being be certified as the performance of a capable person, so that the producer is thereby brought to public notice. It is not the *N. N. fecit* that is to be made

36 Martin Heidegger, *A Dialogue on Language*, cit., p. 45.

37 See Martin Heidegger, *The Origin of the Work of Art*, in Id., *Basic Writings* (New York: HarperCollins, 1993 [Original work published 1950]), pp. 139-212.

known. Rather, the simple *factum est* […]".[38]The work of art confronts us with the extraordinary event of being that emerges from the entity, it strikes us with that prodigious shock (*Stoß*) that requires us to transform our usual way of seeing the world.

Figure 5
Vincent van Gogh,
A Pair of Shoes

The change of view resulting from the impact of the artwork also involves our conception of life and death. If Heidegger focuses on the painting *A Pair of Shoes* in order to stress the dis/continuity between being and entity, "the clearing of beings" (*die Lichtung des Seienden*) and "the opening up of the open region" (*die Eröffnung des Offenen*),[39] Ōhashi shows the chiaroscuro nature of late van Gogh's paintings, in which the *kire-tsuzuki* between life and death, and therefore the experience of *shōji*, are palpable. In the bright yellow of van Gogh's wheat fields we can see an anguished darkness.[40] In line with the Taoist perspective that there is no light that does not generate shadow, in van Gogh brightness always has a dark counterpart, which is polarly connected to it. The abyss of gloom in van Gogh's paintings is not an element opposed to light but is co-essential to

38 Martin Heidegger, *The Origin of the Work of Art*, cit., p. 190.
39 Martin Heidegger, *The Origin of the Work of Art*, cit., p. 196.
40 See K, p. 161.

it. The dis/continuous dynamic of *kire-tsuzuki* seems to cross the boundaries of Japanese culture and manifest itself in the osmosis between light and darkness of the Dutch painter's work, in which the bright yellow of sunny wheat fields is permeated by shadowy pain just as in the expression *shōji* life is permeated by death.

Perhaps this peculiar dynamic can also be recognized in the series of van Gogh's still lives named *Sunflowers*, executed in Paris in 1887. However, in conclusion of this paper, we would like to highlight another possible parallel between *kire-tsuzuki* and western art that Ōhashi does not consider, namely the fundamental relationship between life and death present in Rembrandt's paintings.

According to Simmel, in all portraits of Rembrandt inhabits "*one* future moment, which after all makes life into a totality precisely by breaking it off".[41] This "breaking off" action is the moment of death inherent in all living things. Almost literally anticipating the conception of *kire* developed by Ōhashi, Simmel describes the relationship between life and death in Rembrandt's portraits in the sign of dis/continuity. Referring to the mythological image of the Greek Parcae, Simmel shows how in Rembrandt's portraits life is not simply cut out of death: rather life and death are intimately and polarly linked and are in a relationship of cut and continuity.[42] "A certain sensibility toward the relationship of life and death", writes Simmel in an important passage, "seems to me to exist with him [...] and he seems to possess the deepest insight into the significance of death. I am convinced that this insight depends entirely on one's giving up the conception in terms of the *Parcae*: as if in a certain temporal moment of life's thread, which until then had been continually spun as life and exclusively as life, had been 'cut off', as if life

41 Georg Simmel, *Rembrandt. An Essay in the Philosophy of Art* (New York-London: Routledge, 2005 [Original work published 1916]), p. 71.

42 The Parcae or Moirae in Greek mythology had the possibility to control human destiny (in fact μοῖρα in ancient Greek means "destiny"). Their task was to weave the thread of every man's fate and to cut it off at the hour of death. This "cut" of life by Parcae marks a clear contrast between life and death, which for Simmel must be completely abandoned if we want to understand that death has always been within life.

were predetermined to confront death at a certain point in its course, but only then, in that moment, comes into contact with it. Instead of this conception, it seems to me beyond doubt that death *inhabits* life from the onset".[43]

Anticipating also Heidegger's reflection about "being-towards-death" (*Sein-zum-Tode*),[44] Simmel claims that "Death is related to life not like a possibility that at some point becomes reality, but rather our life only becomes life as we know it, and is only formed as it is, in that we (whether growing or fading, on life's sunny uplands or in the dark shadows of its decline) are always and already *such beings that will die*".[45]

The image of life that grows and fades can be referred again to the metaphor of the flower, which expresses the transience and the *kire-tsuzuki* between life and death. According to Simmel, we must disprove the inauthentic idea that "we die" only in an indeterminate future: "the awareness that we shall die is not simply an anticipation, an idealized foreshadowing of our last hour, but is the inner ever-present reality of each moment".[46] Also in this case the anticipation of the Heideggerian themes of *Being and time* is manifest.

Opposing the traditionally Western idea of death expressed in still life and "dances of death", which indicates the transience and mortality of life in a cautionary and negative sense,[47] Rembrandt does not conceive death as "an enemy [...] coming from afar toward us, but rather death is from the onset a *character indelebilis* of life".[48] This is why Simmel urges us not to consider death as a "skeletal ghost" (*der Knochenmann*) that lies outside of life: "If one grasps death not as a violent creature waiting outside — as a fate coming upon us at a certain moment — if

43 Georg Simmel, *Rembrandt. An Essay in the Philosophy of Art*, cit., p. 71.

44 See Martin Heidegger, *Being and Time* (Albany: State University of New York Press, 1996 [original work published in 1927], pp. 219-246.

45 Georg Simmel, *Rembrandt. An Essay in the Philosophy of Art*, cit., p. 71.

46 Georg Simmel, *Rembrandt. An Essay in the Philosophy of Art*, cit., p. 71.

47 Ōhashi, for example, refers to the still lifes of Jan Brueghel the Elder (1568-1625), as an expressive example of baroque *vanitas* and of the *memento mori* theme. See K, pp. 213-214.

48 Georg Simmel, *Rembrandt. An Essay in the Philosophy of Art*, cit., p. 72.

one moreover comprehends its insoluble, deep immanence in life itself, then the death secretly casting its shadow out of so many Rembrandt portraits is only a symptom of how unconditionally, in his art, precisely the principle of life connects itself to that of individuality".[49] In Rembrandt's portraits such as *Self Portrait with Saskia* (1636), *Man Holding Gloves* (1642), *Titus at his desk* (1655), *Syndics of the Drapers'Guild* (1662) and *Laughing Self Portrait* (1665-1670 ca.), death is immediately felt with and within life as one of its elements. According to Simmel, "those portraits contain life in its widest sense, which also includes death. Everything that is merely life, such that it had estranged itself from death, is life in its narrower sense; it is in a way an abstraction".[50] Particularly in the *Laughing Self Portrait* "the laughing is unmistakably something purely momentary", but "the whole is as if infused by, and oriented toward, death".[51] Some interpreters claim that Rembrandt, in this self-portrait, likens himself to the fifth-century BC Greek painter Zeuxis, who, according to myth, died laughing while contemplating the portrait of a funny-looking old woman that he had just finished painting.[52] Other interpretations conclude that Rembrandt represents himself by referring to the laughing face of Democritus juxtaposed with the bust of the severe Heraclitus or, more generally, that he laughs in the face of his own impending death.[53] At the end of his life, Rembrandt portrays himself with an expression that is both a fierce grin and a serene acceptance of death. It seems a threshold proxemics between laughing and crying. Between life and death there is the most disquieting affinity: the old man's smirk carries with it the cheerfulness of youth, which nevertheless appears marked by the burden of a life of suffering. The element of death in life, which in youth remains hidden and invisible, now emerges on the surface. The precious tissue that glides over the

49 Georg Simmel, *Rembrandt. An Essay in the Philosophy of Art*, cit., p. 79.
50 Georg Simmel, *Rembrandt. An Essay in the Philosophy of Art*, cit., p. 74.
51 Georg Simmel, *Rembrandt. An Essay in the Philosophy of Art*, cit., p. 74.
52 See Ernst van de Wetering, *Self Portrait as Zeuxis Laughing*, in *A Corpus of Rembrandt Paintings* (Dordrecht: Springer, 2005, vol. IV), p. 556.
53 See Corrado Ricci, *Rembrandt in Italia* (Milan: Alfieri & Lacroix, 1918), p. 17.

painter's shoulders is a stream of light that, like a shooting star, consumes its glow and returns to the darkness. It is probably a metaphor for the parable of a fading life.

Figure 6
Rembrandt, *Titus at his desk*

Figure 7
Rembrandt, *Laughing Self Portrait*

It is not possible, at this point, to relate the laughter of Rembrandt's self-portrait to the smile of the *Tiger in the snow* (『雪中虎図』), which represents the self-portrait of Hokusai Katsushika (葛飾北斎, 1760-1849) before he died.[54] We can perhaps only hint at the possible affinity between the sneer of old Rembrandt and the serenity of Hokusai's tiger: in both cases, old age expresses a serene, youthful and playful attitude towards death as an element of life. The incessant circularity of the earthly world and otherworldly world, of life and death, are thus transformed into play (遊び, *asobi*), into a serene hovering between two worlds.

"One of the deepest typical conditions of our worldview",

54 See K, pp. 142-145.

claims Simmel almost in unconsciously Taoist terms, "becomes valid here. Many of our essential determinations of being order themselves into dichotomies such that one concept finds its meaning in the correlation with the other: good and evil, masculine and feminine, credit and debt, progress and stagnation, and numerous others. The relativity of the one finds its limit and form in the other [...]. And so perhaps life and death — insofar as they seem to exclude each other logically and physically — are still only relative opposites, embraced by life in its absolute sense that underpins and embraces the mutual limitation and conditioning of life and death".[55]

The immanence of death in life, which in Rembrandt's paintings seems so close to the idea of circularity and unceasing dis/continuity of life and death contained in the expression *shōji*, is perhaps an indirect and further developable point of contact between the world of Western and East Asian images.

55 Georg Simmel, *Rembrandt. An Essay in the Philosophy of Art*, cit., p. 72.

Raffaele Milani[1]

THE (ORIGINAL) NATURE OF IMAGES

The Beauty of the Place of Origin

In the history of art we find many recurrences of antiquity, since it is a source of instruction and a model for subsequent aesthetic developments. In his studies of Neoclassical and Romantic aesthetics and poetics, Rosario Assunto[2] illustrates that antiquity itself can be experienced as the future. It can be said that memory underpins all innovation and gives authenticity to new and, at times, shocking forms. Antiquity is present in artworks in the play of fantastic forms we find in masterpieces. This presence entails the reinterpretation of images from the Classicism of the Romans to that of the age of Charlemagne, from Humanism to the Enlightenment, from the Renaissance of the modern era to the Renaissance of postmodern era. Even the Greeks reinvented their past in an "archeology of nostalgia", to use John Boardman's[3] expression. Greek antiquity features myth, history, imagination, and personification in an amalgam of meanings and symbols. Classicism is synonymous with values considered to be universal: perfection, proportion, equilibrium, harmony, grace, and the intensity and naturalness of figures. In this sense, we can speak of a future dimension of Classicism, according to Salvatore Settis, who studies the phases of the Western artistic tradition. He argues that the more we see the "classical" not as a dead culture we inherited and for which we

---

1 University of Bologna

2 Rosario Assunto, *L'antichità come futuro* [*Antiquity as the future*] (Milan: Mursia, 1973).

3 John Boardman, *The archeology of nostalgia: how the Greeks re-created their mythical past* (London: Thames & Hudson, 2002) [Italian translation in: John Boardman, *Archeologia della nostalgia. Come i Greci reinventarono il loro passato mitico* (Milan: Bruno Mondadori, 2004)].

can take no credit but as something surprising to be recreated each day and as a powerful stimulus to understand the "other", the more we will be able to mould future generations.[4]

In order to appreciate this perspective, we need to reflect on the imagination and the relationship between art and nature, providing appropriate examples. Antiquity as the future is to be studied in the light of the process in which reality is expressed as form and form expresses reality. In this regard, it is useful to take into account the viewpoints of two different but important authors. The first is that of George Simmel who, in the early part of the twentieth century, stated that the relative heights attained by technical progress had become an *absolute* value in the sense that the splendor of technology and money were smothering "spirituality" and "meditation", qualities that managed, nonetheless, to achieve a sort of vindication by generating a sense of tension and nostalgia.[5] The second is that of Roland Barthes who described the endless resignification of the object observed and in so doing affirmed the overflow of the senses relative to first impressions.[6] The real is thus enriched by the artificial. We could also say, as does Hans Blumenberg with his concept of "metaphorology", that art produces an illusion but it is never simply fantasy. It is the elaboration of elementary or foundational models of thought: the creative process is essentially mythic.[7]

We need to examine the roots of this perspective on antiquity proposed by Assunto, Boardman, and Settis as seen in the

---

4 Salvatore Settis, *Futuro del classico* [*The future of the classical*] (Turin: Einaudi, 2016).

5 Georg Simmel, *Die Herrschaft der Technik*, in: Georg Simmel, *Philosophie des Geldes* (Leipzig: Dunker und Humblot, 1900), pp. 520-535; Georg Simmel, *Die Grossstaedte und das Geistesleben*, originally in *Jahrbuch der Gehestiftung* IX (1903), pp. 188-206 [Italian translation in: Tomás Maldonado (ed. by), *Tecnica e cultura* [*Technology and culture*] (Milan: Feltrinelli, 1987)].

6 Roland Barthes, *Droit dans les yeux* (1977), in *L'obvie et l'obtus* (Paris: Edition du Seuil, 1982) [Italian translation in Roland Barthes, *L'ovvio e l'ottuso* (Turin: Einaudi, 1985)].

7 Hans Blumenberg, *Paradigmen für eine Metaphorologie* (Bonn: Bouvier, 1960) [Italian translation in: Hans Blumbenberg, *Paradigmi per una metaforologia* (Bologna: il Mulino, 1969), pp 107-12].

philosophical, semiotic, and rhetorical interpretation offered by Simmel, Barthes, and Blumenberg. To be more specific, we need to reflect on imagination and nature. If we think of imagination as the act of dreaming, we are sometimes able to gain access to the hidden order of a universal language that nature itself creates and projects all around us: a language, we might say, of both nature and art, that is, of being and doing (of the poietic display of things and events) because nature pertains to art, the expression of living forms, as art pertains to nature, the expression of existent things. It is a language whose properties are multiplicity and mutability; it is a language infused with myths and symbols, facts and metaphors, truth and appearance or fantasy. It is the ecstatic vision that humans experience as part of nature and as the illusion of a dream world. Signs, symbols, and representations surround us and seem to relate to us.

We might say that, like the aesthetic and artistic imaginary, dreams are an experience that frees us from the tyranny of time and space; it is an escape from the world while we are living in it. In this creative mental state, we have the sensation of having an experience that is rich in figures, forms, and analogies: images that flow with the rhythm of a musical score. We can say that we are pleasantly enmeshed in an ecstatic perception. This occurs when something near us attracts our gaze and causes us to have the impression that we ourselves are being observed by the thing that we are contemplating. We discover that we are participating in a transformation: the trees, the hillside, the valley, the mountains, the fields, and everything that comprises the landscape becomes, before our eyes, closer in a sort of fusion, a gesture of love and enchantment. I see myself and I am everywhere. Distance disappears in nearness. This also happens with time and the things of history. Perception becomes illumination rather than description through a kind of doubling of the object in which the visible and the invisible merge, and dreams finds its abode in a sort of intermediate kingdom. A dream is the infinite shadow of the true; in this sense, memory reshapes our future as we go. Sometimes we wonder whether we are dreaming or are awake: this thought comes to us in daylight as well as in the obscurity of wandering, between a dreamed world and a lived world; and the lived world can also become a dreamed world, as the mind surrenders its self-control during the daytime and drifts toward deeper realities. This is the journey through space and time in the aesthetic-artistic dimension.

Thus, magical attractions propel human beings into the search for truth beyond appearances, from the visible to the invisible, starting with the charm of the earth, the sublimity of places, the sacredness of mountains, grottoes, springs, and the elements of nature. In this way, we can feel the enchantment of an original mystical perception of the world around us, alongside and in concert with the mythological and enigmatic vision. The latter implies a broad, new reading of mythology. In his poetry, Rilke interpreted it, but it is also illustrated in painting; for example, Giorgio De Chrico's *Disquieting Muses* or Alberto Savinio's *La maschera del mito* (*The Mask of Myth*), as well as in the films of Jean Cocteau: the modern present returns to the past to affirm it as a model for the future. Also evident, right at the end of the twentieth century, which is dominated by a citationist attitude, but especially in the early decades of the new millennium, are two important examples of how an earlier image can inspire a multitude of images in the present, already clothed in what is to come. The postmodern returns, in a sense, to the past in order to reaffirm it as a template for the future. We discover this in many of Bill Viola's videos, which are inspired by the frescoes of Masolino da Panicale, Pontormo, and Paolo Uccello, as well as in Lech Majewski's film *The Colours of the Passion* (2011), inspired by Bruegel the Elder's *Ascent to Calvary*, which is an interpretation of redemption. In contemporary art the signs of antiquity in its various expressive forms remain.

The nostalgic image of our country of birth is an affective one around which other important images revolve, namely, those of our actual, quotidian existence, as well as those of the ideal life. The sense of belonging to the land and the community is especially strong when we sacrifice these by leaving them behind, which is an action that accentuates the emotional response to our place of origin in the spatial and temporal dimensions, that is to say, the place from which we come and the past we have lived, preserved as they are in our precious memory and imagination, both personal and collective. The home and the land are spirits of the inner world, produced by a mental and sensible interaction (evocations traveling from the sense of sight to those of hearing, smell, taste, and touch). The nature of things and the things of nature, together with the faces of people dear to us, are inextricably embedded in a rich fabric of emotions that we nurture within us in an auto-therapeutic ritual involving a web of elements that reconfigure what has been into faded images that have almost vanished from memory and linguistic sounds, the idiom of the place of which only shadows remain. These images and sensations are all the more powerful when they are experienced from a distance.

The myth, narrative in its widest sense, preserves personal and collective memories. This narrative schema, which is to say the construction of such expressions of the anthropology of the human imagination, prompts reflection on the affective nature of the images from which the evocative pleasure of the representation of origins emerges.

Some examples from the European literary tradition illustrate this nostalgia for the homeland. We could say, as do Edgar Morin and Anne B. Kern[8], that in the increasingly frantic modern era of globalization, our minds and hearts are pushed to extend the image of the place of origin to the planet as a whole, to see it as our Earth-Homeland as we face the ecological crisis of its profound illness and destruction. In the context of this congress, however, I prefer, instead, to reflect on what has always been said and written in the West on the affective feeling of belonging to our place of origin.

We can begin with Homer's *Iliad*, where Achilles announces his decision to return to his home and to abandon the war:

---

8 Edgar Morin and Anne B. Kern, *Terre-Patrie* (Paris: Edition du Seuil, 1993) [Italian translation in: Edgar Morin and Anne B. Kern, *Terra-Patria* (Milan: Raffaello Cortina, 1999)].

> "you'll see (…) / tomorrow my ships will be sailing off, / on the fish-filled Hellespont (…). And if Poseidon, / famous Earthshaker, / gives us fair sailing, / in three days I'll reach fertile Phthia. / There I own many things I left behind / when I made this disastrous trip to Troy. / (…) if the gods keep me safe and I get home, / Peleus himself will find me a wife. / There are plenty of Achaean women / in Hellas and in Phthia (…). From them I'll choose / the one I want to make my cherished wife. / My heart has often felt a strong desire / to take a woman there as my own wife, / someone suitable for marriage" (Bk. IX, vv. 358-400)[9]

In the *Odyssey*, Telemachus replies with the following words to Menelaus, who wants to give him as a gift three horses and a chariot:

> "And whatsoever gift thou wouldest give me, let it be some treasure; but horses will I not take to Ithaca (…) thou art lord of a wide plain (…). But in Ithaca there are no widespread courses nor aught of meadow-land. It is a pasture-land of goats and pleasanter than one that pastures horses" (Bk. IV, vv. 600-609)[10]

We note that to give greater importance to goats than to horses is unheard of for an aristocratic Greek, but Telemachus seems to be unaware of this even as he asserts the superiority of Ithaca.

Also in the *Odyssey*, Ulysses reveals his identity to the Phaeacians:

> "I am Odysseus (…). I dwell in clear-seen Ithaca, wherein is a mountain, Neriton, covered with waving forests (…). Ithaca itself lies close in to the mainland the furthest toward the gloom (…) a good nurse of young men; and for myself no other thing can I see sweeter than one's own land. Of a truth Calypso, the beautiful goddess, sought to keep me by her in her hollow caves, yearning that I should be her husband; and in like manner Circe (…) but they could never persuade the heart within my breast. So true is it that naught is sweeter than a man's own land and his parents, even though it be in a rich house that he dwells afar in a foreign land away from his parents." (IX, vv. 19-35)[11]

---

9 Online translation: http://johnstoniatexts.x10host.com/homer/iliadtofc.html

10 Online translation: https://www.perseus.tufts.edu/hopper/text?doc=Perseus%3Atext%3A1999.01.0136%3Abook%3D4%3Acard%3D593.

11 Online translation: https://www.perseus.tufts.edu/hopper/text?doc=Perseus%3Atext%3A1999.01.0136%3Abook%3D9%3Acard%3D1

Once more, nostalgia for the distant homeland stirs the mind and the heart.

Moving on to the Greek poets, we can mention Tyrtaeus, who describes the bitter destiny of the exile with these words:

> "The pain of leaving one's city and the fertile fields for the life of a beggar, wandering with mother, old father, little children and wedded wife. The man beaten by need and odious poverty is detested everywhere he goes, a disgrace to his family and noble appearance, trailed by dishonor and evil".[12]

The pain of separation from our country, a land we cultivate and care for, is well expressed by Theognis of Megara:

> "Son of Polupaos, I have heard the cry / of the bird that announces to men the most propitious / time for plowing and has pierced my anguished heart / because others possess my fertile fields". (vv. 1197-1202) (my translation)

Among the works of the tragedians, perhaps the best-known passage in praise of the homeland is contained in the chorus of Sophocles' *Oedipus at Colonus* (vv. 668 ff), which I cannot cite in its entirety here. Famous words praising Attica can also be found in Euripides' *Medea* (vv. 643-650), words that are once more attributed to the chorus:

> "Oh home, oh country, ne'er may I / Through long and hard years of poverty, / that bitterest of all distress, / Live on an alien citiless: / Nay, rather, having had my day, / Let death, let death, do me away: / For no woe doth outpass this woe, / One's fatherland no more to know." (vv. 643-650)[13]

Late in the play, we find more of Euripides' famous homage to his country:

> "The Athenians, great from long ago, / And children of the gods in Heaven, / Still for their daily nurture know / The loftiest food of wisdom given / A hallowed and unconquered state; / And, through their bright,

12 In: *Early Greek Poetry* (MI: University of Michigan Press, 1992), p. 48.

13 Translation in: *The Medea of Euripides* (London: Macmillan,1868).

translucent air, / Move ever with proud and jubilant gait, / There, as old rhymes relate, / Where erst Harmonia, of the yellow hair, / virgin nine Pierian muses bare. / There too, the ancient lays run thus, / Once Cypris, quaffing from the wave / Of crystal flowing Cephissus, / O'er all the land her soft breath drave / In tender wafts of scented wind." (Vv. 823-837)[14]

Finally, from a philosophical perspective, we have the following quote from Plato's *Crito* (44b). Preparing for his death, Socrates recalls the very words of Achilles with which I began this brief list of illustrations. A beautiful and regal-looking woman appeared to him in a dream and said to him: "Socrates, you shall arrive in fertile Phthia on the third day" (44b).[15] Here, the return to the homeland coincides with the soul's return to its eternal home: a new world has begun.

The theme acquires an intimate and personal quality in the works of the Latin poets. Some famous examples follow: Catullus: "Sirmio! Eyelet of islands and peninsulas, (…) how gladly and how happily do I see you again" (*Poems* 31, vv. 1-4)[16]; or Horace's *Odes*: "Septimus, you, who are prepared to visit / Cadiz with me, and its tribes (they're not used / to bearing our yoke)" (2.6)[17]; the theme of travels to faraway lands is juxtaposed to that of the return to one's place of origin: "That corner of earth is the brightest to me, / where honey gives nothing away to that / of Hymettus (…) That place, and its lovely heights, call out to me, / to you." (2.6)[18]

Clearly, the "locus classicus" of feeling for the native land is represented by Virgil's first eclogue in its entirety. I quote here only a few lines:

"Happy old man, who 'mid familiar streams, / And hallowed springs, will court the cooling shade. / Here, as of old, your neighbour's bordering

14 Translation in: *The Medea of Euripides*, cit.

15 Online translation: https://www.pitt.edu/~mthompso/readings/crito.pdf

16 Online translation: http://www.perseus.tufts.edu/hopper/text?doc=Perseus%3Atext%3A1999.02.0006%3Apoem%3D31

17 Online translation: https://erickimphotography.com/blog/horace-the-odes-book-2/

18 Online translation: https://erickimphotography.com/blog/horace-the-odes-book-2/

> hedge, / That feasts with willow-flower the Hybla bees, / Shall oft with gentle murmur lull to sleep. / while the leaf-dresser beneath some tall rock / Uplifts his song, nor cease their cooings hoarse / The wood pigeons that are at your heart's delight. / Nor doves their moaning in the elm-tree top."[19]

We can say that the quotations above shed light on the meaning of the notion of "native soil" in the sense that true beauty consists in shining a light on the homeland, or being able to see the foundational image of the homeland within us. The real beauty of an originary landscape lies in the hope of being recognized by the existence of what we are looking at and of being included in that image.

Plotinus (1,6,8) expounds on the gaze eternally directed toward the fatherland, from which we come and to which we belong, a place that welcomes us and which we must cherish. He advises, then, that we run toward the dear fatherland. Just as Ulysses says that he escaped from the sorceress Circe and from Calypso, we must escape the present in order to go where our fathers are. Not on foot, by ship or chariot: we need to detach ourselves from such things and replace corporeal sight with another sense, for the purpose of activating the imaginative faculty that we all possess but few implement. This is the light of beauty that, by gradations, shines in the innermost part of the soul. This is the process of recognition, the image beyond things: the image is anterior to the nature of things themselves and the nature of the essential images behind which emerges the world of appearances. In this way, we arrive at the seat of our origin, purified of material forms, a mental and immaterial patrimony of the consciousness of living, nurturing, belonging, participating, and contemplating, because, as Plotinus tells us, everything leads back to nature (of beauty) as determined by fate.

Finally, with respect to the above comments on interior landscapes and, at the same time, the recognition of external landscapes, we can use Joseph Rykwert's *On Adam's House in Paradise*[20] as a source of guidance and reassurance. Rykwert

19 Online translation: http://classics.mit.edu/Virgil/eclogue.mb.txt

20 Joseph Rykwert, *On Adam's House in Paradise* (New York: Moma, 1972).

conducts a historical study of the mythology of building, retracing the views of architects (from Alberti to Vitruvius and from Alberti to Scamozzi) and of philosophers through a matrix of complex anthropological and symbolic meanings. This is an attempt to reach the image anterior to the house, the original shelter, the seat of humanity from the earliest times, involving an archetypal building described in a multitude of ways in ancient documents. Thus, the original hut becomes both a memory and a place in which to exist and to dwell.

POP AESTHETICS

Federico Farnè[1]

IMAGES OF BEAUTIFUL BODIES IN THE INTERNET ERA

The Heritage of Old-School Bodybuilding

Pumping Iron, a documentary directed by Robert Fiore and George Butler, came out in movie theaters in 1977. The film, which was shown during the 30th annual Cannes Film Festival, follows the last 100 days of preparation of the *IFBB* athletes (*International Federation of Bodybuilding and Fitness*) for 1975's Mr. Olympia competition in Pretoria, where Arnold Schwarzenegger won his 6th consecutive gold medal by defeating his friend, the recently-deceased Franco Columbo. Set in Venice Beach's legendary Gold's Gym and Muscle Gym, the film offers a deep view into the world of professional bodybuilding. In doing so, partly thanks to Schwarzenegger's charismatic presence, it marked the definitive transition of bodybuilding from subculture to the mainstream, a process which had already begun during the 1950s. This transition had a profound cultural impact by influencing the ideal body standards of star actors and top athletes, who from the 1980s onwards made an increasingly large use of bodybuilding to develop their bodies for both promotional and performative purposes. Not only that: on an even broader scale, the rise of bodybuilding went on to completely redefine canonical male beauty standards in Western society.[2]

Bodybuilding's first foray into film production came during the 1950s, when it was introduced to Italian filmmaking through the *peplum* genre, also known as *sword and sandals*. *Peplum* is a historical costume piece sub-genre often set in ancient classical

---

1 University of Bologna

2 For a history of Bodybuilding: Gordon LaVelle, *Bodybuilding: Tracing the Evolution of the Ultimate Physique* (Sandy, Utah: Aardvark Global Publishing, 2011).

or biblical scenarios, with additional elements from fantasy and action films. Its name comes from *peplo*, a Latin word with Greek origins that refers to the typical Hellenic female robe, which was often used in these low budget productions for its convenience. Steve Reeves and Reg Park were the two great icons of this time period, working with Italian directors such as Mario Bava, Anto Margheriti, Umberto Lenzi, Sergio Corbucci, and others.

However, starring actors with muscular and well-defined bodies had a functional purpose in this sort of film genre; whereas from the 80's onwards, the actor's sculpted body started transcending this role-oriented functionality to become the personification of a new male beauty standard based on the body's proportions.

Among the chief promoters of this cultural revolution were Frank Zane and the already mentioned Schwarzenegger. The former won the title of Mr. Olympia for three consecutive years between 1977 and 1979, becoming one of the only three men to ever defeat the Austrian star in an official competition along with Chester Yorton and Sergio Oliva. Zane also became the symbol of change within the so-called *Golden Era*[3] of the bodybuilding movement, moving from a physicality purely focused on muscle mass (hypertrophy) to a more harmonious and better proportioned bodily aesthetic. After all, it is no coincidence that Zane's aesthetic reference, which he refers to in his own books, is that of the symmetry of ancient Greek sculpture. Another indication of this aesthetic shift came during a 1976's exhibition in New York's *Whitney Museum of American*, curated by Butler. Over the course of this exhibition, the bodybuilders posed on rotating platforms for a jury of art critics, who judged them based on

3 The Golden Era of Bodybuilding ranges across a time span that goes from the 1950s to the end of the 1980s. Beyond the great experimentation and innovation in training, with the introduction of new exercises and a full-body programming, the Golden Era is characterized by an aesthetic that emphasizes lean muscularity, a very low level of water retention and a fat mass. below 10%. The athlete's work is focused on creating a body inspired by classical sculpture and great importance is given to the relationship between the width of the shoulders and the waist: the famous V-shape. This aesthetic begins to decline in the 90s, opening up to the "monsters" of the so-called Mass Era.

a comparison with ancient Greek sculpture.[4] But whereas Zane was the one to define a new standard of male beauty based on quasi-objective criteria of precise proportions, Schwarzenegger was the one who carried this new aesthetic to the mainstream through the big screen, thus establishing the foundations of what later became our modern fitness culture. The first blockbuster production that elevated him to worldwide stardom was *Conan the Barbarian* (1982), a film that was built entirely around Schwarzenegger's character by its director John Milius, who recognized the Austrian actor's physicality as being perfect for the role of the protagonist. The next big breakthrough came with 1984's *Terminator*, where Schwarzenegger himself convinced director James Cameron to give him the role of T-800, the time-travelling cyborg assassin that became a worldwide pop-cultural cinematic icon along with his famous line "I'll be back", spoken in a strong German accent.

Schwarzenegger's meteoric rise to Hollywood stardom completely revolutionized the ideal of sex symbol. From that moment onwards, the male actor's body became more and more sculpted with time: hairless and chiseled by diet and exercise, it turned into a completely new and tangible model of masculinity. This new ideal is in contrast with the prior mysterious seductive charm that was expected of a male sex symbol, which transcended any specific physical requirements and was instead based on an indecipherable personal charisma. But the rise of fitness culture created universal criteria, at least within the Western world, that allow us to objectively evaluate male beauty. Just look at *The Most Handsome Actors* chart from imdb.com,[5] one of the most popular cinema-centric websites on the internet. It is no coincidence that the top five actors listed are embodiments of a physical perfection that is clearly inspired by classic bodybuilding. Furthermore, every corner of the internet is overflowing with articles and advertisements promoting a

4 Frank Zane, Christine Zane, *The Zane Way to a Beautiful Body Through Weight Training for Men and Women* (New York: Simon & Schuster, 1979).

5 https://www.imdb.com/list/ls022036831/

variety of shady products and shortcuts for us to obtain the body of our favorite star.

Just as David Le Breton suggested almost twenty years ago, while it is true that the female body still remains the privileged target of

> bodily metamorphosis *ateliers* or of cosmetic marketing, men are becoming increasingly more involved. With the fall of the older prejudices that considered the male body to be but a peripheric aspect with respect to an elsewhere-focused seduction, which comes from his actions, worldly attitude and so on, […] the imperatives of appearance are starting to influence an increasingly high number of men. These men are in turn anxious to seduce and stay young in ways that confound the ideal of bodily aesthetics with a subtle rearranging of their own manliness.[6]

And so, the body, now stripped of that nobility that made it the transient receptacle of the soul, turns away from itself. It becomes a pale alter ego, ready to be continuously re-modelled like an accessory to one's own presence. "This modern version of dualism, which spreads itself through ordinary life, places men against their own bodies, instead of the former spirit/body dichotomy".[7] Dualism does not belong to metaphysics anymore, as was the case during the fifteenth and sixteenth century with Andreas Vesalius and Renee Descartes; instead, it vehemently crosses into the realm of the concrete. In Western societies, the body becomes a hub of identification and individualization. Not only does it imply a difference between the self and the other (individualism) and between the self and the world, but also between the self and itself. To cite once again Le Breton, "the Western body is the border, the objective domain of the sovereignty of the ego".[8] Through his body, rearranged and continuously remodeled, the individual affirms himself. The concept of anatomy shifts from unchangeable destiny to amendable and constantly reversible instance. "The ancient

6 David Le Breton, *Anthropologie du corps et modernité* (Paris: Presses Universitaires de France, 2000), XVII.

7 Le Breton, *Anthropologie du corps et modernité*, cit., p. 5.

8 Le Breton, *Anthropologie du corps et modernité*, cit., p. 172.

sanctity of the body does not represent the rigid identity matrix of one's personal story anymore, but a form to be constantly remodeled".[9]

Such a state of being can lead to paradoxical outcomes. On the one hand, this postmodern and post-metaphysical dualism opens the way to transhumanistic scenarios of complete abandonment of the body, which becomes a shell to leave behind by uploading one's mind into cyberspace. This is the case for WBE (Whole Brain Emulation). On the other hand, we are witnessing an increasing overexposure of the body, which is perceived as a prosthetic of the ego. By constantly looking for a transitory incarnation, the ego tries to ensure the presence of significant traces of oneself. In our contemporary society, the problems of inwardness are resolved through an overt display of outwardness; "in order to embody our existing, we strive to visibly multiply our outer bodily signs".[10] A man has a body, but he is not his own body.

And of course, to better examine this second aspect, fitness culture in general and bodybuilding culture in particular represent privileged vantage points. Unlike other more traditional practices where the goal is to increase one's strength, such as powerlifting and weightlifting, bodybuilding inverts its parameters. Instead of having hypertrophy be just an adaptive means to improve one's performance as a consequence of an athletic gesture, growing muscle mass becomes the end goal to strive for a perfect body: a body that is perceived as seductive and erotic purely from its aesthetic qualities. The physical act of weightlifting along with a rigid diet are just the means to reach this goal. That is one of the reasons that bodybuilding cannot be considered to be a sport.

Originating from Richard Shusterman's pragmatic *somaesthetics*, if we accept the distinction between representational practices, such as cosmetics, and experiential practices, such as yoga, bodybuilding finds itself in a liminal zone between the two, where these two aspects blend into each

9 Le Breton, *Anthropologie du corps et modernité*, cit., p. 172.
10 Le Breton, *Anthropologie du corps et modernité*, cit., p. 175.

other. Indeed, if we consider the body in its "complex ontological structure […] both as a material object in the world and as an intentional subject projected towards the world",[11] we come to an inevitable conclusion. Even though bodybuilding strives for a representational goal, it also produces internal proprioceptive sensations through an increased sense of proprioception and widespread stress on a central nervous system level. Over time, these sensations can also become experiential goals that the bodybuilder pursues.[12] Training the body becomes a way of "thinking through the body".[13] As the American philosopher points out, in fact, if we recognize the somatic-bodily experience as an inevitable and inescapable part of experience, and if we see in philosophy an investigation into the experience and conduct of existence, then we cannot avoid considering somatics - with its efforts and attempts to improve the lived-experience through the exercise of the body - as an essential part of philosophy.[14] Going beyond that stale dualistic rhetoric, of clear Cartesian matrix, for which the brain is trained through intellectual activities, while the body is trained by sports and physical exercises, we discover that the movements of the body have repercussions on brain plasticity, on cognitive processes and, consequently on our thoughts. As Simone Ragazzoni points out: "training means involving oneself in a process of radical transformation that involves the totality of our being: thoughts, emotions, muscles, hormonal rates, neuronal networks and brain matter".[15] The

11 Richard Shusterman, *Body Consciousness: A Philosophy of Mindfulness and Somaesthetics* (New York: Cambridge University Press, 2008), p. 45.

12 An emblematic case in this sense is that of Mishima Yukio 三島由紀夫, whose relationship with bodybuilding is treated in *Taiyō to tetsu* [Sun and Steel] 『太陽と鉄』 (Tokyo: Kodansha 講談社, 1968). For the Japanese author, physical exercise becomes as much experience as orgasmic dissolution. In his view the body, through physical exercise, becomes a vessel for intellectual and material transcendence.

13 Richard Shusterman, *Thinking through the Body. Essays in Somaesthetics* (Cambridge: Cambridge University Press, 2012).

14 Richard Shusterman, *Performing Live. Aesthetics Alternatives for the Ends of Art* (London: Cornell University Press, 2000), 160.

15 Simone Ragazzoni, 'Postura e Pensiero', in *La palestra di Platone*, Kindle ed. (Milan: Ponte delle Grazie, 2020).

point of view of Derrida's disciple seems to be in agreement with the results of research in the field of embodied cognition theory. According to the neurobiologist and dancer Lucy Vincent, this leads to the conclusion "that the functioning of the brain and that of the body are not hierarchical, but inextricably linked. Imposing a certain posture on your body modifies the hormonal rates, but also the intellectual faculties".[16]

Starting from these considerations, at least in the case of bodybuilding, the aforementioned distinction between representational practices and experiential practices does not lead to an effective dichotomy when it comes to the praxis of the discipline. Instead, it can only be applied to a theoretical-critical analysis.

However, for our purposes we will assume the perspective of the pursuer of an ideal corporeal image. So, by focusing on the representational component of bodybuilding, we are necessarily going to overlook those experiential aspects. Despite this, I believe it is necessary to stress that bodybuilding is an all-encompassing discipline even when practiced at an amateur level. It is indeed true that nutrition plays a key role in sport because, as Ragazzoni points out, "a well-trained mind can push the body to the limit, but if the body has no energy, and the muscles and brain are not well nourished, the mind can do nothing, as without food we are unable to think".[17] However, in bodybuilding, diet becomes functional to make the body a work of art, a sculpture. It is no coincidence that in the movie Pumping Iron, when asked if he sees himself as a sculpture, Schwarzenegger answers:

> The good bodybuilders have the same mind that a sculptor has. If you analyze it, you look in the mirror and you say, okay, I need a bit more deltoids, so that the proportion's right, and you exercise and put those deltoids on, whereas an artist would just slap on some clay on each side. For us is more difficult because we work on human body

---

16 Lucy Vincent, *Fate danzare il cervello* (Milan: Ponte delle Grazie, 2019), p. 39.

17 Simone Ragazzoni, 'Mente incarnata e filosofia della nutrizione', in *La palestra di Platone*, cit.

Bodybuilding becomes an analog of body art. This idea seems to actualize the thought of the late Michel Foucault who sees bios as a material to be modeled for an aesthetic work of art.

> What strikes me is the fact that in our society, art has become something which is related only to objects and not to individuals, or to life [...] But couldn't everyone's life become a work of art? [...] From the idea that the self is not given to us, I think that there's only one practical consequence: we have to create ourselves as work of art.[18]

In the interesting and original interpretation of Foucault given by Ragazzoni,[19] the perfect body of the Austrian actor becomes the incarnation of one of the utopias dreamed of by the French philosopher who observes his own image in front of the mirror.[20]

> The human body is the principal actor in all utopias. After all isn't one of the oldest utopias about which men have told themselves stories the dream of an immense and inordinate body that could devour space and dominate the world?[21]

However, if the sensitive-bodily dimension assumes a founding and fundamental role in the construction of a bios that poses itself as a work of art, that of Foucault cannot even be considered a reduction of the aesthetics of the body to mere appearance. And as I have discussed earlier, there is no such reductionism in *Golden Age* bodybuilding either. In contemporary society, how does the emptying that transforms a complex physical discipline into a mere aesthetic appearance take place? Through mass media

---

18 Michel Foucault, *The Foucault Reader* (New York: Pantheon Books, 1984), pp. 350-51.

19 Simone Ragazzoni, 'Foucault e Schwarzenegger', in *La palestra di Platone*, cit.

20 "Still, every morning same presence, same wounds. In front of my eyes the same unavoidable images are drawn, imposed by the mirror: thin face, slouching shoulders, myopic gaze, no more hair-not handsome at all. And it is in this ugly shell of my head, in this cage I do not like, that I will have to reveal myself and walk around." In Michel Foucault, 'Utopian body' (*Le corps utopique*, 1966), in C. A. Jones (ed. by), *Sensorium. Embodied experience, technology and contemporary art* (Cambridge, Massachusetts: MIT Press, 2006), p. 229.]

21 Michel Foucault, 'Utopian body', cit., p. 231.

marketing, the fitness and wellness culture created the idea of a body as a commodity that expanded following the dynamics described by Guy Debord in *The Society of the Spectacle*. The beautiful body is no longer the result of physical effort, of a continuous confrontation with oneself and with one's own limits, nor, even less, the reflection of the Platonic Kalokagathia (καλοκαγαθίᾱ). As well as the other commodity-images spread by the mass media, the image beautiful and perfect body produces "waves of enthusiasm for a given product" resulting in "moments of fervent exaltation similar to the ecstasies of the convulsions and miracles of the old religious fetishism".[22]

Furthermore, the rise of new information and communication technologies have drastically and inevitably revolutionized people's perception of their own bodies as well as those of other people, thanks to the popularity of image-based social networks such as Instagram. The meticulous presentation of one's outer appearance becomes the main focus of online social actors to approach others within a global dimension. That is not all: digitalization, through an interactive extension just as somatic as it is psychic, allows for forms of bilateral cybernetic

22 "The satisfaction which no longer comes from the use of abundant commodities is now sought in the recognition of their value as commodities: the use of commodities becomes sufficient unto itself; the consumer is filled with religious fervor for the sovereign liberty of the commodities. Waves of enthusiasm for a given product, supported and spread by all the media of communication, are thus propagated with lightning speed. A style of dress emerges from a film; a magazine promotes night spots which launch various clothing fads. Just when the mass of commodities slides toward puerility, the puerile itself becomes a special commodity; this is epitomized by the gadget. We can recognize a mystical abandon to the transcendence of the commodity in free gifts, such as key chains which are not bought but are included by advertisers with prestigious purchases, or which flow by exchange in their own sphere. One who collects the key chains which have been manufactured for collection, accumulates the indulgences of the commodity, a glorious sign of his real presence among the faithful. Reified man advertises the proof of his intimacy with the commodity. The fetishism of commodities reaches moments of fervent exaltation similar to the ecstasies of the convulsions and miracles of the old religious fetishism. The only use which remains here is the fundamental use of submission." In Guy Debord, *The Society of the Spectacle* (New York: Zone Books edition, 1994), p. 45.

exchanges that are absent from more traditional kinds of mass-media. All these aspects lay down the foundations for a diffused aestheticization process. On the one hand, this turns the body into a ubiquitous entity. On the other hand, this new dynamic replaces various kinds of intermediation processes in favor of new forms of direct virtual contact. This leads to the progressive emancipation of sexuality from the organic, as has been theorized by philosopher Mario Parniola.[23] And with digitalization comes a generational shift in role models.

The perfect body of an actor or athlete represents a distant ideal, whose aesthetic perfection seems unreachable to the fan. Thus, that body is pervaded with the last remnants of a fading metaphysics. In contrast, the relationship between follower and influencer completely overthrows this paradigm. The Internet eliminates the very concept of distance or at least, creates the illusion of breaking down the barriers, simulating a direct relationship between who gets followed and who follows. The influencer is separate from myself, but at the same time seems like a potential version of myself. That is because the influencer represents the everyman who rises up to become an ideal; but instead of being an unreachable ideal, it is an ideal that could potentially be similar to myself.

Such a relational dynamic is based on parasocial psychological mechanisms. As if through a pane of semi-reflective glass, I get the impression that the other person is looking at me, even though they are actually looking at their own reflection. A recent article from weekly magazine and popular entertainment website Variety reported the results of a survey conducted in the USA. These results strongly suggest that among generation Z and younger millennial responders, Youtubers and influencers are better-known and perceived more positively than famous actors, athletes, or singers.[24] Another issue that vehemently re-emerges

23 Mario Perniola, *Il Sex appeal dell'inorganico* (Turin: Einaudi, 1994).

24 Todd Spangler, 'YouTuber PewDiePie Is More Liked Than LeBron James Among Gen Z Males, Study Finds', in *Variety*, October 5 (2019), https://variety.com/2019/digital/news/pewdiepie-lebron-james-gen-z-influencer-study-1203393503/.

from social networks is that of the authenticity of the body image. A similar question had already appeared in cinema: from 1960s Italian mondo movies by Paolo Cavara, Gualtier Jacopetti and Franco Prosperi, to fake-snuff series such as Japanese Guinea Pig, which aired from 1985 until 1992, without forgetting great exploitation classics such as Ruggero Deodato's *Cannibal Holocaust* (1980). By re-actualizing this body-authenticity question, social networks on the one hand manage to separate it from its more extreme connotations. On the other hand, they make this issue so pervasive that it bursts into our increasingly interconnected lives, becoming part of our daily experience.

The various Instagram profiles of the numerous fitness and bikini models alike showcase perfect bodies that, despite appearing as such only at the moment of photoshooting, create an illusion of continuity between the materiality of tangible experience and the virtuality of the web. The athlete's body, whether caught in his practice routine or during mundane daily life activities, is often immortalized during a peak week, under favorable lighting conditions, and with the right angle and poses to perfectly display muscle lines. And in the middle of this aestheticizing indifferentiation, we look around in astonishment and ask ourselves: what is real?

Kyōko Itō-Morales 伊藤モラレス杏子[1]

THE CHANGING IMAGE AND ROLE OF *ONI* IN JAPAN

app *Oni kara denwa* (Call from an *oni* app)

Oni (鬼, demons) have been present in life in Japan ever since the country was formed. At the present time, remnants of *oni* tradition can be seen in every aspect of Japanese life: eg. "*oni wa soto* (鬼は外, demon outside!)" at the *setsubun* (節分) festival in February, countless proverbs and idioms referring to *oni*, local festivals celebrating *oni*, literature, music and theatrical productions involving *oni*, and so forth. Even New Zealander Michael Leitch, the Captain of Japan's National Rugby Team, commented "we have to be *oni*" to express the strength of his fighting spirit in an interview before the last match of the elimination round of the 2019 Rugby World Cup 2019.[2]

Oni is an imaginary creature, often described as a hideous and terrifying evil monster. Yet, depictions are not always negative; *oni* sometimes represent the positive image of something with extraordinary qualities, for example *kisai* (鬼才, genius). This mixture of positive and negative associations comes from the *oni*'s complex origins and its long history of transformation, which have been influenced by various religions, local beliefs, popular thoughts, global trends, and other factors. When we examine the path taken by *oni* in detail, we may be able to understand how the image of *oni* has been transformed and what philosophical message it has been carrying. Therefore, the present study aims

1 University of Granada

2 Nakayasu Masato 中安真人, 'Fukuchō riichi, minagiru jishin… oni ni naru' [Recovered Leitch, Overflowing Confidence…we will be oni] 「復調リーチ、みなぎる自身…鬼になる」, in *Yomiuri Shinbun* 読売新聞, 13 October 2019, available online at: https://www.yomiuri.co.jp/rugbyworldcup/20191012-OYT1T50375/ Accessed 9 August 2020.

to complete the following two objectives: 1) a review of the transformation process of the image of *oni* throughout Japanese history and 2) an analysis of the accompanying philosophy.

Origin: Oni *as a Horrible Demon*

In order to research the roots of *oni* in Japan, we analyze the related studies into three principle streams from which *oni* developed its characteristics: the Japanese line, the Chinese line, and the Buddhist line.[3] The Japanese line is based on primitive thoughts. People's fear of destructive powers such as lightning and earthquakes led to the conception of these natural shocks as *oni*. Ancient people had no clear distinction between *kami* (神, gods, divinities) and *oni*; whatever possessed horrible or extraordinary power were *kami* and *oni*.[4] *Toyoko-kami* (豊子神, Gods from the other land/dead land) or *marebito* (賓, foreign travelers) with awesome powers, which were not always negative but sometimes had "happiness-bringer" features, were considered *kami*, and therefore could be *oni* as well.[5] In fact, the

3 Although Noriko Reider categorizes the sources for tradition into four main streams, relatively few studies claim a direct relationship between *Onmyōdō* and *oni*. Moreover, the author considers that the *Onmyōdō* stream is less notable in today's image of *oni*. Therefore, we use a framework of three origin streams. For a deeper analysis, please refer to Noriko T. Reider, *Japanese Demon Lore: Oni from Ancient Times to the Present* (Logan: Utah State University Press, 2010), p. 2.

4 Nakao Satoshi 中尾聡史, Morikuri Shigekazu 森栗茂一, Fujii Satoshi 藤井聡, 'Onidensetu kara miru doboku gijutsusha no ichizukeni kansuru minzokugakuteki kenkyū' [Folkloric Study about Civil Engineer in the Stories of Oni] 「鬼伝説からみる土木技術者の位置づけに関する民俗学的研究」, in *Jissen seisakugaku* 実践政策学, 3-2 (2017), p. 176. See also Rokugō Manzan Nihon Isan Suishin Kyōgikai [Rokugo Manzan Japan Heritage Promotion Council] 六郷満山日本遺産推進協議会, *Oni ga hotoke ni natta sato "Kunisaki" Zukan* [The Village where Oni became Gods: Kunisaki, a pictorial book] 『鬼が仏になった里「くにさき」図鑑』, (n.d.), available online at: https://www.onie.jp/zukan/kunisaki_oni_zukan_J.pdf, p. 34. Accessed 13 August 2020.

5 Noriko T. Reider, *Japanese Demons and Lore: Oni from Ancient Times to the Present*, cit., p. 3.

modern image of *oni* as an evil entity was formed along with social changes much later.[6] Another source for *oni* within the framework of its Japanese roots can be found in the myths of The *Kojiki* (古事記), in which dead Izanami, the female creator of Japan, transforms into an ugly *oni* named Yomotsushikome (黄泉醜女) because her husband Izanagi who visited her in the underworld broke his promise not to look back, and that made her furious and ashamed.[7] The last source of *oni* from the Japanese tradition is the ancestors' spirits, which stay in the mountains around their former home villages to protect the lives of their descendants. Because they cannot be seen, they were called *onu* or *on* (隠, hidden) and eventually came to be called *oni*.[8] Overall, *oni* as derived from Japanese roots present a mixture of positive (protector, happiness-bringer) and negative (terrifying and furious) characteristics.

The second stream feeding into the creation of *oni* was imported from Chinese tradition. In Chinese *guǐ* (鬼) means the sprits of the dead (死霊, *shirei*) or ghosts (幽霊, *yūrei*). In ancient China, it was believed that when a person died, he or she first became a *guǐ,* and then was placed into one of the two categories of good spirits, or divinities (善鬼), or evil spirits (悪鬼). The latter was considered to cause disasters and lure people into a diabolical path. Later these were commonly called *guǐ* (鬼).[9] When Chinese lexigraphic characters were introduced into Japan and the meaning and image of 鬼 spread, *oni* started to

6 Nakao Satoshi, Morikuri Shigekazu, Fujii Satoshi, 'Onidensetu kara miru doboku gijutsusha no ichizukeni kansuru minzokugakuteki kenkyū', cit., p. 176.

7 Noriko T. Reider, *Japanese Demon and Lore: Oni from Ancient Times to the Present*, cit., p. 4.

8 Rokugō Manzan Nihon Isan Suishin Kyōgikai, *Oni ga hotoke ni natta sato "Kunisaki"*, cit., p. 34.

9 Yoshimura Kōji 吉村耕治, Yamada Yūko 山田有子, 'Nihonbunka to chūgokubunka ni okeru oni wo arawasu iro -wabunka no kiteini mirareru in'yōgogyōsetsu-' [Colors Associated with Demons in Japanese and Chinese Culture: The Theory of Yin-Yang and the Five Elements Considered as a Basis of Japanese Culture] 「日本文化と中国文化における鬼を表す色ー和文化の基底に見られる陰陽五行説ー」, in *Nihon Shikisai Gakkaishi* 日本色彩学会誌, 42-3 (2018), p. 114.

appear in different forms of art and entertainment: literature, paintings and performing arts. The early form of typical image that we have of *oni* today — an ugly creature with one or more horns, commonly black but also blue, red, or yellow-skinned, and quite often wearing a tiger skin— was formed during these periods.[10] This visual appearance had its roots in Chinese *gui-shen* (鬼神, ghosts and spirits), but later Buddhism adopted the image of *gui-shen* and incorporated into its teachings. *Gui-shen* came to Japan around the seventh century with Buddhism and gave a shape to Japanese *oni* that at that time did not have a clear visual appearance.[11] In sum, Chinese tradition delivered a negative and frightening image of *oni* and this lore is still shared among countries and regions considerably influenced by China such as Korea, Taiwan, Vietnam and Laos.[12]

The Buddhist line represents the third source of *oni*. As stated above, the visual picture of *oni* came to Japan with Buddhism. As part of Buddhist teaching, *oni* were introduced to Japan as hideous supernatural creatures that dwell in the depths of Buddhist hell to punish those who have acted against divine justice while they lived. The origin of Buddhist *oni* can be found in Indian *yasha* and *rasetsu*. *Yasha* were monsters who were said to live by absorbing human's vital energy and *rasetsu* were another type of evil being who fed upon sinners' bodies in hell. As Buddhism developed, *yasha* were incorporated into its teachings and high-class *yasha* were promoted to heaven, while low-class *yasha* remained in hell as *oni*. The image of *oni* as hell's prison guards spread over Japan and Buddhism played a role to exorcise fear from people and expand its teachings.[13] The *Jigoku zōshi* (地獄草紙, volumes collecting paintings depicting

10 Noriko T. Reider, *Japanese Demons and Lore: Oni from Ancient Times to the Present*, cit., p. 7.

11 Noriko T. Reider, *Japanese Demons and Lore: Oni from Ancient Times to the Present*, cit., p. 9.

12 Shirokawa Takuma 白川琢磨, 'Oni to dentō bunka' [Oni and Traditional Culture] 「「鬼」と伝統文化」, in *Nanakuma no mori* 七隈の杜, 11 (2015), p. 18.

13 Noriko T. Reider, *Japanese Demons and Lore: Oni from Ancient Times to the Present*, cit., pp. 10-12.

hell) in *Rokudōe* (六道絵, Paintings of the six paths), frequently painted during the periods from Heian to Kamakura reflect the influence of Buddhism and are typical examples of the power of art in religions.[14] Even in the present day, we can encounter many *jigokue* (地獄絵, paintings of hell) in Buddhist temples, and probably the author is not alone in having been horrified during the process of being taught Buddhist morality through these images.

Transformation: Oni, *from a horrible to a loveable creature*

Having assimilated diverse origins and influences, *oni* from their earliest appearances in distinct communication materials such as literature, tales, paintings, and plays were described as cruel and frightening supernatural creatures. At the same time, they began to play an important role in carrying a philosophical message of respect for nature, which has been notably marked by the Japanese line, or of the divine justice of Buddhist teachings. However, the image of *oni* did not remain fixed in its initial form forever; rather it enjoyed a long journey of transformation. We will now explore the process by which the image of *oni* developed.

Dating back to medieval times, when many visual and written images of *oni* were created as forms of literature and performing arts,[15] there are two major attributes represented in depictions of *oni*: cannibalism and transformation.[16] First, let us look at the cannibalism. This aspect is considerably influenced by Indian Buddhist *yasha* and *rasetsu*, which add the image of terrifying appearance of *oni* wandering in search of human flesh.

14 Richard Shusterman, 'Arts and Religion', in *The Journal of Aesthetic Education*, 42-3 (2008), pp. 1-18.

15 Noriko T. Reider, 'Transformation of the Oni: From the Frightening and Diabolical to the Cute and Sexy', in *Asian Folklore Studies,* 62-1 (2003), p. 135.

16 Noriko T. Reider, *Japanese Demons and Lore: Oni from Ancient Times to the Present*, cit., pp. 14-18.

There are such stories in *Ise monogatari* (伊勢物語), *Shutendōji* (酒呑童子), and *Nihonkoku genhōzen'aku ryōiki* (日本国現報善悪霊異記), among others. Still, in those stories, rarely can we find the descriptions of moments when *oni* actually eat human beings. Rather when a disappearance or murder occurs, people cast suspicious eyes on *oni* because they are supposed to be responsible for those affairs. In this sense, *oni* represent human phobias towards invisible, mysterious and supernatural occurrences, which are also sometimes called *kamikakushi* (神隠し, hidden by the gods). The second attribute is the power of *oni* to transform themselves. Examples can be found in the aforementioned *Nihonkoku genhōzen'aku ryōriki,* or in other works such as *Konjaku monogatari* (今昔物語) and *Rashōmon* (羅生門), an example of *Nō* (能) drama. *Oni* may appear as a beautiful young women or talented gentlemen. However, of these, there are more works emphasizing the ability of *oni* to transform into women to use female sexuality to complete their ambitions.[17] In these writings, *oni* maintains the primitive features represented by its cruel and terrifying actions.

The following stage in the development of the image of *oni* was their weakening, in other words, the transformation of *oni* into creatures that can be defeated. Examples of transformed *oni* of this type are found in *Issunbōshi* (一寸法師) and *Momotarō* (桃太郎). In those tales, *oni* are still horrible and frightening beings, yet now the protagonists fight against them and even conquer them. Moreover, in their defeat, *oni* offer their vanquishers fortunes and happiness. That is to say, the new role of *oni* is to bring about happiness.[18] In the tale of *Issunbōshi*, the hero defeats an *oni* and wins a magic mallet, which transforms the tiny Issunbōshi into a normal-sized man, in addition to granting him treasures. In *Momotarō* as well, the vanquishing of *oni* enables Momotarō to return happily to his home flush with wealth inherited from *oni*. Perhaps, this storyline still survives in contemporary Japanese

17 Noriko T. Reider, *Japanese Demons and Lore: Oni from Ancient Times to the Present*, cit., p. 18.

18 Noriko T. Reider, *Japanese Demons and Lore: Oni from Ancient Times to the Present*, cit., pp. 24-29.

life in the form of *Setsubun* (節分), which is celebrated every February. Screaming "*oni wa soto, fuku wa uchi*" (「鬼は外、福は内！」, "*oni* outside and happiness inside!") and throwing dried beans at an *oni* (a person dressed as an *oni*) that characterize this event presents a clear example in which *oni* are treated as beatable and happiness-bringing actors. There are also customs and festivals where *oni* are treated as warmly welcomed guests because they actually help people to get rid of misfortune and bring them happiness. In Kunisaki (国東), Kyūshū, *Shujō onie* (修正鬼会) is celebrated on January 7th of the old calendar.[19] In this region, *oni* are believed to be *hotoke* (仏, Buddha) who help your wishes to come true, deliver happiness to you, and are like your longtime friends. Originally, the Buddhist-rooted *oni* had nothing to do with a friendly and positive creature. Still, the syncretization of Shintoism and Buddhism in these areas has successfully transferred *oni* into a god-like, but reachable and familiar, character.[20]

In the modern period, *oni* has come to have an even more amiable existence. A representative book to be mentioned here is *Naita akaoni* (泣いた赤鬼, *The Red Oni who Cried*) written by Hamada Hirosuke (濱田廣介).[21] Originally published with the title *Oni no sōdan* (おにのさうだん) in 1933 in a monthly journal for children, this story has been published with minor revisions over and over up to this day. It has been even used as teaching material for *kokugo* (国語, Japanese as a mother language class) and *dōtoku* (道徳, ethics class) in primary school education.[22] The red and blue *oni* appearing in this text are human-like delicate, sensitive, and warm-hearted beings. Because the friendly red

19 Rokugō Manzan Nihon Isan Suishin Kyōgikai, *Oni ga hotoke ni natta sato "Kunisaki"*, cit.

20 Shirokawa Takuma, "Oni' to dentō bunka', cit., pp. 22-28.

21 Noriko T. Reider, 'Transformation of the Oni: From the Frightening and Diabolical to the Cute and Sexy', cit., pp. 145-146.

22 Imaizumi Takeo 今泉岳雄, 'Jibun no monogatari toshite "naita akaoni"o yomu' [Discussion about "Naita Akaoni" from the Viewpoint of One's Own Story] 「自分の物語として「泣いた赤おに」を読む」, in *Tōhoku bunkyō daigaku tanki daigakubu kiyō* 東北文教大学短期大学部紀要, 6 (2016), pp. 1-2.

oni represents the marginalized stranger who makes all efforts to be welcomed into a community, and the blue-*oni* teaches us the value of self-sacrifice, this work has been a favorites in the Japanese education system for a long time,[23] which has played an important role in changing the portrait of awful *oni* to that of a humanized creature[24] throughout all generations in Japan.

The gentle image of *oni* was softened even more when several children's songs about *oni* were released. Besides *Mamemaki* (まめまき, *Bean Throwing*), one of the more popular children's songs, which describes *oni* as a beatable creature, *Oni no pantsu* (鬼のパンツ, Oni's Pants) (author unknown, children's song, around 1975) and *Akaoni to aooni no tango* (赤鬼と青鬼のタンゴ, *The tango of the red oni and the blue oni*) (lyrics by Katō Tadashi 加藤直, composed by Fukuda Wakako 福田和禾子 and sung by Bitō Isao 尾藤イサオ, 1978) present *oni* with fun and humor. This process of the infantilization of *oni* brings them to a new and difference space where *oni* have become one of a number of loveable characters like *Hello Kitty* or *Doraemon*. This progress has probably served as a bridge to promote *oni* for commercialization. Now they are frequently used in manga, anime, commercial goods, and as mascots for *machi okoshi* (町おこし, town revitalization), among other applications. Consumer culture has de-monopolized the long-established symbolic value[25] of the original *oni* as a guardian of divine justice.

Instrumentalization: Oni *as a tool on demand*

We may assume that the unique sources of *oni*, that is, the mixture of their complex roots and original characteristics (both positive and negative), enabled the image of *oni* to be converted

23 Imaizumi Takeo, 'Jibun no monogatari toshite "naita akaoni"wo yomu', cit., pp. 3-9.

24 Noriko T. Reider, 'Transformation of the Oni: From the Frightening and Diabolical to the Cute and Sexy', cit., p. 146.

25 Mike Featherstone, *Consumer Culture and Postmodernism* (Los Angeles, London, New Delhi, Singapore: SAGE Publications, 2007), p. 96.

from that of a cruel horrible supernatural being to a human-like, cute, and loveable creature. Still, recent commercialization of *oni* looks disturbing to some extent, since they no longer function as a philosophical brake to control morals in Japanese society. In order to examine this trend, we turn now to the example of commercialization and instrumentalization of *oni* by analyzing the telephone application called *Oni kara denwa* (鬼から電話, Call from *Oni*).[26]

Oni kara denwa is a smartphone application developed by Media Active, Inc. and its purpose is to ease the parental effort involved in the raising of kindergarten-aged children. Between its release in 2012 and the summer of 2020, it was downloaded more than twenty million times, and the application was being used at the later date by one in every 6 people with children under 6 years old.[27] Basically, this app is used to frighten and scold children. The mechanism is very simple and effective; after downloading the app, parents open it when their children misbehave. The app then generates a phone call from a terrifying *oni* designed to frighten the child into correcting his/her behavior. There are also different versions with other horrible characters such as ghosts, vampires, zombies and *namahage* (なまはげ). Sasaki, the creator of the application, says he was originally inspired by the *namahage*, which is a terrifying *oni*-like creature who serves a similar child-rearing function in a traditional festival in Akita prefecture.[28] Some of the factors behind the extraordinal success of this app include the increase of nuclear families with busy lifestyles, the dependence of socially isolated young families on apps for child discipline, and a general and widespread demand for effective and quick solutions to everyday problems.[29] However, parent users do not always have a defensible reasons for using it. They may

26 https://www.onikara-denwa.com/ Accessed 13 August 2020.

27 https://www.onikara-denwa.com/collabo.html Accessed 13 August 2020.

28 Koizumi Hiroyuki 小泉裕之, 'Oni kara denwa "kora!" [Call from Oni "Hey!"] 「鬼から電話「こら！」」, in *Nikkei Style*, 31 May 2013, available online at: https://style.nikkei.com/article/DGXDZO55603110Z20C13A5EL1P01/ Accessed 13 August 2020.

29 '"Oni kara denwa" kodomo wo shikaru apuriga daininki' ["Call from Oni" an App to Scold Children Becomes Very Popular] 「「おにから電話」子ど

rely on the app when they want children go to sleep quickly so that they can start playing videogames or when kids are bothering adults because they want attention, showing a willingness to use it to shut up children as quickly as possible without trying to understand the needs being expressed. Unfortunately, there is no space for *oni* and its philosophy to reconsider the rightness of use of fear. Clearly, the popularity of this app exhibits the instrumentalization of *oni*: *oni* as a tool on demand.

Let us compare the original *oni* with the ones in this application. *Oni* had been autonomous entities, possessed of god-like supernatural power, making them unreachable, frightening but respectable creatures. These were the very reasons why *oni* were considered the watchdogs of divine justice, figures who brought either punishment or happiness to those who had earned one or the other. The *oni* in the app is merely an instrument; it is no more than a controllable object with no capacity to act flexibly, therefore nothing but a consumer's servant. Hence, the educational philosophy traditionally accompanying *oni* has disappeared.

There are criticisms about the popularity of the *Oni kara denwa* app. Essentially there are two groups of people who express doubts concerning the practical value of this application. On one hand, psychologists of early-stage child development warn of the danger of its use because children facing the fear of *Oni kara denwa* are neither protected by their parents to ease the experience of horror nor punished by philosophically-validated *oni* with a capacity to be flexible.[30] Small children have not yet developed enough to understand the well-learned punishment quickly. Old *oni* used to give people (including children) time and a chance to reflect and understand their own faults, sometimes with the help of Buddhist monks, sometimes with parents. That was why *oni*

もを叱るアプリが大人気」, in *Huffpost*, 4 June 2013, available online at: https://www.huffingtonpost.jp/2013/06/04/onikaradenwa_n_3382396.html Accessed 13 August 2020.

30 Usui Mafumi 碓井真史, *"Oni kara denwa" no kōka to tsukaikata: shikarikata no shinrigaku* [The effect and use of "Call from Oni": Psychology of Scolding] 『「鬼から電話」の効果と使い方：叱り方の心理学』, 14 April 2013, available online at: https://news.yahoo.co.jp/byline/usuimafumi/20130415-00024405/ Accessed 13 August 2020.

could act flexibly and even brought happiness later. Now *oni* in the application do what their masters demand: scare children. There is no aftercare because *oni* does not have this function any longer. Children are not being attended by their parents either, because they are the very people who bring about the fear, regardless of whether their reasons are valid or not. This is the concern raised by psychologists. At the same time, religious groups, particularly Buddhists, have also express their worries regarding the app.[31] Their arguments are quite similar to those of psychologists. In addition, they are naturally concerned about the instrumentalization of *oni* as a simple frightening object, something which ignores Buddhist ethical teachings completely. Thus, despite the outstanding sales of *Oni kara denwa*, it sparks the need of a thorough review on the use of the *oni* 's terrible image for purely commercial purposes.

In order to respond the criticisms, Media Active, Inc. has taken corrective actions and adopted several characters that express positive messages. The new characters are superheroes from TV series', famous actors and athletes whom children admire, and beloved seasonal characters like Santa Claus. Thanks to these new cast members, *Oni kara denwa* now offers tools to promote good behavior in children that are not limited to scolding, but can also encourage them to be good boys and girls so that their favorite characters may praise them. Thus, the selection of whether to use fear or praise to correct children's behavior has now been left to the choice of service consumers, who are the parents. Nonetheless, the fact that *oni* and other personalities are simply tools on demand has not been changed.

Role of original philosophy of oni *in consumer society*

In this work, we have examined the long journey of Japanese *oni*, starting with their origins, then proceeding to the processes by which their image transformed from a horrible monster to a

31 Nihon bukkyō hoiku kyōkai 日本仏教保育協会, *Hotoke no ko* [Child of Buddha] 『仏の子』 (Tokyo: Senkyōsha 宣協社, 2015).

loveable creature as well as the communication materials used (paintings, literature, local and national festivals and music), and finally examining present trends. Throughout most of these developmental stages, *oni* have played the role of messengers of divine justice. However, contemporary tendencies toward instrumentalization in our consumption-based society endangers the morally driven philosophy of *oni*, a condition demonstrated by the example of the smartphone application *Oni kara denwa*. Although it is natural that images and the philosophies attached to them evolve along with social change, it is sometimes necessary to question and reflect on the nature of these transformations. By doing so, as far as *oni* are concerned, we can rediscover why *oni* were created, why they are still with us, what message they want to transmit to us, and how we should live with them. Recalling the philosophical role of *oni* may help us to seek an adequate balance of between the development of their image and extreme instrumentalization to which they have been subject.

Acknowledgements

The author thankfully acknowledges the valuable corrections and constructive suggestions she received from Robert and Judi Dey for this work.

Olga Kopylova[1]

STYLE NEGOTIATED

Transformations of the Visuals in Manga-to-anime Adaptations

Introduction

Since Japanese popular culture began its rapid advance abroad in the 1990s, quite a number of tutorials have been printed in English on 'drawing manga and/or anime'. Notably, books like *How to Draw Manga: Basics and Beyond!*[2] or *Mastering Manga with Mark Crilley*[3] do not aim to explain actual steps of creating comics. Rather the reader is expected to learn about some homogenous visual style, or at least a number of traits that are common and recognizable enough to make a drawing (usually a character image) sufficiently 'manga-esque'. Such generalizations might not be surprising in textbooks for the would-be-practitioners, but it is more perplexing to see manga mentioned as a "particular comics style" in an academic publication.[4] As any experienced reader can attest, graphic narratives produced in Japan display great variety in terms of their visuals, and these variations play an important, if not central, role in the experiences and practices of consumers and producers alike.

This significance has been at least partially recognized by Japanese scholars and critics. Entire movements and genres,

---

1 Tohoku University

2 Katagiri Ryō, Sengoku Hiroyuki, and Onishi Yukio, *How to Draw Manga: Basics and Beyond!*, by Japanime Co. Ltd. (Saitama: Manga University, 2019).

3 Mark Crilley, *Mastering Manga With Mark Crilley* (Canada: Impact Books, 2012), Kindle.

4 Charles Forceville, Elisabeth El Refaie, and Gert Meesters, 'Stylistics and Comics', in Michael Burke (ed. by), *Routledge Handbook of Stylistics* (New York: Routledge, 2014), pp. 485-499.

such as *gekiga*[5] (劇画) or *shōjo* (少女) manga, have been defined by their visual aspects, namely quality of lines,[6] stylistic deformations (such as 'starry' eyes) and page layout,[7] as well as visual properties of verbal text and interplay of words and images on a page.[8] Anglophone discussions of visual style in comics

5 *Gekiga*, known for its realistic thrust, went through a boom in the 1960s and still persists as an obscure, but well-read subcategory of mainstream manga today. Considering that themes and genres handled in *gekiga* are as varied as sites and formats of publication, it indeed seems reasonable to define it primarily as a visual style.

6 Takeuchi Miho 竹内美帆, 'Sen kara toraenaosu "gekiga": Saitō Takao wo chūshin ni' [Rethinking gekiga through the linework: with focus on Saitō Takao] 「線から捉えなおす「劇画」——さいとう・たかをを中心に」, in Jacqueline Berndt, Yamanaka Chie, and Leem Hye Jeong (ed. by), *Global Manga Studies*, vol.3 (Kyoto: Kyoto Seika University International Manga Research Center, 2013), pp. 175-199; Takekuma Kentarō 竹熊健太郎, 'Dōgu to tacchi no hyōgen hensen-shi: koseitekina "sen" wo umidasu no wa, jidai ka, dōgu ka?' [The history of changes in tools and style: are idiosyncratic lines the product of their time or tools?]「道具とタッチの表現変遷史——個性的な「線」」を生み出すのは、時代か、道具か？」, in *Manga no yomikata* [How to Read Manga] 『マンガの読み方』, Inoue Manabu 井上学 (ed.by) (Tokyo: Takarajima-sha 宝島社, 1995), pp. 38-51.

7 Fujimoto Yukari 藤本由香里, 'Takahashi Macoto: The origin of shōjo manga style', in Matt Thorn (trans.), *Mechademia* 7 (Minneapolis: University of Minnesota Press, 2012), pp. 24-55; Thierry Groensteen, *Comics and Narration*, Ann Miller (trans.) (Jackson: University Press of Mississippi, 2013); Itō Gō 伊藤剛, *Tezuka izu deddo: hirakareta manga hyōgenron* [Tezuka is Dead: Postmodernist and Modernist Approaches to Japanese Manga] 『テヅカ・イズ・デッドーーひらかれたマンガ表現論へ』 (Tokyo: NTT Shuppan NTT出版, 2005); Fusanosuke Natsume 夏目房之介, 'Koma no kihon-genri wo yomitoku: dokusha no shinri wo yūdō-suru komawari to iu majikku' [Basic panelling principles: the magic of panel layouts that shape readers' response]「駒の基本原理を読み解く——読者の心理を誘導するコマ割りというマジック」, in *Manga no yomikata*, cit., pp. 168-195.; Takahashi Mizuki 高橋瑞木, 'Opening the Closed World of Shōjo Manga', in Mark W. MacWilliams (ed. by), *Japanese Visual Culture: Explorations in the World of Manga and Anime* (New York: M. E. Sharpe, 2008), pp. 114-136.

8 Giancarla Unser-Schutz, 'Language as the visual: Exploring the intersection of linguistic and visual language in manga', in Hans Coppens, Nele Noppe (ed. by), *Image [&] Narrative*, Vol 12-1 *Visual Language of Manga* (2011), pp. 167-188, WEB; Ōtsuka Eiji 大塚英志, 'Naimen no hakken to sōshitsu: shōjo manga ni okeru "kotoba" no hen'yō' [Finding and losing the interior: transformations of verbal text in shōjo manga] 「内面の発見と喪失——少女まんがにおける「ことば」の変容」, in *Sengo-manga no hyōgen kūkan: kigōteki shintai no jubaku* [The expressive space of postwar manga: the spell

usually cover the same parameters,[9] with particular emphasis on graphic (or 'drawing') style, which is understood to include the amount of details, distribution of blank spaces, depth, and lighting in addition to the aforementioned linework and levels of stylization.[10] Most of Anglophone discussions, however, have so far gravitated to individual authors and their idiosyncratic style,[11] as opposed to Japanese research and criticism, where considerable attention is paid to so-called 'group styles'. There is also a related tendency in Japanese comics studies to focus on readership as much or even more than on particular authors and to treat visual style as the means of identity formation (for both artists and readers) or communication, rather than just an instrument of highly individualized self-expression.[12]

The current chapter follows this direction as it addresses visual style both as a vehicle of communication and as something communicated. However, contrary to the majority of previous publications grounded mostly in semiotics, historical research, art

---

of symbolic bodies] 『戦後まんがの表現空間: 記号的身体の呪縛』 (Kyoto: Hōzōkan 法藏館, 1994), pp. 56-71.

9 Jan Baetens, Hugo Frey, *The Graphic Novel: An Introduction* (New York: Cambridge University Press, 2015); Lukas Etter, 'Visible Hand? Subjectivity and Its Stylistic Markers in Graphic Narratives', in Maike Sarah Reinerth and Jan-Noël Thon (ed. by), *Subjectivity Across Media: Interdisciplinary and Transmedial Perspectives* (New York: Routledge, 2017), pp. 92-110; Charles Forceville et al., 'Stylistics and Comics', cit., 2014; Pascal Lefèvre, 'No Content without Form: Graphic Style as the Primary Entrance to a Story', in Neil Cohn (ed. by), *The Visual Narrative Reader* (London: Bloomsburry, 2016), p. 67-88.

10 It should be noted that narratological or semiotic analyses of page layouts or various operations with text and images outnumber those concerned with stylistics.

11 Jan Baetens and Hugo Frey, *The Graphic Novel*, cit., pp. 134-161; Lukas Etter, 'Visible Hand?', cit.; Jared Gardner, 'Storylines', in *SubStance* Vol.40-1, Issue 124: *Graphic Narratives and Narrative Theory* (Madison: University of Wisconsin Press, 2011), pp. 53-69; Hannah Miodrag, 'Chaptear Eight: Style, Expressivity, and Impressionistic Evaluation', in *Comics and Language: Reimagining Critical Discourse on the Form* (Jackson: University Press of Mississippi, 2013), pp. 197-220.

12 Takeuchi Miho, *Biteki tōya to shite no manga: bijutsu kyōiku, hyōgenron, tekusuto bunseki* [Manga as aesthetic Bildung: art education, manga expression, textual analysis] 『美的陶冶としてのマンガ——美術教育、表現論、テクスト分析』, Ph.D. thesis (Kyoto: Kyoto Seika University, 2017).

theory, or literary analysis, the discussion here is informed by media and fan studies. The last thirty years has seen the digitization of production and consumption processes, the rapid development of international fan communities, and, most importantly, the arrival of convergence culture, where narratives, characters and fictional worlds, on the one hand, and increasingly active, "participatory" audiences, on the other hand, move actively across platforms and media.[13] In popular culture today material aspects of visual style pose new challenges, while its functions are realized on a much larger scale and in increasingly complex ways. Interactions between various parties that utilize visual style have also grown more prominent and multifarious – this holds particularly true for environments like the Japanese otaku market,[14] where numerous media share visual conventions, codes, and styles and where transmedial adaptations are a matter of course. To look into visual style in such a context requires attention to immediate materiality of the media in question (i.e. drawing tools and support) and to their conventions (such as predominance of serialized narratives or focus on character image), but also to corresponding industries (including specifics of both creative labour and production processes), and, finally, to individuals and communities at play.

Challenges of cross-platform reproduction of an established style have been largely ignored in scholarly and critical discussions, which more often focus on a singular medium of the graphic narrative and on solitary labour of a particular "author-artist".[15] This article is but a single step into this yet unexplored terrain. It starts with a brief summary of the ways style can serve as the means of communication in contemporary popular cultural environment. Considered next are more specific issues that have to do with treatment of style in manga and anime, these

13 Henry Jenkins, *Convergence Culture: When Old and New Media Collide* (New York: New York University Press, 2006).

14 'Otaku market' can be defined as a site of production, dissemination and consumption of anime, manga, video games, and other Japanese popular media (as well as goods and services) that share common aesthetics, narrative tropes and genres, and maintain strong material and conceptual links with each other.

15 Lukas Etter, 'Visible Hand?', cit., p. 97.

two pillars of otaku-oriented franchise development in Japan. Central to both parts is graphic style, with aspects like panel layout or lettering omitted from the discussion. Besides space constraints, this narrow focus is warranted by the importance of line as the basic structural unit and the default expressive means of the medium, equally valued by artists and readers. Hopefully, the following observations will inspire more multifaceted analyses of visual style in transmedia environment and further exploration of the relevant topics within and outside Japan.

Style and Communication: The Reader's Perspective

The verb 'communicate' has two principal connotations: 1) 'to exchange (ideas, thoughts, information, etc.)', and 2) 'to transmit (feelings, emotions, messages, etc.)'. The communicative value of style is utilized first and foremost in the second sense. One does not need to seek strict correspondence between artists' stylistic choices and any specific message to acknowledge that a drawn picture is always in and of itself an interpretation of the depicted object.[16] The reader's impressions are shaped by style as well as by narrative content, and sometimes more by the former than by the latter. Beyond this rather banal point, all drawings reveal the process of their own making, albeit to a different extent. The final image, and especially the line, retains "the gestural movement of the artist",[17] or the inherent dynamism, which can be more or less pronounced. It follows that the drawing mediates 'face-to-face' contact between the reader and the artist,[18] or, to be more precise, the 'graphiateur'. The latter term, coined by Philippe Marion and popularized by Jan Baetens,[19] designates a "singular and

16 Jan Baetens and Hugo Frey, *The Graphic Novel*, cit., p. 138; Pascal Lefèvre, 'No Content without Form', cit.

17 Paul Atkinson, 'Movements within Movements: Following the Line in Animation and Comic Books', in *Animation-an Interdisciplinary Journal*, 4-3 (2009), pp. 265-281, WEB.

18 Maaheen Ahmed, 'Comics and Authorship: An Introduction', in *Authorship*, 6-2 (Ghent University, 2017), WEB; Jared Gardner, 'Storylines', cit.

19 Jan Baetens, 'Revealing Traces: A New Theory of Graphic Enunciation', in

individual subjectivity" imagined by the reader, which resides not only in the visual interpretation of the depicted object or scene (revealed through the enunciative act of 'graphiation'), but also in material traces of the drawing hand.[20] The graphiateur is therefore conceptualized as an abstract figure, which, however, still maintains a connection with the actual artist on a physical level.[21] This duality makes the concept highly useful in the context of manga production in Japan.

It is common knowledge that the majority of mainstream manga series are the product of collaborative labour, which involves the manga artist, her assistants, editors (who will likely change several times before the series is over), and, sometimes, a scenario writer.[22] The input of each participant may vary, but assistants in particular contribute directly to the final drawing – a fact habitually acknowledged in both interviews and on manga pages.[23] At the same time, the majority of the team members (barring scenario writers) tend to stay in the background, whether in fan talk or in official accounts;[24] and the entire series is typically

---

Robin Varnum and Christina T. Gibbons (ed. by), *The Language of Comics: Word and Image* (Jackson: University Press of Mississippi, 2001), loc. 1822-1952, Kindle.

20 Jan Baetens, 'Revealing Traces: A New Theory of Graphic Enunciation', cit., loc. 1877.

21 Jared Gardner, 'Storylines', cit.

22 Bryan Hikari Hartzheim, 'Chapter 2: Manga Production and Shueisha's Weekly Shōnen Jump', in *Inside the Media Mix: Collective Creation in Contemporary Manga and Anime*, Ph.D. thesis (Los Angeles: University of California, 2015), pp. 49-126; Jennifer S. Prough, 'Chapter Four: Affective Labor: Gender, Generation, and Consumption in the Production of Shōjo Manga', in *Straight From the Heart: Gender, Intimacy, and The Cultural Production of Shōjo Manga* (Honolulu: University of Hawai'i Press, 2011), pp. 89-109; Sharon Kinsella, 'Chapter 6: Creative Editors and Unusable Artists', in *Adult Manga: Culture and Power in Contemporary Japanese Society* (Richmond: Curzon Press, 2000), pp. 162-201.

23 Sakurai Gamon 桜井画門, for instance, painstakingly documents his assistants' input at the end of each volume, down to objects drawn and percentage of the work done within each panel.

24 Even publications and programs that go behind the scenes of manga production tend to focus on principal artist as the key creator. See, for example, *Weekly Shōnen Jump* 40th anniversary collection of interviews edited by Kadokura Shima 門倉紫麻: *Manganō no kitaekata* [How to Train the Manga Mind] 『マ

attributed to one principal artist, a creative position that is widely publicized and marketed. Venerated veterans and new stars alike are usually known for their trademark graphic style[25] as much as for the stories signed with their name, and readers often seek the 'hand', or 'touch' (タッチ), associated with a certain artist.[26] Thanks to its abstract quality, the concept of graphiateur can accommodate multiple participants in manga production, while its emphasis on "a physical encounter with both a particular pen and a particular hand"[27] reflects the importance attributed to both styles and author figures.

As evident from the outline above, the drawing in a graphic narrative can in itself be perceived as a vehicle of communication insofar it becomes an expression of a particular worldview and a site of bodily encounter between the graphiateur and the reader. On the level of production, visual style in mainstream Japanese manga emerges as an outcome of communication and negotiation between different parties, from below-the-line assistants to the publishing house. Another area where graphic style features prominently is fandom, where it becomes the means for an amateur creator[28] to share her views and preferences, carve

ンガ脳の鍛えかた』 (Tokyo: Shueisha 集英社, 2010); or the TV documentary *Urasawa Naoki no manben* [Urasawa Naoki's Manben] 『浦沢直樹の漫勉』, NHK (2015-2020).

25 Which also should be called the most personalized aspect of visual style in commercial manga production where editor's input affects first and foremost page layout, framing and text placement.

26 For instance, reviewer Minami Nobunaga 南信長 not only introduces "the greatest" and "most interesting" manga authors for the benefit of his regular readership in his book-length recommendation list, but he takes time to reconstruct a network of visual influences for the mentioned artists. See *Gendai manga no bōkensha-tachi: Ōtomo Katsuhiro kara Ono Natsume made* [Adventurers of Modern Comics: From Katsuhiro Ōtomo to Natsume Ono] 『現代マンガの冒険者たち——大友克洋からオノ・ナツメまで』 (Tokyo: NTT Shuppan NTT 出版, 2008).

27 Jared Gardner, 'Storylines', cit., p. 67.

28 The following part focuses on amateur artists who actively participate in a certain fandom. Nowadays, it is common for professional artists, as well as veteran fanartists, to off-handedly draw a fanart piece or two in reaction to public hype, as a part of a flashmob, or simply for self-promotion. Obviously, their self-identity, as well as their relationship with fan community, is constructed differently from those dedicated amateurs.

a distinct place for herself in the community and, on more advanced levels, shape others' tastes and shared 'truths'.

According to Marjorie Cohee Manifold,[29] the initial stage of typical fanartist[30] development involves imitative drawing, with a newcomer struggling to master the style of the source work.[31] Copying and studying different styles is, of course, an essential part of art education. However, for fanartists it can be the goal, rather than the means. Apart from immediate pleasure of reproducing the object of one's fascination, imitative drawing facilitates integration of a novice fan into the larger fan community, which would encourage or even demand adherence to the source style. A successful copyist enjoys social acceptance and a sense of belonging based on shared aesthetic preferences. On the other hand, accomplished fanartists already recognized and respected in their fandom would usually abandon copying in favour of invention and strive to develop their own style.[32] They would also use their cultural capital and skills to "contribut[e] to conversations",[33] reinterpret the source material or establish new conventions in the fandom.[34] It must be noted, however, that masterful imitation is generally appreciated as much as

29 Marjorie Cohee Manifold, 'Fanart as Craft and the Creation of Culture', in *International Journal of Education through Art*, 5-1 (2009), pp. 7-21, WEB.

30 Manifold operates with a broad definition of 'fanart', which includes "drawing, painting, sculpture, photography, photo manipulation, videos, crafts, textiles, metal smithing, and fashion" and is based on "a specific TV show, movie, book, or other media event not owned or created by the artist" (Fanlore 2020). The current discussion, on the other hand, adheres to a more narrow understanding of fanart as similarly derivative art "that is drawn or painted either traditionally or digitally" (ibid.). See https://fanlore.org/wiki/Fanart (accessed on Sep. 22, 2020).

31 Marjorie Cohee Manifold, 'From Amateur to Framauteur: Art Development of Adolescents and Young Adults within an Interest-Based Community', in *Studies in Art Education*, 54-1 (Alexandria: National Art Education Association, 2012), pp. 37-53 and pp. 41-42.

32 Marjorie Cohee Manifold, 'From Amateur to Framauteur: Art Development of Adolescents and Young Adults within an Interest-Based Community', cit., pp. 45-46.

33 Marjorie Cohee Manifold, 'Fanart as Craft and the Creation of Culture', cit., p. 17.

34 Marjorie Cohee Manifold, 'Fanart as Craft and the Creation of Culture', cit., p. 13.

skilful innovation, and new interpretation might mean drawing a completely new scene in the style of the source work.

Manifold's observations sum up experiences of three hundred fan creators from all over the world – one can assume that they largely apply to Japanese manga fandoms, too. In Japan, however, fan activities gain another dimension due to the specifics of the manga industry, that is, an established tradition of cultivating new artists directly from the readership.[35] Already in the late 1950s rental comic books included a letter page, and readers were encouraged to submit copies of their favourite panels and drawings in the style of particular authors. Artists like Saitō Takao commented on submissions, persistently referring to the quality of lines – or of drawing style in general.[36] The tradition was not limited to *gekiga* or rental books either: *shōjo* manga magazines of the same period likewise encouraged readers to submit fanart – often an imitation of a particular image was required.[37] These practices radically closed the distance between artists and readers – who all partook in the same aesthetics and representational techniques. They also served to educate the readers, fostering future creative workers for the same magazines. Besides, letter pages allowed fanartists (both individuals and groups) to exchange post addresses and thus find like-minded amateur creators.[38] In other words, periodicals specializing in manga facilitated communication between readers and artists (as well as editors) in order to hold the interest of their young readers, consolidate fan loyalty, and secure new hands for the industry. They also gave their readers the opportunity to communicate with their peers and in doing so contributed to the formation of fan community.[39]

---

35 Bryan Hikari Hartzheim, *Inside the Media Mix*, cit.; Jennifer S. Prough, 'Chapter Three: Raising Readers, Rearing Artists: Fabricating Community in Shōjo Manga Magazines', in *Straight From the Heart: Gender, Intimacy, and The Cultural Production of Shōjo Manga*, cit., pp. 57-88.

36 Takeuchi Miho, 'Sen kara toraenaosu "gekiga"', cit., pp. 189-191.

37 Fujimoto Yukari, 'Takahashi Macoto: The origin of shōjo manga style', cit., pp. 24-55.

38 Takeuchi Miho, 'Sen kara toraenaosu "gekiga"', cit., p. 190.

39 It must also be noted that online communication utilizing visual style

As demonstrated in this section, graphic style in mainstream manga serves multiple purposes in more or less direct ways. It can become an instrument of self-expression and an individual voice, but it is also a collective property, which both facilitates interpersonal communication on various levels of production and consumption and is shaped by it. These processes come to the fore in the context of contemporary popular culture that thrives on ceaseless proliferation of characters and narratives across works and platforms. This movement brings together multiple media, industries and creative personnel, necessitating dialogue and negotiation on all levels of production. Illustrative examples of resulting visual transformations of shared materials (most prominently, characters) come from manga-to-anime adaptations, which are discussed in the next part of this chapter.

Manga-to-Anime Adaptations and Visual Style

The anime industry continues to rely heavily on stories and characters created and developed in other media, and manga has always remained the primary source of new narratives. Because of the affinity between the two media, manga-to-anime adaptations inevitably bring forth the issue of style, particularly important for the already-existing fan base. It goes without saying that the collaborative process of anime-making is very sophisticated compared with manga production and depends on

grows in both scale and variety. First, widely recognized elements such as pictograms and pictorial runes (such as sweatdrops representing anxiety, depression, fear, etc.) or methods of exaggeration (e.g., so-called 'super deformed') can become a lingua franca shared by thousands of users across the world. Likewise, a certain set of stylistic traits can become representative of a certain platform or social network, as exemplified by the notorious 'Tumblr Red Nose Syndrome.' Numerous international flash mobs involve playing with styles associated with a certain artistic tradition, a specific work, or an acknowledged artist. Finally, peer artists, professionals and amateurs alike engage in friendly exchanges and collaborations where they imitate or juxtapose each other's manners of drawing. All these practices go beyond a single community, indeed beyond the fandom per se, bringing together creators of all backgrounds and interests.

the coordinated efforts of numerous active players at all stages. Therefore, in adaptation projects, visual style becomes a subject of negotiation between various "creative stakeholders",[40] media, and the market (with aesthetic preferences of the target audience always taken into account).

Unsurprisingly, transformations of style necessitated by medium specificity proliferate even when the media involved are as visually close as anime and manga. Only certain aspects of the overall visual style can be retained in a typical adaptation. One such aspect is the drawing style, and particularly the way characters are depicted, including the quality of the line, the amount of detail, and the manner of stylization.[41] Universal focus on characters is practically inevitable. First, since the success of Tezuka's *Astro Boy* in 1963, fictional characters have remained the major driving force behind transmedia franchise development in Japan;[42] second, in collaboratively produced serial graphic narratives character drawings are the most representative with regards to the (main) artist's individual style. Efforts to reproduce that style, however, are always compromised and challenged by the specifics of anime production, conventions that operate in the industry, strategic choices and interests of various parties involved, etc. Because of space constraints, technical challenges that (re-)shape the graphic style of the work will be mostly omitted from the discussion. It is important to remember, however, that creative choices made by media workers are usually intertwined with practical considerations.

To start with the obvious, character drawings in the TV anime tend to be less detailed than their manga prototypes. Such simplification cannot be avoided when numerous episodes have

40 Derek Johnson, *Media Franchising: Creative License and Collaboration in the Culture Industries* (New York: New York University Press, 2013).

41 Since pictograms and pictorial runes are used to convey emotional states and reactions in a stylized manner, they can be subsumed in the drawing style; the diversity of such devices and frequency with which they are used tend to coincide with the manner and level of stylization (in other words, heavily cartoonized drawings signal the increased possibility of popped veins representing anger).

42 See Marc Steinberg, *Anime's Media Mix: Franchising Toys and Characters in Japan* (Minneapolis: Minnesota University Press, 2012).

to be animated on an extremely tight schedule. Original video animation (OVA) and anime films (both original and "theatrical versions" of popular TV series[43]) are less restricted in terms of time and budget, but impose higher demands on image quality. One may therefore discover radically different amount of details in animated adaptations of the same work, depending on their format. Creative choices and proclivities of industry workers in general are shaped around such technical requirements. For instance, in an interview for "Animage" prominent character designer Onda Naoyuki (恩田尚之) recounts how he decided to streamline his designs (essentially, reducing the amount of lines) when working on the OVA adaptation of Atsushi Kamijo's *To-y* in 1987.[44] Onda frames this choice as personal change of taste, another step in his artistic progress. When interviewed as a character designer for *Ergo Proxy* (Manglobe, 2006), Onda takes a more pragmatic (and less positive) attitude: eliminating lines is necessary to make the image 'moveable' – on the downside, simplified, more abstract drawings too often feel sterile.[45] Onda's remarks are not necessarily in opposition: rather they demonstrate how the individual creativity of official producers is entangled with practical demands and modified by compromises.

Not only the amount of lines, but their parameters tend to change in manga-to-anime adaptations. As mentioned already, a line is understood as a graphic trace that allows the reader to feel the presence of the graphiateur (typically superimposed on the artist

---

43 *Gekijōban* (劇場版, theatrical versions) either summarize or expand the narrative of some pre-existing TV animated series or OVA.

44 Onda Naoyuki 恩田尚之, 'Dai 156 kai: kono hito ni hanashi wo kikitai' [№156: We would like to ask this person] 「第156回 この人に話を聞きたい」, by Oguro Yūichirō 小黒祐一郎, in *Animage* 『アニメージュ』 (Tokyo: Tokuma Shoten 徳間書店, 2013), pp. 90-93 and p. 91.

45 Onda Naoyuki, 'Genba no shōgen: Voices from staff: 6' [Testimonies from the production site: Voices from staff: 6] 「現場の証言｜Voices from staff: 6」, in *Toppu kurieitā ga oshieru kyarakutā no tsukurikata: samurai chanpurū, ergugo purokusī ni miru animēshon seisaku genba* [Character-making taught by top creators: animation production sites seen through Samurai Champloo and Ergo Proxy] 『トップクリエイターが教えるキャラクターの創り方——『サムライチャンプルー』『エルゴプロクシー』に見るアニメーション制作現場』, (Tokyo: MC Press MCプレス, 2007), pp. 142-143.

in charge of the manga series). Obviously, this presence is lost, or rather replaced, in adaptation. After all, the act of graphiation is based entirely on the physical act of drawing, so the graphiateur a viewer encounters on screen would be different from the one she keeps meeting on page.[46] With that said, in theory anime can still approximate a sense of immediacy (by using rough lines or otherwise revealing "the movement of production")[47] and peculiar characteristics of the linework (which in itself imparts an image with a certain atmosphere, mood, and aesthetics). This, in fact, happens regularly in scenes that involve intense action or comedy, where the immediacy of the rough, sketch-like drawing, with uneven mobile lines, broken outlines, and irregular shapes re-emerges in full force. In addition, some mainstream anime, including the widely popular *Demon Slayer: Kimetsu no Yaiba* by Ufotable (2019), do employ unconventional character outlines of varying thickness. Similar experiments will most likely continue to emerge along with technological advances (for example, it is now possible to change the texture and feel of the line art without redrawing it).

On the whole, however, the application of unconventional lines in TV anime is still rather limited, and despite the diversity of lines in mainstream manga, the majority of the adapted titles get a much more generic look on screen. What is the reason? At least a partial answer lies in the demands of production. It is true that neat, even lines greatly simplify the work of in-betweeners,[48] allowing them to keep a pace consistent with incessantly

46 It must be noted that much like in manga, despite its 'materiality' the act of graphiation in animated series cannot be unequivocally attributed to a single creator. While prominent animators are often entrusted with entire sequences down to in-betweens, their final work is still checked by animation director in charge of the episode, chief animation director, chief director and so on (the amount of people involved varies depending on studio and project), all of whom may add corrections.

47 Paul Atkinson, 'Movements within Movements', cit., p. 272.

48 In-betweeners supply intermediate drawings between key animators, who draw the keyframes, and assistant animators, who do the final cleaning. See Tom Sito, *Drawing the Line: The Untold Story of the Animation Unions from Bosko to Bart Simpson* (Lexington: The University Press of Kentucky, 2006), p. 378.

pressing deadlines. That said, animated TV series drawn by uneven energetic lines had reportedly been more widespread until Miyazaki Hayao (宮崎駿) established the neutral-line paradigm in his animated film *Lupin the Third: The Castle of Cagliostro* (1979). Miyazaki's innovation was allegedly intended to hide traces of individual animators and solidify the director's visual interpretation of characters. In other words, it privileged the personal touch of the director and character designer over those of key animators.[49] While Miyazaki's approach proved successful on the level of a single animated movie and even set a new standard for the industry, it hardly affected the visibility of key animators, as evidenced by never-ceasing enthusiasm of so-called *sakuga* (作画) fans.[50] With this in mind, the current tradition in mainstream anime to neutralize lines may be seen as the great equalizer of various creative interests: it downplays all idiosyncratic traces, so as not to remind the viewer of any specific hand on the level of linework – at the same time various participants in anime production get an opportunity to show their hand in other aspects of the moving image, be it character forms or animated sequences. The quality of line in adaptations might therefore result as much from negotiation between creative workers in the two industries (whose hand is visible in the final product, how is it visible, or should it be visible at all?), as from material differences between the two media.

The last set of visual transformations discussed here has the least to do with medium specificity – they are determined entirely by the adapting side. More often than not anime, as well as other media,

49 Anime director Kitakubo Hiroyuki 北久保弘之, 'BS anime yawa: *Ashita no Joe*. Dezaki Osamu' [BS Anime Night Talk: *Ashita no Joe*. Dezaki Osamu] 「BSアニメ夜話 『あしたのジョー』出崎統」, NHK, 8 Sep. 2004, 22-28 min.

50 From 作画, or 'animation'. *Sakuga* fans have been known to collect and analyse outstanding animated sequences (initially from Japanese animated films and series, but increasingly from all over the world), but their interests encompass all aspects of anime production and all visual aspects of the final product (for an extended introduction into the movement see Kevin Cirugeda, 'The Joy of Sakuga', *Anime News Network*, 30 Sep. 2015, https://www.animenewsnetwork.com/feature/2015-09-30/the-joy-of-sakuga/.93579 (accessed 22 Sep. 2020).

retain the designs of the source manga, but are not necessarily drawn in the same way. In other words, the manner and level of stylization (again, first and foremost in character models) may undergo more or less radical changes. Motivations of the adapting side vary greatly and include both creative and commercial concerns, though on most occasions it is hard to draw a line between the two. Nevertheless, one can tentatively distinguish between projects that prioritize visual novelty and creative reinterpretation of the source aesthetics, those aimed to test and develop new technologies, and those where graphic style is recalibrated in order to better suit the tastes and preferences of the target audience.

An example of the first approach is the adaptation of Oshimi Shūzō's (押見修造) *The Flowers of Evil* by studio Zexcs (2013), entirely produced through rotoscoping. Rotoscope animation is employed regularly in anime to deal with complicated movements, but on a rather limited scale.[51] Tracing not just bodies of live actors, but even their faces resulted in a realistic but decidedly uncanny look far removed from conventionally cute character images of the source work. While radical transformations like this would often signal a new take or a critical commentary on the adapted material, director Nagahama Hiroshi (長濱博史) allegedly aimed for more efficient means of expression, rather than new readings.[52] Despite Nagahama's determination to reproduce the dark mood and psychological nuances of the story, as well as Oshimi's open approval and support of the adaptation, it met backlash from the manga fans and mixed responses from regular anime viewers – a reaction predicted and factored in by the producers (ibid.). If anything, *The Flowers of Evil* successfully marked its uniqueness in the oversaturated anime market of the 2010s.

51 Ōya Yasunori 應矢泰紀, 'Rotosukōpu-ron' [Rotoscoping Theory] 「ロトスコープ論」, lecture, (Kyoto: Kyoto Seika University, 2015).

52 Anime 'Aku no Hana' Gensakusha Oshimi Shūzō to kantoku Nagahama Hiroshi to taidan [Interview with the creators of The *Flowers of Evil:* author of the source work Oshimi Shūzō and director Nagahama Hiroshi] 「アニメ「悪の華」原作者・押見修造と監督・長濱博史が対談」 on Natalie (https://natalie.mu/comic/pp/akunohana, accessed 9 Jan. 2021).

3DCG animated adaptations like *Ajin* (2016) and *Drifting Dragons* (2020) by Polygon Pictures or *Land of the Lustrous* (2017) and *Beastars* (2019) by the studio Orange are equally experimental in exploring new approaches to animation, but they tend to pursue more traditional aesthetics. Since the turn of the new century, the anime industry has been increasingly fascinated with computer graphics and their potential to expand the expressive range of the medium, to streamline the production process. and to reinforce anime's position on the international market. At the same time, the characteristically flat 'traditional' anime look is considered a crucial selling point.[53] Against such a background, adaptation projects like those listed above gain double significance: on the one hand, they become testing grounds for new technologies and techniques, on the other hand, they utilize already popular manga titles to promote 3DCG animation and win over more conservative viewers.

At the commercially oriented end of the spectrum, the adaptation might, for instance, change the mood and look of the source work by restricting or, conversely, expanding its expressive arsenal. Following the same line, the style of the source work may be reinterpreted if it appears too old-school. This is not limited to adaptations of the old classics: with any long-running manga series the artist's style is prone to evolve over the years. For instance, the manga *Berserk* had been running for two decades and counted more than three hundred chapters when Studio 4°C set out to adapt the first part of the story into three animated films (*Berserk: The Golden Age Arc*, 2012-2013). Character designer Onda Naoyuki thus faced a dilemma: which stage of Miura Kentarō's (三浦建太郎) artistic development should he work with? The answer came from Miura himself,

53 For a range of professional opinions regarding the history, current state, and future possibilities of the 3D CG animation in Japan, see the series of interviews by producer for Toei Animation Noguchi Kōichi 野口光一 (Mar. 2012-present) on EE.jp (http://www.enhanced-endorphin.jp/, accessed 22 Sep. 2020).

who recommended Onda to use the seventeenth and eighteenth volumes for reference.[54]

This section closes with a case involving almost all of the points discussed above – the 3D CG animated adaptation of Sakurai Gamon's (桜井画門) *Ajin: Demi-Human* by Polygon Pictures (2016). At the initial stage, character designer Moriyama Yūki (森山佑樹) and modelling director Kataama Mitsunori (片甕満則) needed to deal with Sakurai's rather rapid progress from a 'cute' graphic style towards more realistic representation.[55] They also had to take into consideration director Seshita Hiroyuki's (瀬下寛之) vision of the series. Seshita reportedly aimed for a "documentary-like" look (which required more realistic character models), but was eager to retain the "anime-esque charm".[56] The latter must have been a serious issue considering the lingering distrust among anime viewers towards Japanese animation made fully in 3D. In the end, the desire to make Polygon's 3D animation more recognizable as typical 'anime' seems to have won, and the adaptors set as a baseline the 'cute' graphic style of the first two manga volumes. It arguably diverged from Seshita's intended atmosphere, but, one suspects, lent itself better to 3D modelling and animation. In a manner of compromise, Moriyama and Kataama opted for more naturalistic proportions and introduced two tiers of stylization, with older and more peripheral characters depicted more realistically than the young protagonist and his friends.[57] The last decision must

54 Onda Naoyuki, 'Onda Naoyuki, Iwataki Satoshi intabyū' [Interview with Onda Naoyuki and Iwataki Satoshi] 「恩田尚之・岩瀧智インタビュー」, by Okamoto Atsushi 岡本敦史、Oguro Yūichirō 小黒祐一郎 (5 Feb. 2013), in *Anime Sutairu* 003 [Anime Style 003] 『アニメスタイル003』, (Tokyo: Media Pal メディア・パル, 2013), pp.172-181.

55 It took Sakurai approximately two volumes (from volume 3 to 5) to completely change the level of character stylization.

56 Seshita Hiroyuki 瀬下寛之, 'Seshita Hiroyuki Ajin sōkantoku intabyū' [Interview with Ajin's chief director Seshita Hiroyuki] 「瀬下寛之『亜人』総監督インタビュー」, by Shimanuki Taisuke 島貫泰介, in *Bijutsu Techō* 『美術手帖』, vol.68-1039 (Tokyo: Bijutsu shuppan-sha 美術出版社, 2016), pp. 20-23.

57 'Kataama Mitsunori (zōkei kantoku)×Moriyama Yūki (kyarakutā dezainā) taidan' [Conversation between Kataama Mitsunori (modelling director) and Moriyama Yūki (character designer)] 「片甕満則（造形監督）x森山佑樹（キャラクターデザイナー）対談」, by Shimanuki Taisuke 島貫泰介, in *Bijutsu Techō*, 68-1039, cit., pp. 24-27.

have reflected an old convention in the otaku market and related media: the age of a character and their role in the plot determine the level of stylization and the amount of detail in its representation. To summarize, the final look of *Ajin* characters was determined by the interplay between creative concerns (trying to match the visuals to the tone of the story), marketing choices (aiming for standard cuteness), technical requirements (the necessity to adapt the manga image to an anime image to a 3D model), and the visual conventions of otaku culture. Meanwhile, Sakurai continued to push for realistic (though not photo-realistic) representation and eloquent lines. As a result, at present the visuals of the source work have very little in common with the visuals of the adaptation.

Conclusion

The key point of this chapter is simple: style matters. It matters as a signature that distinguishes a particular artist, an implied author, a creative group, a 'school', or a period. It matters as an expressive device that tunes up and shapes the narrative text as much as the story content. It also matters as a platform of communication between individuals, groups and communities. Producers and consumers, professionals and amateurs, official and fan content creators (delineations that are becoming increasingly vague in the contemporary media environment) all become involved in debates over the visual style of particular works, reinterpret and repurpose their visuals, develop new styles and are swept away by them. Likewise, intermedial adaptation, which is part and parcel of current trends in transmedia franchise development, always involves exchange and negotiation between various creative interests, media, and audiences. Negotiation leads to a chain of compromises ultimately taking the form of a concrete work. Changes of style in manga-to-anime adaptations are therefore inevitable, necessitated not only by marketing strategies of the adapting side, but also by technical limitations and the current conventions of the adapting medium. At the same time, they are not by default detrimental and in some cases could arguably even benefit the source work, if only by attracting new readers. Audiences unfamiliar with the adapted title may follow traces of the familiar 'hand' they associate with character designer, key animator, or even director into an unknown territory, just as manga readers habitually do with their favorite artists. Fans of the source work may either embrace changes or reject them, but any reaction leads to discussions within the fan community and reinvigorates it.

It follows that media and fan studies alike can benefit from addressing issues of style in the bustling otaku market and its works and franchises. The same applies to comics studies within and outside Japan, where research in style has so far remained at a somewhat nascent stage. Many questions are left to be investigated. For instance, if so much tends to change in the adaptation process (as is hopefully clear from the discussion above), how can anime viewers even start to evaluate 'visual fidelity'? Why are some works acknowledged as successful interpretations of the source style, even as others are criticized for unwelcome divergences? Furthermore, how does medium specificity figure in negotiations of style that take place in intermedial adaptations? Since the focus of this article is on the relations between style and communication, it emphasizes the human factor – at the same time, it has barely scratched the surface on issues concerning various technical nuances. Exploring this topic further will no doubt be beneficial for comics research, manga studies, and animation studies. Many possible paths of inquiry traverse media and disciplines — one only needs to follow where they lead.

STUDENT PAPERS

Luca Contardi[1]

ABANINDRANATH TAGORE AND OKAKURA KAKUZŌ

A Brief Comparison on Biographical, Technical/ Methodological, and Theoretical Grounds

This paper has the aim to present the two figures of Abanindranath Tagore and Okakura Kakuzō 岡倉覚三, both leading thinkers in their own countries with respect to the reassessment, creation, and rediscovery of tradition and national identity, the former – Aban – being the founder of the Bengal School of Painting and considered the long-awaited representative of the re-enactment of artistic tradition, and the latter – Okakura – being the promoter of the ideology of Pan-Asianism and of the *Nihonga* 日本画 school of painting.

The purpose of this paper is to try to shed light on the relationship between the two, highlighting not only the several similarities that allow the drawing of a comparison between them, but also focusing on those features that, on the contrary – even signaling the direct influences that can be detected – mark a shifting, a re-thinking, or an overtaking of concepts previously shared and compared.

The comparison will be managed on three different levels. The first of these is biographical, underlining some communal elements in their life-stories – something which can be considered as possibly coming out of simple casualty, but which in fact has clearly led the two to share similar experiences and thus shaped their thought and approaches in a similar manner. The second is technical/methodological, in regards to the reception and incorporation in Abanindranath's way of painting in a specific technique – later called the 'wash technique' – derived from the Japanese *Nihonga* school, a technique whose purpose was actually

1 University of Bologna

counter-posed in its usage. The third and final comparison will be done on the theoretical level, showing the extent to which the thought of Okakura influenced that of Abanindranath, and how the latter's developed divergently, being rooted in a different political, social, and cultural context.

Biography

Abanindranath Tagore was born in 1871, member of the famous Tagore household, whose cultural, intellectual, and social relevance would be established by the granting in 1913 of the Nobel Prize for Literature to Rabindranath Tagore, cousin of Aban.[2] First trained in Western oil painting techniques, Aban decided to abandon this pursuit after his encounter with Mughal and British miniature paintings. He turned from oil to more traditional methods and began to take up traditional themes such as Indian mythology. A turning point in his life-story was his encounter with E.B. Havell in 1896, when the Englishman was appointed principal of Kolkata Government School of Art, laying the foundation for the turn of academic training towards more traditional attitudes. Having sold all the Western works of art in the school collection and bought in turn examples of Mughal paintings, Havell also started to exhibit Aban's works, arranging to have him appointed vice-principal of the school in 1905. Revolutionizing the pedagogical approach then common, Aban grounded training at the school on the creation of an evocative environment and atmosphere in which students' creative individuality could be nurtured. Promoting with his fellow students the so-called Bengal School of Painting, Aban is credited with the initiation of Modernism in India, and he became emblematic of the re-enactment of the tradition of Indian painting.[3]

2 To be precise, first cousin once removed. Aban's father (Gunendranath) was Rabindranath's first cousin.

3 See Tapati Guha-Thakurta, *The making of a new 'Indian' art. Artists, aesthetics and nationalism in Bengal, c. 1850-1920* (Cambridge: Cambridge

For his part, Kakuzō Okakura was born in 1862 in a low-status samurai family whose interest had turned to the silk trade with the West. During his study at the University of Tokyo, he met Ernest Fenollosa, an American professor who introduced him to German idealism and who came to have a strong influence on his thought. After university, Okakura found himself employed by the Ministry of Education in the art section and, along with Fenollosa, he started a long battle to revise artistic education and tastes in Japan towards a reappropriation of traditional methods and practices. In 1889, the new Tōkyō Bijutsu Gakkō 東京美術学校 (or Tokyo School of Fine Arts) was founded, following the new principles laid out by Okakura and Fenollosa. Okakura, having been appointed principal of the school, gave birth with his students to the new *Nihonga* school of painting, which promoted a synthesis between Eastern spirituality, as represented by traditional styles (like that of the *Kanō* School, Kanōha 狩野派), and Western techniques.[4]

Looking at these brief sketches of their lives, it is quite easy to see some similarities. Both men were born in family contexts split between the local culture and contact with the outside world; both were strongly influenced by a Western figure who introduced them to the Orientalist/nationalist discourse, affecting the development of their personal ideas; and both give birth to the cultural enactment of a resistance and had (partial) success in their revisionary attempt.[5]

Technique

The first physical encounter between Okakura and Abanindranth took place in 1902, when the former was a guest in the house

University Press, 2008).

4 Fred G. Notehelfer, 'On Idealism and Realism in the Thought of Okakura Tenshin', in *The Journal of Japanese Studies* 16-2 (1990), pp. 320-1.

5 For a wider comparison and account on their lives, see Debashis Banerji, *Art in Japan e India: A Comparative Study of Okakura Kakuzo and Abanindranath Tagore* (CooperJal, 2007, e-book).

of Surendranath, another member of the Tagore family. Despite being brief, the meeting was actually fruitful to such an extent that Okakura agreed to send Aban two of his most talented students for a six-month cultural exchange in Kolkata, where they were supposed to teach Japanese painting techniques to Indian pupils. The two students were Yokoyama Taikan 横山大観 and Hishida Shunsō 菱田春草, and they reached Kolkata in 1903. Shunsō had formulated a specific style called *mōrōtai* 朦朧体 (murky/blurred style), "attempting to bring Western techniques emphasizing space and light into Nihonga by reducing or eliminating the reliance on line, and particularly outlines."[6] The usage of strong lines had been a particular feature of Japanese art, and in order to overcome it he used techniques such as *karabake* 唐刷毛 (he dripped paint on a wet surface, then brushed it with a dry brush) to obtain tonal gradation and hues. This wash technique was used "to put down pigment in subtle ways, so that colours or tones seemed to melt into one another without perceptible transitions, lines or edges."[7] Drawing directly from the *mōrōtai* style developed by Shunsō, Abanindranath created his own personal version of it, teaching it to his students in Kolkata. Starting from a pencilled outline, he applied as many as fifteen transparent washes. Once dried, he immersed the work in a basin of water so as to fix the colours naturally. He then wet it from behind repeatedly to achieve the desired colour. To finish, he added either transparent or opaque colours. "Although giving the impression of a misty haze, the colours also conveyed a sense of depth and space."[8] Beside these characteristics, Aban's adaptation of the *mōrōtai* wash technique, more than aiming at creating a sense of depth, space and luminosity (not necessarily implied in his composition), actually "translated its natural atmospheric effects to a suffusion of mood

6 Penelope Mason, *History of Japanese Art* (Upper Saddle River, New Jersey: Pearson Prentice Hall, 2005), p. 365.

7 Tapati Guha-Thakurta, *Abanindranath, known and unknown: the artist versus the art of his times* (Kolkata: Centre for Studies in Social Sciences, 2009), pp. 9-10.

8 Natasha Eaton, 'Swadeshi Color: Artistic Production and Indian Nationalism, ca. 1905-1947', in *The Art Bulletin* 95-4 (2013), p. 624.

as the subjective envelope of the image". This created a strong connection with his idea of colour as the main medium through which to give a specific mood to the painting - mood which was at the core of the Indian artistic peculiarity, whose aim was to suggest a specific emotion as linked and derived from the image.

It is therefore clear that the specific purpose underlying the usage of the wash technique was counter-posed: for *Nihonga*, it was a specific way to incorporate Western artistic features such as depth, following a dialectic of mixing Japanese and Western tools to reach an higher synthesis; for Abanindranath, on the contrary, it was a way to obtain the effect of giving the image some uniform extension of mood, so that it can clearly convey the 'emotional' message implied in the artistic composition – a dynamic that allows his technique to get closer to the aim as prescribed by the Indian tradition. Moreover, Shunsō and Taikan made use of this experimental technique for a short time, discarding it shortly after their return to Japan[9]; while Abanindranath made it one of the most important features of his main works of art, using it – in varying degrees – throughout his career.

Theory

The second meeting between Abanindranth and Okakura occurred some ten years later, in 1913, again in Kolkata. Okakura was seriously ill, and was actually to die in a few months' time, after his return to Japan. During his stay in India, despite his illness, Okakura intended to visit Orissa, a region to the south of Bengal widely renowned for its temples, and Abanindranath joined him on his trip.[10] When in Puri, they visited the Jagannath[11] Temple, one of the most important sites in India for the Hindu faith and also one of the few temples to which access inside was

9 Shigemi Inaga, 'The Interaction of Bengali and Japanese Artistic Milieus in the First Half of the Twentieth Century (1901-1945): Rabindranath Tagore, Arai Kanpō, and Nandalal Bose', in *Japan Review*, 21 (2009), p. 152.

10 Debashis Banerji, *Art in Japan and India*, cit.

11 One of Vishnu's avatara.

(and still is) strictly prohibited to non-adherents to the religion. Nevertheless, Okakura managed to enter the temple, and this is how Abanindranth describes the event:

> Sri Okakura of Japan paid his last visit to this country. His health had broken down with a malignant disease, but he had not given up his pursuit of art, nor holding appreciative discussion on art. The said foreigner had come to visit a place of pilgrimage in India. His intention was to have a look, before he returned from the distant foreign country to his own room and took to his deathbed, at the interior of the temple of Jagannath and see how it was decorated inside with works of art. [...] Jagannath had summoned my brother artist of the foreign land. Lord Jagannath may summon, but his mace-bearer [the entrance guard] may not grant [access], for he [the guard] wields the power to prevent [access] even [to] the Viceroy of India! How could one give him a slip? One artist held counsel with another. The counsel was held in secret, but the friend went out in broad daylight like a king to pay his homage to Jagannath. That was what the Great Artist of the Universe had intended, our visiting artist might be a foreigner, but on the day of the visit his movements should not be restricted. [...] With this favour of heavenly bliss my friend proceeded homeward unhurt. I still remember his last word on the day of the parting: 'I am blessed, extreme delight did I get, now let me depart with pleasure towards the other shore', said he. That was the history of a true devotee of art, though a foreigner.[12]

What is meaningful in this account is the credit assigned to Okakura as the epitome of the real appreciator of art who continues to pursue art and finds the strength to persist in this pursuit even in his illness and despite every hindrance. Aban even imagines Jagannath himself coming to grant Okakura access to a usually-forbidden space, conceding a sort of divine endorsement. This stands in sharp contrast with what Abanindranath says about Indian people who, on the contrary, are apathetic towards their own art and do nothing either to protect it, causing their decay, or to make it flourish again. In this sense, they "*do not achieve any right to art*" anymore.[13]

This passage resonates profoundly with what Okakura wrote in his most renowned text, *The Ideals of the East*, written during

12 Abanindranath Tagore, *The Bageswari Lectures of Art,* Part I (Kolkata: Pranoti, 2006), pp. 11-12 (Lect. 1).

13 Abanindranath Tagore, *The Bageswari Lectures of Art,* Part I, cit., pp. 10-13 (Lect. 1).

his first stay in India in 1902 and edited in 1903. In the text, Okakura first declares the key concept of Pan-Asianism, that is the idea that every country of Asia and their people and cultures share a common and intertwined background, a sort of cultural humus from which all the diverse expressions had sprung and thrived – diverse but springing forth from the same soil.[14] The famous opening lines of the text goes:

> Asia is one. The Himalayas divide, only to accentuate, two mighty civilizations, the Chinese with its communism of Confucius, and the Indian with its individualism of the Vedas. But not even the snowy barriers can interrupt for one moment that broad expanse of love for the Ultimate and Universal, which is the common thought-inheritance of every Asiatic race, enabling them to produce all the great religions of the world, and distinguishing them from those maritime people of the Mediterranean and the Baltic, who love to dwell on the Particular, and to search out the means, not the end, of life.[15]

These few lines clearly express the core of Okakura's thought: to essentialize "Asia" for its "love of the Ultimate and Universal" in opposition to the "West's love [...] of the Particular". This, of course, can be read in terms of the Orientalists' general divide between spiritual East and materialist West.[16] In his thought, Okakura was actually deeply influenced by Ernest Fenollosa, who, as Okakura's philosophy professor, had played a key role in his cultural and intellectual education. The two had eventually worked together and collaborated for several years, resulting in Okakura being imbued with Fenollosa's way of thinking.

14 The delineation of the concept of 'Asian solidarity' has its roots in the aftermath of the First Opium War (1839-1842); it had been autonomously delineated both in the West (as a threat to Western countries' interests in Asia, the so-called 'Yellow Peril') and in the East (as a way to oppose the Western imperial threat). Okakura's cultural specification highlighted the fact that the concept could be a "*significant factor in international relations*". For further information see Christopher W.A. Szpilman, Sven Saleer, 'Pan-Asianism as an Ideal of Asian Identity and Solidarity, 1850-present', in *The Asia-Pacific Journal* 9-1 (2011), pp. 1-28.

15 Kakuzo Okakura, *Ideals of the East, with Special Reference to the Art of Japan* (New York: ICG Muse, 2002), p. 1.

16 Debashis Banerji, *Alternate Nation of Abanindranath Tagore* (New Delhi: SAGE, 2010), pp. 39-40.

Fenollosa's thought had been first publicly made evident in 1880, during a lecture – later to become known by the title of *An explanation of Truth in Art* - held before the Ryūchikai 龍池会, an exclusive Japanese art club, in which he marked his 'conversion' toward the support of traditional Japanese art. Fenollosa, in the lecture, openly attacked the Western style and strongly praised traditional Japanese art. Using the Hegelian dialectical model, he argued that the universal spiritual ideals of Asia lay at the core of Japanese art and stood in contrast to the West's preoccupation with realism, materialism, and technical facility. Moreover, submitting to the concept of the evolution of the spirit in time, he placed the Hegelian spirit's roots in the Japanese past, assigning a central role to Japan's spiritual heritage in shaping the cultural history of the world: it was Japan's due to make a synthesis out of the global confrontation. Eastern spiritualism, on the one hand, identified with traditional Japanese art, must be combined with Western technical achievements, on the other, in order to create a higher culture to be shared in both the East and the West.[17]

Acknowledging Fenollosa's thinking as the intellectual framework, it becomes clear where Okakura's thought came from. Accepting this Hegelian structure and this simplistic thesis-antithesis logic, Okakura, in *The Ideals of the East*, followed up on what Fenollosa had said, adding more precise insight into the Asiatic context. For him, the two core values of Asiatic tradition were Indian spirituality – transmigrated to Japan through Buddhism – and Chinese humanism – carried by Confucianism, which happened to be unified in a remarkable and superior synthesis under the peculiar genius of the Japanese race. Since India and China had not had the capacity and the strength to oppose to their conquerors over the centuries, something which resulted in the loss of their high achievements, it was now Japan's duty as '*living museum*' and '*spiritual repository*' of Asia to be the voice of the continent.[18]

17 Fred G. Notehelfer, 'On Idealism and Realism in the Thought of Okakura Tenshin', cit., pp. 321-2.

18 Fred G. Notehelfer, 'On Idealism and Realism in the Thought of Okakura Tenshin', cit., pp. 331-3.

To further support his idea, Okakura introduced another concept into the discourse: that of Advaitism, a Sanskrit term referring to a specific Vedāntic school of Indian philosophy. The concept had then come to be widely known thanks to Vivekananda, an Indian monk who was actively preaching Hinduism around the world during those years, presenting it as a unifying religion based on tolerance. Vivekananda's Advaitism, or non-dualism, was a Hindu Monist school related to spiritual practices aimed at realizing the unreality of the world and the permanence of a transcendental consciousness which was unrelated to the phenomenal world.[19] More than strictly referring to the Indian philosophical school, Okakura's use of the term implies a more or less a generic view of the notion of 'spirituality', that is the very idea of 'universalism' that he places as the true essence of Asia and which implies the capacity of accepting the new without discarding the old – but overtaking it. Therefore, on the one hand Japan had preserved the artistic ideals (as summoned throughout Asia) in its practices and collections; on the other hand, India had managed to maintain the living philosophical ideal in its spiritual practices, as proved by Advaitism.

> The strange tenacity of the race, nurtured in the shadow of a sovereignty unbroken from its beginning, that very tenacity which preserves the Chinese and Indian ideals in all their purity amongst us, even where they were long since cast away by the hands that created them [...] holds Japan to-day intact, in spite of this sudden incomprehensible influx of Western ideas. To remain true to herself, notwithstanding the new colour which the life of a modern nation forces her to assume, is, naturally, the fundamental imperative of that Adwaita idea to which she was trained by her ancestors. To the instinctive eclecticism of Eastern culture she owes the maturity of judgment which made her select from various sources those elements of contemporary European civilization that she required.[20]

Okakura himself explains the concept of Advaitsm (as he perceived it) in a note to the text, which reads as follow:

19 Debashis Banerji, *Alternate Nation of Abanindranath Tagore*, cit., pp. 40-41.
20 Kakuzo Okakura, *Ideals of the East*, cit., pp. 222-3.

> Adwaita idea – The word adwaita means the state of not being two, and is the name applied to the great Indian doctrine that all which exists, though apparently manifold, is really one. Hence all truth must be discoverable in any single differentiation, the whole universe involved in every detail. All thus becomes equally precious.[21]

Since Okakura considered Art as the "expression of the highest and noblest of our [Japanese] culture",[22] it is plausible to say that "Okakura was planning to realize in the artistic world what Vivekananda was realizing in the spiritual world".[23] As an evident clue of this, we should consider the clear symmetry "between Vivekananda's spiritual synthesis of the world religions and Okakura's idea of self-realization and the actualization of Oriental art history."[24]

If, on the one hand, Vivekananda was promoting Hinduism as the 'universal religion' capable of including in itself all the other religious experiences under the banner of tolerance (or inclusivism), on the other hand Okakura proposed a similar vision with reference to Japanese art, which had already been capable of acquiring in itself the other Asiatic artistic expressions. Yet, in Okakura's vision this concept is intertwined with that of Hegelian dialectics: Japanese art would also acquire Western styles and techniques, overrunning any contemporary expressions and reaching for a new superior synthesis.

Okakura came to know Vivekananda's thought thanks to Josephine MacLeod, a wealthy American woman who attended lectures delivered by him in Tokyo on the topics that would eventually merge in *The Ideals of the East*. MacLeod had become a disciple of Vivekananda in 1894, when the two had met in New

---

21 Kakuzo Okakura, *Ideals of the East*, cit., p. 235.

22 Shigemi Inaga, 'Okakura Kakuzō's Nostalgic Journey to India and the Invention of Asia', in Susan Fisher (ed. by), *Nostalgic Journeys: Literary Pilgrimages Between Japan and the West: Proceedings of a Conference Held in Vancouver, British Columbia, September 1999 in Honour of Kinya Tsuruta* (Vancouver: University of British Columbia, 2001), p. 121.

23 Shigemi Inaga, 'Okakura Kakuzō's Nostalgic Journey to India and the Invention of Asia', cit., p. 121.

24 Shigemi Inaga, 'Okakura Kakuzō's Nostalgic Journey to India and the Invention of Asia', cit., p. 121.

York, and from that moment on she had been actively propagating his ideas in the West. She was also responsible for Okakura's first trip to India in 1901 and for his encounter with Vivekananda, whom he was determined to convince to join him at his school in Japan[25] – an aim he could not attain, as Vivekananda died in 1902.[26]

During his stay in India, lasting from December 1901 to October 1902, Okakura was hosted in Kolkata by Surendranath Tagore, nephew of the renowned Nobel-Prize winner Rabindranath Tagore.[27] Okakura only got to know Abanindranath Tagore shortly before his departure, but despite the brevity of the encounter, Aban was deeply influenced by their meeting, both on the technical side (as already stressed) and on the theoretical one. Okakura was at that time translating into English the still-unpublished text of *The Ideals of the East* with the helping hand of Sister Nivedita (born Margaret Noble), an Irish woman deeply devoted to Vivekananda who wrote the introduction to the English edition of Okakura's first book. Despite the fact that Aban and Okakura were not to meet again in person until 1913, Okakura started sending regular copies of his art-history journal, *Kokka* 国華, to the Tagore mansion after his return to Japan, thus keeping open a window through which Aban could follow what was going on in the artistic intellectual milieu of Japan.

Leaving the technical aspect aside, Okakura's deep influence on Abanindranath was put on full display some twenty years later, during the 1920s, when Aban was appointed Bageswari Professor of Indian Fine Arts of the University of Kolkata and delivered – within ten years – twenty-nine lectures on Indian Aesthetics and Philosophy of Art. These lectures, known as the Bageswari Lectures, were collected, translated into English, and

25 Okakura had already tried to convince Vivekananda to participate in a World Conference of Religions he was trying to organize in Kyoto, in the light/on the basis of the 1893 International Religious Parliament held at the Chicago World's Fair, which had make Vivekananda renowned all over the world.

26 Shigemi Inaga, 'Okakura Kakuzō's Nostalgic Journey to India and the Invention of Asia', cit., p. 120.

27 Surendranath was the eldest son of Satyendranath, one of the eleven brothers and sisters of Rabindranath.

edited in 1947, and became quite renowned in India. The Lectures are significant because they mark a shift in Aban's theoretical approach. By then in his fifties, Aban presented himself as a sort of free thinker, arguing in a very personal way and selectively using his knowledge to delineate and validate his own thought. If in previous contributions he had been focusing on the analysis of quotes from traditional Sanskrit texts as a starting point from which to personally elaborate, now he used quotes only as a warranty of his ideas.

From the Lectures it becomes apparent how much Okakura's ideas had influenced Aban's (back then still being defined) thought on Art. From the passage quoted above, it is clear that Aban agreed with Okakura as to the derogatory vision he had of Indian people. Aban fiercely attacked the way Indians had managed their own artistic heritage, saying that they must completely change their attitude towards what was left of their past in order to regain any right to it. It was not just like in a hereditary blood lineage but was instead a right one must earn by caring, nurturing, and reenacting the heritage itself.

Abanindranath also partly accepted the Hegelian dialectics implied in Okakura's thought. He shared and strongly advocated the idea that the 'old' must be known, comprehended, and assimilated, but just in order to go beyond it, by means of accepting the new that can come from external influences as well as from experimentation – so that the art can progress. Aban, nevertheless, read this dynamic in a diachronic sense, diverging from Okakura's view on the basis of the different historical and political paths of India and Japan. As a matter of fact, he placed this mixing of old (read, tradition) and new (read, experimentation and foreign influences) as the core of the evolution and progress of Indian art. Placing this mixing not only in the future - as a way of surviving – but also in the past – as a defining feature - Aban assumed hybridity as the steam engine at the nucleus of Indian art.

> No great thing did ever move along an uneven path fearing hybridization. [...] Afraid of hybridization we may confine the artist within the bounds of rules of Indian art according to Hindu scriptures and thereby save the art from hybridization, but when the awfulness of rigid technique would

> give rise to the symptoms of death and decrepitude all over art it would be beyond the power of Lord Shiva himself to cure it and make it beautiful. […] You can never tell how many things from the Greeks, the Mughals, from China and Nepal went to make Indian art![28]

Since it had worked in the past, it could now work as well in present times, acquiring what comes also from the West: the artist should not discriminate on the basis of the techniques' provenance; he studies and apprehends them, and then he picks the most suitable ones for his/her specific purpose.

> Techniques have to be acquired from all corners. […] From all sides India has acquired techniques of art, social systems and modes of livelihood. The root of Indian art and India is united with a joy of acquiring the techniques of building up an India that is greater than Hindu India, and an Indian art that is greater than Hindu Indian art. […] This is the great aspect of Indian art, in this respect there rest the dignity and glory of Indian art.[29]

This ability to expand and hybridize is what made Indian art thrive for such a long time. The art itself dies when it lacks the willingness to be influenced from the outside.

Abanindranath went further in his reasoning: along with the formation of a Nation as a geographical and political entity, its cultural characteristics go on shaping, both exteriorly (manners, clothing, food) and interiorly (ideals, ways of thinking), leading to definition of a national unity and tradition. As a synthesis of the differences, this will eventually result in a national art, basing on whose features one can define Chinese, Indian, and European art. This categorization, however, is only rooted in an external basis, dealing with specific time, space and objects.

---

28 Abanindranath Tagore, *Bageswari Lectures of Art,* Part I, cit., pp. 214-5 (Lect. XII). Abanindranath was replying to what Akshay Kumar Mitra had written in an article in the journal *Bharatbarsha*: "Hybridism in art is rising its head in the nae of procedures of Indian art and so it is necessary to make attempts to preserve its Kaulinya (the purity of its high descent of birth), but the path to defend it is very uneven." (Abanindranath Tagore, *Bageswari Lectures of Art,* Part I, cit., pp. 213-4.)

29 Abanindranath Tagore, *The Bageswari Lectures of Art,* Part I, cit., pp. 217-8 (Lect. XII).

> We find differences in physical appearance, in complexion and in language to take place as a law of nature, and so [we] determine division among races between men based on that. We go to ascribe differences between the art of one country and that of another also in the same way. But these external differences are not the ultimate truth either as regards humanity or as regards human art – the truth in which all men are the same, all art, irrespective of Aryan or non-Aryan races, are the same also come before our eyes and our mind.[30]

If one has to delve into it, it becomes apparent that considering the core of art in its profound significance, no categorization can withstand. This core is recognized by Abanindranath in the Indian aesthetic key concept of *rasa*.

> Manner and style arise along traditional custom and convention and practice [...] All the several arts of the world are the same with this predominance of rasa.[31]

> The marriage of art with the nation is a marriage by force (rākshasa bibāha), [in] national art [...] no rasa can be found there.[32]

Indian Aesthetics has always considered the artistic expression as a way to communicate a specific emotional content, which can be detected in every work of art[33] and should be perceived by the spectator. To attain this, the work of art must contain some specific features which, through different phases, allow one to reach specific 'stable emotions'. These will eventually develop into '*rasa*', or the peculiar taste and mood of the art itself, as perceived by the viewer. Drawing from this aesthetic tradition,

---

30 Abanindranath Tagore, *The Bageswari Lectures on Art*, Part II (Kolkata: Pranoti, 2008), pp. 385-6 (Lect. XXII).

31 Abanindranath Tagore, *The Bageswari Lectures on Art*, Part II, cit., pp. 283-4 (Lect. XXII).

32 Abanindranath Tagore, *The Bageswari Lectures on Art*, Part II, cit., p. 287 (Lect. XXII).

33 To be more precise, Indian philosophers had initially applied this notion only to drama and poetry; it was during the 20th century that some thinkers like A.K. Coomaraswamy started to try and include in this vision also figurative arts, such as paintings – in general, everything that was conceived in the West as '*fine arts*'.

Aban developed his own peculiar notion of *rasa*. Discarding all those features prescribed in the traditional treaties, he considered it as the specific mood implied in the composition that allows one to create a sort of heart-connection between the object that is represented and the subject who is perceiving it through the link of the emotional content as conveyed in the work of art and as experienced by the viewer.

Abanindranath did not direct even a single attack against Japan's perceived artistic superiority, since it was believed to have come naturally from its national progress as a leading power in Asia. But, Aban says, the two aspects, art and politics, are not intertwined or even related.

> It never happens that the art of the nation grows accordingly as the nation grows. Modern Japan is great as a nation, but from the point of art modern Japan stands defeated before that 'uncultured Japan' as a poet remarked. A nation is not a mother of its art, nor can it ever be; a non-formal marriage (gāndharva bibāha) never takes place between a nation and art, it is with the artist that the marriage takes place.[34]

So the case of Japan itself is used as an example to challenge the nationalistic categorization: its rising as an imperial power is not matched by an equivalent growth in artistic expression, denying once again any correlations between art and nation.[35]

In Aban's vision based on *rasa*, 'spirituality' as the main feature of Asian art, which strongly distinguishes it from its Western materialistic counterpart, is easily discarded as a sort of simplistic easy way out, through which it had cancelled the field of comparison between East and West, at the same time creating a new one on

34 Abanindranath Tagore, *The Bageswari Lectures on Art*, Part II, cit., p. 288 (Lect. XVII).

35 Abanindranath was not the only one who was training to overcome the 'nationalistic' categorization of art at that time: his struggle was shared by some other renowned Indian thinkers of that time, who were trying to highlight the connection and profound unity of art in its different expressions like Benoy Kumar Sarkar. See Benoy Kumar Sarkar, 'Viewpoints in Aesthetics', included in the reader: Nalini Bhushan, Jay L. Garfield (ed. by), *Indian Philosophy in English. From Renaissance to Independence* (Oxford: Oxford University Press, 2011).

which Asian art can shift on its own while putting itself on a higher level. As a matter of fact, the fact of being 'spiritual', according to Aban, does not necessarily imply that a work of art is good:

> Indian art, whether ancient or modern, has a form of its own. Its merit and demerit, its superiority of inferiority may be judged only by that form. It is wrong to think that it would pass as a great thing in world art if we would base it on the certificate of spiritualism. A thing of beauty easily established itself as a thing of beauty without depending on quality. [...] What is ugly can never become handsome even with the clearance certificate of the formless.[36]

Abanindranath, as should be clear, was trying to set the comparison between Eastern and Western art again on a shared field, at the same time also trying to cope with the way to resolve the alleged clash. He eventually proposed to go beyond the dichotomy of beautiful and non-beautiful, focusing instead on the idea that the true artist, the true art, is the one which can exceed this external distinction (between beauty and non-beauty) reaching out for the goal of attaining a work of art which can contain '*rasa*'. That is, a work of art which is capable of creating a connection with the heart of the spectator, creating a bond, a tie, between the object itself as represented and the subject perceiving and comprehending that object, discerning and recognizing in the process of creation of art the same process of creation of the world. That is, recognizing a profound and essential unity in the diversity of expressions.

In this, it is apparent that Abanindranath is not so methodologically distant from the significance of the vision

36 Abanindranath Tagore, *The Bageswari Lectures on Art*, Part II, cit., p. 312 (Lect. XVIII). It is worth mentioning that Abanindranath was speaking in the 1920s, when European *avant garde* artists were much better known in India (than at the beginning of the century), as were their different artistic research approaches and goals. Academicism had been partially overtaken by then, and so had *mimesis* (that is, naturalistic imitation) as the main purpose of artistic expression. Nonetheless, during the time of Okakura's first trip to Europe and USA in 1886, some of these renovating forces were already at work. For an analysis of Okakura's blinding prejudice during the trip, see Fred G. Notehelfer, 'On Idealism and Realism in the Thought of Okakura Tenshin', cit., pp. 325-6.

of Okakura's '*Adwaita*'. As a matter of fact, the Indian school of philosophy that Abanindranath was most influenced by was Bengal Vaishnavism, whose Advaitic basis sees phenomena as the differentiation of One Person who has multiplied Himself into the many for the sake of Play. Ontologically, here, phenomena are informed with the intense emotionalism of the moods of Divine Love, and so it is through emotions – as transmitted via works of art and perceived by the viewer in the vision of the work of art – that the viewer/the onlooker manage to perceive the unity.

What is different from the vision of Okakura is the core idea that this possibility, this trait of art is actually applicable to all the different artistic expressions of the world, while Okakura, in his Hegelian dialectic, was convinced that this specific feature would have been what Japanese art – being the only one to possess it – could specifically bring in the new artistic synthesis coming out of the encounter of East and West. Moreover, it is clear that Okakura's vision is intrinsically – and more than anything else – political, in the sense that his thought programmatically gives much relevance to Japan and its culture in terms of a nationalistic view. Being political, his thought is also not very 'artistic': the concepts he explained are based more on ideas than on facts, usually combining also some approximate, rash references and rough errors in the field of art history. In brief, it can be said that Okakura "sacrificed historical accuracy in favor of philosophical assertion."[37] The project of Abanindranath, on the other hand, whilst rising from a cultural milieu of nation-building, is based on a technical and practical necessity (being himself an artist), and is clearly more interested in reflections on the statute of art than in any political statement.

This different vision is clear also in the technical dimension: for Aban, the 'wash technique' was a method to clearly express the mood of the composition, of the work of art (through colour)

37 Shigemi Inaga, 'Okakura Kakuzō and India: The Trajectory of Modern National Consciousness and Pan-Asian Ideology Across Borders', in *Review of Japanese Culture and Society, Vol. 24, Beyond Tenshin: Okakura Kakuzo's Multiple Legacies* (University of Hawaii Press, december 2012), pp. 47-8.

to allow the communication of the emotion implied in the work itself. In this way, through the communication of emotion as a global language, Aban reaches his goal of considering artistic expression in a universal, shared dimension.

References

Michele Marra, 'Hegelian Reversal. Okakura Kakuzō', in Michele Marra, *Modern Japanese Aesthetics: A Reader* (Honolulu: University of Hawai'i Press, 1999), pp. 65-71.

Midori Wakakuwa, 'Japanese Cultural Identity and Nineteenth Century Asian Nationalism: Okakura Tenshin and Swami Vivekananda', in Brij Tankha (ed.), *Okakura Tenshin and Pan-Asianism. Shadows of the Past* (Folkestone: Global Oriental, 2009), pp. 22-6.

Raman Siva Kumar, *Paintings of Abanindranath Tagore* (Kolkata: Pratikshan, 2013).

Giacomo Barbini[1]

BEYOND METAPHOR, IN THE MAKING OF POETIC WORD

A Comparative Analysis between Heidegger's, Bashō's and Kyoto School Aesthetic Perspectives

This article will attempt to define the specificities and differences that emerge from a comparison between the interpretation that the philosopher Martin Heidegger makes of Hölderlin's poetry and the poetics of the Japanese seventeenth-century *haiku*[2] 俳句 poet Matsuo Bashō (松尾芭蕉, 1644-1694), of which Tomio Tezuka (手塚富雄, 1903-1983) – professor of German literature – can be considered the spokesman in the dialogue that the two thinkers had in 1954. Particularly, we will try to bring out the relationship between the status of reality of things and the power of the poetic word which indicates them. This investigation, theoretically, aims to show how the overcoming of the metaphor in the poetic word is the necessary prerequisite, in both examined perspectives, to realize a non-representative, namely non-metaphysical, thinking of reality. In this regard, according to the illustrious scholar of Japanese aesthetics Michele Marra, we must posit a status of postmodernity (i.e. intellectual dismantling of Western epistemology) ante-litteram for the non-Western culture whose premodern world has developed independently from Western influences. In addition, he claims that this intellectual practice of dismantling Western epistemology by means of its own philosophical tradition (*tetsugaku* 哲学) is exactly what is currently occurring among Japanese intellectuals.[3] Among these we will particularly examine those who belonged to the well-

---

1 University of Bologna

2 For further references to *Haiku* see *Haiku: Japanese literature*, in *Encyclopaedia Britannica*, https://www.britannica.com/art/haiku.

3 Michele Marra, 'Japanese Aesthetics: The Construction of Meaning', in *Philosophy East and West*, 45-3 (1995), pp. 367-368.

known philosophical Kyoto School (*Kyōto-gakuha*京都学派), of which Tezuka was a member.

The framework for this transcultural investigation can be outlined on two different sides. On the one side is Tezuka, who in his work *An Hour with Heidegger* claims that his main intellectual interest focuses on the German philosopher's discussions on poetic language, since the latter considered what is most essential about human existence to be concentrated in language. In this regard, Tezuka is focused on Heidegger's understanding of human existence in language on the basis of instances where language comes forth purely and with forceful energy, as happens in the best poetry. On the other side is Heidegger, who asked Tezuka for a reading and an explanation of a *haiku* by Bashō, – mentioned below – which he had read previously and by which he had been very impressed:

Higher than the lark,
ah the mountain pass!
– quietly resting.

We know from the Reinhard May's English translation of Tezuka's report about the dialogue with Heidegger that the German philosopher felt a vast world in such a simple expression and observed that what is simple is not without content. From this first insight into Japanese poetic words, the concepts of "vastness' and 'simplicity with contents" come out, which trace the inquiry of the two interlocutors on the original meaning of the Japanese word that stands for "language". In other words, they attempt to discover how language – and so the process of thinking or without-thinking – actually works and in what consists its power of referring to and letting things appear.

Poetic word as a verbal painting: appearance, emptiness, movement

First, in order to compare and understand differences and similarities, one must consider the relation between appearance and essence. In the Japanese language, these concepts are matched by two words, respectively *shiki* 色 for appearance and *kū* 空 for essence, which from Buddhist philosophy have been absorbed into the Japanese "life-world" (or ordinary meanings of life), to represent the "so-called *shiki soku kū* 色即空 and *kū soku shiki* 空即色way of thinking". On this point, Tezuka remarks that "*shiki* would be colour and colouring, and, by extension, appearance; and though *kū* originally means emptiness, or sky (*sora* 空), it also means the open (the opened-up world)".[4] Therefore, since where there is appearance (*shiki*), there is emptiness (*kū*), the appearance begins to approach what is essential. In this theoretical framework Japanese art is conceived as an art of space, essentially oriented to the empty nothing and limitlessness. The empty nothing, here conceived in the sense of primordial way of being of all things, or a state of pure potentiality, implies that aesthetic beauty is achieved when this "empty nothing" is suggested by what appears. Since the essence of Oriental poetry is said to be like a painting, *haiku* therefore can be said to be a "verbal painting"; in this regard Ryūnosuke Akutagawa[5] (芥川龍之介, 1892-1927) states that "a not negligible characteristic of Bashō's haikai is precisely the peculiar technique with which he was able to express a similar pictorial taste".[6] The way in which the Buddhist concept of "voidness" is concerned with the expression of beauty in Zen art allows us to understand in what sense *haiku* is named "verbal painting". Moreover, it can be useful to take into account also Shin'ichi Hisamatsu's (久松真一, 1889-1980) theory of the Formless Self, which emerges from his

4 Reinhard May, *Heidegger's Hidden Sources* (London: Routledge, 1996), p. 62.

5 For the sake of completeness, it is worth noting that Akutagawa, who was a strong supporter of classical poetic tradition is the author of the two short stories that inspired the Akira Kurosawa movie *Rashomon*. Besides the eponymous story, the movie is also based on Akutagawa's short story of 1922 *In a Grove*, which provides the characters and plot. The movie itself is one of the main topics discussed by Heidegger and Tezuka during their dialogue in 1954. For this, a subtle cultural linkage provides support to my inquiry.

6 Ryūnosuke Akutagawa, *Note sparse su Bashō*, in *Bashō, Il romitaggio della dimora illusoria*, trad. it. a cura di Lidya Origlia (Milano: SE, 2005), p. 91.

conversation with Heidegger about *Art and Thinking.*[7] While in the West an artwork is conceived as an objectification of reality, a substantialized entity, something formal, complete in itself and meaningful, in Zen culture – Hisamatsu claims – we must consider as artistic those works which let things appear bringing them to presence, and in doing so they manifest their source as a formless ground of the non-being, that is a space of givenness where a process of a potential coming to being of something continuously happens. The beauty of an artwork, then, consists in this movement of coming to being, namely the appearing of the movement of Formless Self in something which is figurative, and since the highest beauty is where no form or structure remains, the art of Zen is not limited to a restricted field.[8] The *haijin* 俳人 (haiku poet) – as well as the Japanese painter – does not fill in the space, but emphasizes the void, that is the spaces between things (or sounds): it is not the thing to be important, but the empty background in which it is placed. Emptiness does not mean absence or deprivation, but the inexhaustible potential space for the appearance of existence. The void as a space of potential appearing recalls the totality, conceived as the way of grasping the particularity of things. In other words, everything must be framed in the relational interdependence that unites it to the others; therefore, no distinction is drawn between plants, animals or humans. The *haiku* can be said to be the way through which such empty space emerges in poetry: an empty mirror does not symbolize anything and does not attribute any meaning through words, and therefore there can be no interpretation of the reality to which it refers. The *haiku* merely portrays an image, an event, an impression in the immediacy of the moment: one can only say that something simply happens.[9]

7 For further references to Shin'ichi Hisamatsu and the School of Kyoto see "The Kyoto School", in *Stanford Encyclopedia of Philosophy*, https://plato.stanford.edu/entries/kyoto-school/#IdeMemWhoBelWha, first published Mon Feb 27, 2006; substantive revision Tue Apr 9, 2019.

8 See Martin Heidegger, 'Art and Thinking, protocol of a colloquium on May 18, 1958', Eng. Trans. Carolyn Culberstone and Tobias Keiling, in *Philosophy Today*, 21/03/2017.

9 See Leonardo V. Arena, *Haiku* (Milano: Rizzoli, 1995), pp. 13-17.

The nature of poetic word: from dualism of metaphor to hinting and freeing things

Tezuka's translation of *kū* (empty) as "the open" – of which Heidegger was enthusiastic as an interpreter of Hölderlin – provides a clue to the proximity between the two thinkers as for the revealing power of poetic words in Hölderlin and Bashō, in other words its capacity to lead humans closer to the being or no-being of things.[10] Heidegger affirms that in spite of Platonic metaphysics, in which there is a division of reality into two levels (i.e. the Idea and its mediation through the sensory level), the kind of relationship between essence and appearance in the Japanese tradition is more that of a unity. Nonetheless, by interpreting *shiki/iro* as a metaphorical image which stands for what can be perceived by the senses i.e. *aistheton*, and *kū* as another metaphor standing for the supersensuous (or what shines through) i.e. *noeton*, Heidegger runs into a conceptual reduction of the Japanese language. In the essay "A Dialogue on Language" – an artful report in the form of a dialogue about the meeting with Tezuka – the philosopher seems to justify himself observing that the metaphysical distinction of Western aesthetic experience is rooted deeply within the nature of the German language itself. These roots represent the semiotic conception of language, whose structure is supported by the basic elements of sound and script on the one hand, and signification and sense on the other. Therefore, metaphor is a linguistic reproduction of a kind of thinking well-rooted within metaphysical dualism, due to the fact that on the one hand we have an image, which acts as a sign, and on the other hand the meaning, or what the image refers to.

Heidegger, on the contrary, believes that the fundamental characteristic of word is to hint or beckon to; that is its power to free a thing from its meaning (as its representative concept) like the expression "house of being" does towards the nature of language. Therefore Tezuka – according to Heidegger's

10 Reinhard May, *Heidegger's Hidden Sources*, cit., p. 62.

report – appreciated the translation of the Sophoclean *Charis* with “graciousness”, inasmuch as it indicates a way of naming things in which the thing is freed. In other words, as an example of a kind of language that is not denotative and representative of an essence and the intrinsic qualities of a thing, but which indicates the original movement of intense magnificence, a profound insight into the being of the thing, a joyful rapture of the consciousness which feels, called by what has not yet been said or thought of the thing and which it claims for it. This original movement of calling for naming is matched with the essence of *iki* いき in Japanese culture, or “the breath of the stillness of luminous delight”, where “delight” is understood literally and not metaphorically, as what “ensnares, carries away onto stillness”.[11] The “breath of the stillness” is this open and empty space, the source from which all things come to being and inhabit language. The essence of appearing has to be seen as the reality of presence in its essential origin and this kind of experience allows us to overcome the subject-object relation.

Compared to what has been said, the fundamental characteristic of the word in *haiku* poetry is the capacity of holding the presence and the power of void. The Italian philosopher Giangiorgio Pasqualotto shows that within *haiku* some words are implied, for example *ya* [や] and *kana* [かな], that he calls “words of void”,[12] inasmuch as they manifest the anattā character (or void of its own consistency, *muga* 無我 in Japanese) of the elements denoted by the words that surround them, because they make explicit the yūgen 幽玄 character of the structure in which these elements are arranged, which is indefinite but therefore itself infinitely definable. In the *haiku* it is precisely the emerging of void that makes possible every word and every sound (that is the

11 Martin Heidegger, ‘A Dialogue on Language’, in *On the Way to Language*, Eng. Trans. Peter D. Hertz (San Francisco: Harper & Row, 1971), p. 44.

12 On a formal level, their function is to introduce a pause, which generates a moment of silence; otherwise in terms of meaning their function is to “allow the interpenetration of the elements and, at the same time, the opening of the structure that connects them”. See Giangiorgio Pasqualotto, *Estetica del vuoto: Arte e meditazione nelle culture d’Oriente* (Venezia: Marsilio, 2013), p. 111.

same of everything and every event), so that *haiku* can be said to be the starting condition for every determination and also the dimension in which this latter ends in dissolving itself, insofar as "the void to which the words of haiku hint is void as the condition of the infinite possibilities of other words".[13]

We are made aware by Tezuka himself of how what has been argued so far is at work in the Japanese words which encode the nature of language:

> *Kotoba* 言葉 is connected with *koto* 事 (meaning 'matter') of *kotogara* 事柄 (meaning 'event' or 'affair'). The *ba* [ば] is a sound transformation (sequential voicing – *rendaku* 連濁) of *ha* [は] and has connotations of 'many' or 'dense', as with leaves of a tree. If this is right, then the *koto* of 'language' and the *koto* of 'matter' are two sides of the same coin: things happen and become language (*kotoba*). The word *kotoba* may have roots in ideas of this kind.[14]

Heidegger, in the aforesaid 'A Dialogue on Language', identifies *kotoba* as the "beckoning delight" from which the leaves of a blossom, like cherry blossoms, stem. In other words, he refers to the event in which every single thing – uniquely, in each unrepeatable moment – delights someone by its beckoning, or its gift of giving themselves to presence, as a calling, a message, or invitation to be named by someone with words. Furthermore, in order to corroborate his theory of "ontological difference" between Being and things in their mutual appearance and concealment in poetic language, Heidegger reports that Tezuka said that the irreducible "more" that *shiki-kū* concepts have, if compared to the metaphysic concepts *aisthesis-noeton*, consists of that "open space" that serves as "the source from which the mutual interplay of the two comes to pass". Such space of mutual interplay between *shiki* and *kū* is *koto*, in the meaning of "[…] holding way over that which needs the shelter of all that flourish and flowers", so that "Language, heard through this word, is:

13 Giangiorgio Pasqualotto, *Estetica del vuoto: Arte e meditazione nelle culture d'Oriente*, cit., p. 112.

14 Reinhard May, *Heidegger's Hidden Sources*, cit., p. 60.

the petals that stem from koto".[15] Here, language should not be understood metaphorically as blooming: flower is not a metaphor for 'word', but the word intends to be literally a flower, due to the fact that both have the same movement, this surfacing to the open or such bringing itself to the light and appearance. Precisely, in this regard, the two interlocutors claim to feel "a concealed kinship" between their way of thinking, because their path and language are so completely different from one another that this ensures that each authentic tradition refers to one another.[16] Tezuka reports that, while translating Heidegger's lecture on Hölderlin's elegy *Homecoming* into Japanese, he felt that "the wellspring of reality from which those two fundamentally different languages arise was the same".[17] This same wellspring is meant to be the poetic word as a freeing word in the form of a hint, respectively the "absence of Being" and the "void": one that doesn't seek for general concepts under which German and Japanese can be subsumed, in this way overcoming the metaphorical distinction between image/sign and meaning, and the denotative function of language.

Ontology of difference: appearance in the word and concealment in the thing

In this first part we have drawn an essential connection between the process of "coming into being" of reality and the power of poetic word that "let it be", in the sense of the original source common to all languages, that which Heidegger calls the "Saying" and Tezuka "Kotoba". In the second part, we will try to trace differences and specificities between the two theoretical perspectives, regarding the nature of non-metaphorical poetic language and thinking, in its capacity to overcome the metaphysical dualism of aesthetic experience of reality, above all that between subject-object and sensuous-supersensuous. We can see the starting point of this inquiry when Heidegger, during

15 Martin Heidegger, 'A Dialogue on Language', cit., pp. 46-47.
16 Martin Heidegger, 'A Dialogue on Language', cit., p. 40.
17 Martin Heidegger, 'A Dialogue on Language', cit., p. 24.

the dialogue, being satisfied by the definition of language hinted by *kotoba*, replies that the latter then could mean "thing". Tezuka underlines that such an attempt clearly showed Heidegger's effort to force the word into a preconceived idea; but since he could not contradict this interpretation, he replied: "In my opinion it could mean thing as well as affair ".[18] Before going deeper into the analysis, it is useful to emphasize the analogy between Heidegger's thought and Japanese thought, regarding the pre-eminence of Being understood as a non-metaphysical becoming rather than as a metaphysical foundation. As for Japanese philosophy, we know from M. Marra that:

> For the impact that Buddhism had on medieval Japanese culture, Karatani is free to argue that rejection of the dualities of one and many, inner and outer, subject and object, and mind and body has been at the core of Japan's philosophical tradition since time immemorial. [...] Karatani argues that the lack of an original metaphysical apparatus explains the preeminence in Japan of the process of becoming (*naru* 成) over an absent presence of Being.[19]

Similarly Heidegger, who searched for a method to get rid of metaphysics, shares the idea that once foundation of Being (*sonzai* 存在) has been ungrounded, Being starts ontologically making sense as the constitutive possibility of "not-being any longer". The philosopher argued that:

> Being cannot be thought of as presence, since the only organ that can actualize it – thought – remembers Being as what has already disappeared (*an-denken*), a void moment of absence. Being is a trace of past words, a message transmitted (*Überlieferung*) from generation to generation of mortal entities; it is contained in the process of becoming, and identifies with the fleeting rhythm of existence, nothingness (Jap. *mu* 無).[20]

The issue at matter here is that for Heidegger, inheriting Greek tradition, there is an essential relation between Being and Saying,

---

18 Reinhard May, *Heidegger's Hidden Sources*, cit., p. 60.

19 Michele Marra, 'Japanese Aesthetics: The construction of Meaning', cit., pp. 368-369.

20 Michele Marra, 'Japanese Aesthetics: The construction of Meaning', cit., p. 370.

which needs to be rethought by means of poetic experience. For this purpose, he comments on Stefan George's poem *The Word*:

> So I renounced and sadly see:
> where word breaks off no thing may be.[21]

With "thing", Heidegger means anything that in anyway has being, any being as such. The word is what first brings that given "thing", as the being that is, into this "is". The "word" is what holds the "thing" there and, so to speak legitimates its being a "thing". Indeed the word itself is what keeps the thing as thing, and as keeper, the essence of the word is the relation itself.[22] The poet's "renunciation" consists in making a step back into the sphere of human being, no longer represented by calculated reasoning and progress toward, but by turning back to where we already are.[23] Therefore, in order to overcome metaphysics, thinking necessarily needs to follow poetry and turn back to the present moment, to the reality where we already are, by which we mean the continuous movement of being of things in the act of appearing into words that simultaneously corresponds to concealing itself into things as appearances. The word for Heidegger does not have an essence represented by a concept, therefore it is not itself a thing, the word is rather a process, it is the power to endow the thing with being. In this regard, the philosopher claims that no-thing is where the word is lacking, inasmuch as a thing is not until, and is only where, the word is not lacking but is there, so Word and Thing are different. According to this, the word shows what is there and yet is not, and itself belongs to what is there first of all, so that that the word function of giving being is concealed within itself.

The word itself is the giver of being in the form of saying that has no being in itself, but gives a meaningful hint. Hence, the word has to be understood as "no-thing", nothing that is, which

21 Martin Heidegger, 'The Nature of Language', in *On the Way to Language*, cit., p. 77.
22 See Martin Heidegger, 'The Nature of Language', cit., pp. 82-83.
23 See Martin Heidegger, 'The Nature of Language', cit., p. 85.

shares with "is" the property of not being a being. In other words neither the 'is' nor the word attain to "thinghood", nor does the relation between 'is' and the word, because it gives an 'is' in each given instance. Heidegger summarises all this in the sentence "the being of language speaks as the language of being". Here, the word being as object no longer means – as Plato does – the essence of a thing, which implies the concept, the idea, or the mental representation by means of which we grasp what a thing is. At the same time being as subject has the function of a verb, like "it is in being" which means "it persists in its presence" and in its persistence, that is its most distinctive property, moves all things and so concerns us in all things. The language, then, belongs to being insofar as the being persists within and in terms of language, so that "what moves all things moves in that it speaks".[24] Heidegger intends to overcome the metaphysical representation of reality given by the Greek conception of *aletheia* or the unveiling of being in the things meant as present and so hiding itself as soon as they come to be represented by a word linked to a concept. He rather believes that what is "properly worthy of thought" is the coming into presence of the thing by means of the power of poetic word, which lets its nature of a "soundless gathering call" speak. It basically means that, since this event or movement of coming to light is due to that formless, potential background, each appearing is characterized by the sonorous nature of the word. Such a call of the thing to be named starts from the persistence into poetic word of its formless sound nature; that is equivalent to say that the thing has a soundless abiding heart. Such givenness, interpreted as the very being of a thing, refers to the fact that the things do not have an essence and so a meaning that can be represented, but that they are free. This essential freedom of their unique and singular gift in each given instance is what bounds them in an intimate relationship with humans, who are irresistibly ensnared to wonder upon that. This relationship calls humans to respond by means of a word which does not pretend to grasp or say the

24 Martin Heidegger, 'The Nature of Language', cit., p. 95.

essence of a thing, but which hints at its concealment and recalls the absence of communication of the essence in terms of "what is not a thing", referring to that formless and potential terrain of sound, to the movement of appearing, or the background preceding everything that comes into being.

Meontology: the presence and effectiveness of void in the poetic word

On the other side, according to the general Buddhist conception about the distinction between reality and language, since reality is a product of human consciousness, it cannot ground itself in the stability of meaning, which, on the contrary, is relative and illusory; therefore, linguistic activity as a temporary means to represent what in reality fails to prove its own existence, is discredited. Then for Zen Buddhism, "Since there is no truth in representation, what we take as reality is nothing but the product of 'a wordly logic' (*zokutai* 俗諦), while Buddhist truth (*shintai* 真諦) cannot become an object of representation".[25] With this in mind is easier to understand why in the Japanese intellectual tradition, compared to what has just been said about the relationship between event, thing and poetic word in Heidegger's thought, the effectiveness of the void in *haiku* is due to the presence of a subjective void and an objective void. These two voids are related to two Japanese expressions, respectively "*fūga no makoto*" 風雅の誠 and "*zōka no makoto*" 造化の誠 which Toshihiko Isutzu (井筒俊彦, 1914-1993) has translated as "genuineness of aesthetic creativity" and "genuineness of cosmic creativity". The first genuineness is the subjective one of the poet which makes him capable of grasping the nature of things and the event of their occurrence with three verses, which is but a particular way of the second, the objective one of the event itself, in others words the cosmic genuineness of nature. The latter, it

25 Michele Marra, 'Japanese Aesthetics: The construction of Meaning', cit., p. 372.

can be said, has its specificity in the void as the absence of a subject, as perceived in the most famous Bashō's poems:

An ancient pond
A frog jumps in
The sound of water.[26]

We observe that the poet is not there; he does not describe and comment on an event, but rather records it as if his mind was a clean mirror. The poet – Pasqualotto claims – in order to accept the genuineness of the objective event empties his intellectual and sentimental intention, so making his verses 'empty' and transforming them into natural events, and so equivalent to the event they describe.[27] The presence and effectiveness of the void in poetry is due to the encounter between these two genuineness (i.e. the 'subjective' one of the poet and the 'objective' one of the event). We could claim that these two voids collapse into a single void that is determined as poetry and as event. The other core aspect is the relation between the interdependent subjectivity and void in the composition of an event, which does not have a single, defined subject, but is rather three equivalent and contemporary events. This happens as none among them is the "strong" subject, and so the centre of action, but rather each does not make sense without the other. From what has been argued emerges that what acts is their relationship, which is operative only if each of the terms and events is not conceived as a closed and fixed subject.

Similarly to Heidegger – even in a different fashion – a crucial element in Bashō's poetics is the role played by the sound dimension of poetic word, which doesn't speak by means of metaphors or by apprehending the meaning of a thing to which the word as a sign refers to. The sound, according to Heidegger – as we noted – is said to be the original, permanent, potential and

26 See Thomas Hoover, *Zen Culture* (New York: Random House, 1977), pp. 205-206.

27 See Giangiorgio Pasqualotto, *Estetica del vuoto: Arte e meditazione nelle culture d'Oriente*, cit., p. 109.

formless background of the word which differs from the form it assumes when it makes a thing coming into being. The core difference is that the use of onomatopoeia, or the presentation of an action through its sound like the *plop* of the appearing of a frog, indicates both the immediacy of the appearing of an event and the identity between the sound, the event and the poet himself, who is so mentally absorbed (*samādhi*) in the happening of the event that he "may prefer to say that he himself becomes the sound".[28] Then we understand that the relationship between the word and man-poet who listens to this is also different. This relationship, from Heidegger's side, is a hermeneutic one, based on "listening from language itself" by means of pondering the words, in order to preserve the absence of the Being, which gives itself from time to time in a unique way: appearing in the word and concealing itself in the things. On the other side, Bashō conceives this relationship as an actual occurrence, like in the case of an evening broken by a splash. During this unique event, the poet's inspiration must be genuine and suggest its own lines as the moment occurs, recalling the Zen practice of eschewing deliberation and rational analysis, as nothing must come between object and perception at the critical moment.[29] The Zen idea of enlightenment as a fleeting instant implies that "this instantaneous perception moves directly from his senses to his innermost understanding, without having to travel through his interpretive faculties".[30] Therefore "whereas the antilogic *kōan* anecdotes were intended to lead up to this moment, Bashō's haiku were the moment of enlightenment itself".[31] We suggest that *kōan* 公案 and *haiku* belong to some extent to those Zen meditation practices that lead the practitioner to the condition of grasping the interrelatedness of opposites through "a particular training of the mind called 'mushin' 無心 or 'no-mind', which introduces the practitioner to a mental stage preceding the formation of

28 Roben Aitken, *A Zen Wave: Bashō's Haiku and Zen* (New York-Tokyo: Weatherhill, 1982), p. 27.

29 Thomas Hoover, *Zen Culture,* cit., pp. 205-206.

30 Thomas Hoover, *Zen Culture,* cit., p. 206.

31 Thomas Hoover, *Zen Culture,* cit., pp. 205-206.

meaning".[32] We apprehend from Michele Marra that the medieval Japanese philosopher Dōgen (道元禅師, 1200-1253) called this privileged access to enlightenment "without thinking" (*hishiryō*, 非思慮), which he distinguished from not "thinking" (*shiryō*, 思慮) and "not-thinking" (*fushiryō*, 不思慮). Furthermore, the peculiarity of "without thinking" consists in a nonconceptual and pre-reflective mode of consciousness, which makes the individual able to perceive reality as it is (*genjōkōan*, 現成公案), "without letting (rational) consciousness and the construction of categories intervene in the modification and distortion of reality. [...] Reality is then perceived in its phenomenological aspect of constant transformation (*mujō*, 無常), which resists reduction to the grammatical rules of logic and rejects the grammaticalization of conceptual categories".[33] To sum up, in that *haiku* tradition is related to Zen culture, that relationship between poetry and thinking – so crucial for Heidegger – is based on a mental stage preceding the formation of thinking called "without thinking", namely a pre-reflective mode of consciousness, which makes an individual perceive reality as it is.

Phenomenology of sound and voice: Kotoba and Saying

We are now able to give a first answer to the issue we raised at the beginning, namely why Tezuka replied to Heidegger that *kotoba* refers to both 'thing' as well as 'affair'. This is because in the poet's intentional void, the word becomes identical to the thing it describes – which is felt more like a singular and immediate event, namely an event composed of multiple interrelated elements or factors. On the contrary, Heidegger relating *kotoba* with "thing" was trying to comprehend the Japanese essence of language within his idea of ontological difference between the "thing" named by words and their act of appearing from the original, sonorous, formless background

32 Thomas Hoover, *Zen Culture,* cit., pp. 205-206.

33 Michele Marra, 'Japanese Aesthetics: The construction of Meaning', cit., p. 371.

of the word that gives an "is" to them. According to this, Heidegger in the work *The Nature of Language* points out that the vocal sounds are the very nature of language since they are demonstrable for any language at any time, and this allows us to get into the specificities of what he means for non-metaphoric language. Now, in this theoretical framework we can understand Tezuka's report about Heidegger's request to hear that *haiku* by Bashō: "And so what he wanted to hear from me was something of the Japanese language – not just something about Japanese language, but the language itself".[34] Heidegger states that the experience of the true nature of sound and speech tone is limited when vocal sound and written character (being experienced in its physiological production of sound as a physical element of language mainly associated with the body) are conceived within of the metaphysical boundaries of the sensuous and so as to be opposed to the so-called meaning and sense-content esteemed as the true spirit of language. Within this argument, the philosopher refers to a different way of speaking in different areas of Germany, which he calls "modes of the mouth". These differences are not related exclusively to the movement patterns of the speech organs, but by the fact that "the landscape, and that means the earth, speaks in them, differently each time".[35] Therefore, Heidegger claims, the mouth is not just a biological organ but body and mouth are part of the flow and growth of the earth in which the men as mortals flourish and from which they receive the soundness of their roots, so if the man loses the earth, he also loses the roots. In this regards, the following are some Hölderlinian poems whose expressions, namely "flower of the mouth", "the sky's blooms may blossom", and "words like flowers", lead us to the "concealed kinship" between the Japanese way of thinking about the enigma of language (i.e. petals that stem from *koto*), and Heidegger's understanding of the power of poetic word as the original source of saying.

34 Reinhard May, *Heidegger's Hidden Sources*, cit., p. 60.
35 Martin Heidegger, 'The Nature of Language', cit., p. 98.

Fifth stanza - Germania
And secretly, while you dreamed, at noon,
Departing I left a token of friendship,
The flower of the mouth behind, and lonely you spoke.
Yet you, the greatly blessed, with the rivers too
Dispatched a wealth of golden words, and they well unceasing
Into all regions now.

First stanza - Walk in the country
Therefore I even hope it may come to pass,
When we begin what we wish for and our tongue loosens,
And the word has been found and the heart has opened,
And from ecstatic brows springs a higher reflection,
That the sky's blooms may blossom even as do our own,
And the luminous sky open to opened eyes.

Fifth stanza - Bread and Wine
Such is man; when the wealth is there,
and no less than a god in Person
tends him with gifts, blind he remains, unaware.
First he must suffer; but now he names his most treasured possession,
Now for it words like flowers leaping alive he must find.[36]

According to Heidegger, "Language is the flower of the mouth. In language the earth blossoms toward the bloom of the sky" and this is "how the nature of language as Saying, as that which moves all things, here announces itself".[37] In order to paraphrase his words, we could say that language above all corresponds to its sound nature, in its formless, open, and potential ground, which is the prerequisite for saying, therefore for making everything that is between earth and sky be. The expression "Being speaks through Sound" recalls its manifestation in things through the appearance of words, and the expression "Words like flower" adds that the appearance of words determines the encounter of earth and sky as "world regions". Since the movement of a flower growing from earth is the same of that of every single word of the mouth that arise

36 Martin Heidegger, 'The Nature of Language', cit., pp. 99-100.
37 Martin Heidegger, 'The Nature of Language', cit., p. 99.

from sound, Heidegger says: "It would mean that we stay bogged down in metaphysics if we were to take the name Hölderlin gives here to 'words like flowers' as being a metaphor".[38] According to what has been said so far, overcoming metaphysical thinking, in fact, goes hand in hand with not making reality appear through metaphors in language, which basically implies that the world and therefore all things are made to appear mainly by means of the sound of language, which calls them with words. The "Saying" is precisely this movement, understood as the source of calling that arises like the earth. Hence, this sound of the voice in its power to make things ring out, is in harmony with the structure of the world or "earthiness". In addition to this, Heidegger conceives a "neighbourhood" of the "modes of saying", particularly between poetry and thinking, which is generated by a movement of "nearness" in the sense of "digression", intended to bring the thought process back exactly to where we already are and not forward. In conclusion, "Saying" is the essential nature of language, whose essential being is to make appear and set free in the means of offering what is called the world, lighting and concealing it.

The aesthetic of wandering and the bodily subjectivity

Symptomatic of the comparison of the poetic spirit of the two poets taken into account is the peculiar relationship with Nature, from which a certain kind of knowledge and language arises. In regards to this, Heidegger analyzes some of Gottfried Benn's general statements about Hölderlin lyrics, which he defines as "nothing more than a 'herbarium', a collection of dried-up plants". First of all, the philosopher argues that the "like" in the expression "words like flowers" is not a secondary statement (e.g. metaphoric function) with the function of adducing and comparing with something else, but it gives back the "Saying" which has the function of keeping the source of its being, characterized by "the gentle force of a singular and

38 Martin Heidegger, 'The Nature of Language', cit., p. 100.

innocent capacity to hear". For Bashō, on the other hand, the art of poetry, intended to reach the very essence of things, was intimately connected with an aesthetics of wandering, representing, at least initially, an estrangement from everyday experience. Thus, "poetry more than a result of a technique to creating good haikai, it was primarily a practice dependent on a flash of insight and its immediate articulation in language, whose propitious circumstances, from Bashō's peripatetic life seems precisely to be: wandering".[39] In this regard, consistent with Buddhist thought, we must consider that language - conceived as a reconstructive practice of experience -, putting the results of retrospective analysis into grammatical form, reduces experience to conceptual categories. It leads to the distortion of reality, as language cannot grasp that immediacy of experience. Buddhist philosophical tradition, on the other hand, by applying a deconstructive practice that suspends the metaphysical correspondence between mind, meaning, and the method that is supposed to unite them, leads to "a truth as an insight into a non-differentiating and non-objectifying wisdom (*prajña*) that frees the interpreter from the danger of thinking of categories as absolutes".[40] The element of immediacy of the experience achieved by Bashō in wandering suggests that the poetic knowledge contained in his poetry is based on the somatic experience of reality. On this matter, the philosopher Thomas Heyd argues that the act of wandering practiced with intensity is based on continuous choices in the placement of the feet and hands, which determine the balance and imbalance of body weight; or again in the acceleration and management of momentum of one's body mass and in the articulation of one's body position with the physical environment. The Wanderer's subjectivity has a somatic experience through the bodily encounter with the non-conceptualizable dimension of reality

39 Thomas Heyd, 'Bashō and the Aesthetics of Wandering: Recuperating Space, Recognizing Place, and Following the Ways of the Universe', in *Philosophy East and West*, 53-3 (2003), p. 292.

40 Michele Marra, 'Japanese Aesthetics: The construction of Meaning', cit., pp. 370-371.

of branches, slippery-muddy areas, volcanic rocks, sand, rivers, and so on. Therefore, we deduce that such a bodily experience involves a volitional commitment that imprints this peculiar intentional level of consciousness (i.e. corporality) with a series of textured images that are visual, tactile, olfactory, kinaesthetic and gustatory, cognitive events; and "It is this cognition of space as composed of perceptually significant places that gives reality to abstractions, like space represented on a map or in a story.[41]

The next step for our discussion consists in clarifying the linking between metaphor as a cognitive event and the bodily experience. The Japanese professor of linguistics Masako K. Hiraga, who applies a cognitive understanding of *haiku*, reports that thanks to G. Lakoff, M. Johnson, and M. Turner's research on the cognitive account of poetic metaphor, we are made aware that:

> Linguistic metaphorical expressions are possible because there are metaphorical concepts that correspond with the linguistic expressions. Moreover, what is insightful and powerful in this view is that metaphors are based on the concepts that emerge from our bodily experience such as space, location, and physical experiences. That is, metaphors arise from an understanding of our own physical experiences.[42]

Bashō, believing that poetic inspiration came from paying close attention to natural processes, used to recommend to his students: "Go to the pine tree if you want to learn from a pine, things about a pine, and go to the bamboo if you want to learn from bamboo, things about bamboo". Dohō – one of his students – comments: "Learn means to enter into the object, perceive its delicate life, and feel its feeling, whereupon a poem forms itself". The process of knowing nature, then, was a matter of apprehending nature for what it is, but from a personal perspective.[43] Therefore, "the

41 Thomas Heyd, 'Bashō and the Aesthetics of Wandering: Recuperating Space, Recognizing Place, and Following the Ways of the Universe', cit., p. 297.

42 Masako K. Hiraga, '"Blending" and Interpretation of Haiku: A Cognitive Approach', in *Poetic Today*, 20-3 (1999), p. 464.

43 See Thomas Heyd, 'Bashō and the Aesthetics of Wandering: Recuperating Space, Recognizing Place, and Following the Ways of the Universe', cit., p. 299.

issue is that in coming to know nature for oneself one comes to know how oneself and the rest of nature fit together" so that we may have a representation of "landscape in human emotion, and human emotion in landscape".[44] Poetic metaphors, of such kind, which find their very source in direct and literal experience, both bodily and cognitive, can be defined as 'Beyond Metaphor', that is, beyond the dichotomy of image/meaning. Those different metaphors, from what has been discussed so far, seem to be at work in the kind of poetry that brings the poet's mind back to being present to the earthly energy of appearing either – in the case of Bashō and Japanese Zen Culture – through direct bodily experience of the immediacy of a thing-event, becoming almost the thing itself, or – in the case of Heidegger as an interpreter of Hölderlin – through listening and pondering from language itself the movement of the givenness of the thing, which calls to be named by a single word arising from the sound power of the mouth. This happens in the same way a flower arises from the earth power of letting appear and conceal in that given appearance.

Poetic spirit and poetic dwelling: the transpersonality of poetic knowledge

In Bashō's poetry, the going beyond metaphor and by the metaphysical distinction between subject and object, image and meaning, the thing itself as it is and its conceptual elaboration, is based on a "transpersonal theory of poetry", since poetry is a product of man's close communion with nature, which presupposes the dissolution of the poet's ego.[45] Such a theory has its core in the idea of "poetic spirit", which Basho defines:

44 Thomas Heyd, 'Bashō and the Aesthetics of Wandering: Recuperating Space, Recognizing Place, and Following the Ways of the Universe', cit., p. 299.

45 Makoto Ueda, 'Bashō and the poetics of "Haiku"', in *The Journal of Aesthetics and Art Criticism*, 21-4 (1963), p. 424.

> It is a spirit which seeks beauty in nature, which tries to escape from the collisions of everyday life. Anyone who wishes to become a happy artist should strive to gain this spirit, because it is in this way that he learns to assume an aesthetic attitude toward life.[46]

In this statement, we can hear a resonance with the Heideggerian idea of "poetic dwelling", based on the relation of "being near" to the world, taking a step back where we already are and not forward. This aesthetic attitude towards life is the intimate and ineffable call to man in his living on earth, due to the belief that "Beauty in nature is a manifestation of the creative force of the supreme being which flows through all things in the universe, animate and inanimate". In these words, we hear what Heidegger says about the power of the poetic word as what gives being to the thing, mainly "what moves everything between earth and sky". Bashō believes that such "energy of the universe is 'transpersonal' in the sense that it has no personal emotion such as joy or anger, grief or hatred, which springs from egoism", but at the same time even "man, being part of the universe, also has transpersonal energy within him, an energy which he shares with the cosmos. It is this energy which every poet must work with in his creative activity".[47] Bashō calls such a retuning of the individual creative 'poetic spirit' with that creative and transpersonal energy of the cosmos, namely *hosomi* 細み, or the practice of burying itself in external object with "delicate sensitivity", a term that resonates with the Heideggerian "innocent capacity to hear". Such an attitude allows the poet – with a concentrated mind – to feel the subtle mist rising over the life of a natural object, as if it were an invisible vibration that occurs in the poet's heart as a response to the smallest stimulus of nature.[48] We can feel *hosomi* from the following haiku:

I wonder whether
Seabirds too are asleep
On Lake Yogo tonight

46 Makoto Ueda, 'Bashō and the poetics of "Haiku"', cit., p. 423.
47 Makoto Ueda, 'Bashō and the poetics of "Haiku"', cit., p. 424.
48 Makoto Ueda, 'Bashō and the poetics of "Haiku"', cit., p. 426.

The Japanese professor of comparative literature Makoto Ueda, observing that a *haiku* poet does not use images of nature to express his emotion, letting natural objects express their feelings, reveals a phenomenological specificity of *haiku* poetry. Indeed, in the aforementioned *haiku* the lonely cry of the seabird is what causes a vibration in the poet's heart, so that the cause-effect relation must not be reversed. For Bashō, the fact that "a poet should suppress his personal sentiment and submerge himself within an outside object is in a way a warning against the pathetic fallacy".[49] The poetic principle of *hosomi*, understood as transpersonal knowledge and poetic creativity, overturns the cause-effect relation and thus allows us to overcome the metaphysical distinction between subject and object. What has just been said shows an affinity with that Heideggerian gift of the thing, calling the poet to meditate on the poetic word, letting the language speak from himself. Bashō believes that all aspects of living will become subjects for aesthetic appreciation, if the human condition is viewed from a detached perspective. The latter is called *sabi* 寂: the feeling of detachment, or tone of loneliness, which is appreciable in the following *haiku*:

Cherry blossom guardians –
Their white heads
Bumping together

Thomas Heyd comments that "here Bashō is reframing the human experience of coming to the end of life, from a broad, 'objective' perspective. Just as the impending fall of the blossoms may be tolerable, and even aesthetically pleasing, so, perhaps, may old age".[50] Ueda in this regard states that *sabi* consists in an atmosphere of loneliness marked by quiet, the vast, or the swift where personal emotions like joy, sorrow, love, anger and jealousy are absent. In other words, it is the atmosphere of impersonal nature, and there is not the emotion of human life, so

49 Makoto Ueda, 'Bashō and the poetics of "Haiku"', cit., p. 427.
50 Thomas Heyd, 'Bashō and the Aesthetics of Wandering: Recuperating Space, Recognizing Place, and Following the Ways of the Universe', cit., p. 295.

this loneliness is not that of a man who has lost his dear one, but that kind exemplified by "the rain falling on large taro leaves at night, or the loneliness emerging out of a cicada's cry amid the white, dry rocks, or the Milky Way extending over the rough sea, or a huge river torrentially rushing in the rainy season",[51] directly appreciable in the following haiku:

Loneliness—
Standing amid the blossoms,
A cypress tree

In this scene loneliness is evoked by the cypress, so it does not refer to a man's personal emotion but describes an impersonal atmosphere. Here, we observe that the ultimate interrelatedness of all things and experiences is revealed by a peculiar attitude to the use of synaesthesia. Therefore we realize that the poetic world of *haiku* includes all existing things, elegant or not elegant, as they are all part of nature (e.g. warbles, blossoms, and the moon, and at the other sight a muddy crow, a bird's droppings, or a horse's dung), and likewise it takes part in all aspects of human life. Then, we understand the unique state of consciousness of a *haijin* (*haiku* poet), which consists in being a bystander (or spectator), who calmly and smilingly has only to observe. While the latter detaches himself from worldly desires, he lives among all things, events, and feelings of human life, not fleeing from the world of ordinary men, but staying in the middle of it in order to understand and share the feelings of ordinary men.[52] The world of *haiku*, then, through the poetic principles of *sabi* allows us to experience that atmosphere of "vastness" and "simplicity with content" which Heidegger himself – as mentioned above – felt. Moreover, by means of *hosomi*, it offers itself as that metaphorical transcending of language into a cognitive apprehension of reality due to the close and intimate interrelation of all things, which

51 Makoto Ueda, 'Bashō on the Art of the Haiku: Impersonality in poetry', in Nancy G. Hume (ed. by), *Japanese Aesthetics and Cultures A Reader* (Albany: State University of New York Press, 1995), pp. 157-158.

52 Makoto Ueda, 'Bashō on the Art of the Haiku: Impersonality in poetry', cit., p.167.

allows a transposition of the emotional experience from one plane of reality to another.

Conclusion

As we approach the conclusion, it is necessary to note that also in Bashō's poetics there is a crucial reference to the flower, which is a key element in providing us with the second answer to the problem we have set ourselves, namely why Tezuka replies to Heidegger that *kotoba* refers both "thing" as well as "affair". With this purpose in mind, we read from Bashō that poetic creativity "[i]s the poetic spirit, the spirit that leads one to follow the ways of the universe and to become a friend with things of the seasons. For a person who has the spirit, everything he sees becomes a flower, and everything he imagines turns into a moon".[53] Considering it semantically, *kotoba* (petals that stem from *koto*) allows one to feel the loneliness we have analysed, in which plants, animals, humans are enclosed trans-personally and interdependently. It tells us that, when the poetic language reflects the creative energy of the universe as an empty mirror, each of the elements portrayed is in relation (Tezuka's "affair") with the others so as to constitute an event: an appearing which is empty of its own consistency and, therefore, literally identical to petals which stem from *koto* like cherry blossoms. Therefore, since these elements are empty in themselves, there is a pure identity between word and thing, man and thing, man and word, creator of universe and creative poetry: elements that are endowed with the same degree of reality. Since poetry created in immediacy and in the void of intentionality is made equal to the creative event itself of the universe, without any difference on the degree of reality, and as inconsistent in both, everything we see that is not endowed with its own consistency can become a flower, so it can be transposed in any other, being all tied up in a relationship of

53 Makoto Ueda, 'Bashō on the Art of the Haiku: Impersonality in poetry', cit., p.153.

interdependence between the elements. Everything we imagine can then turn into a moon; in the same way, the three verses of Bashō, reflecting the void of subjective intentionality, have the power to generate the same perceptual sensations aroused during and by the event itself. Ultimately, this parallelism that echoes Holderlin's "word like flower" – which makes us understand what Heidegger claims as the essence of language known as *Saying* – shows more clearly that concealed kinship between their non-metaphoric way of thinking – as examined in the first section –, precisely because – as our comparative inquiry about the nature of word and flower has underlined – their path and language are completely different. In other words, this divergence is based on an "ontological difference" between word and thing in Heidegger and on a "meontological identity"[54] between these two in the Japanese philosophical perspective that was considered.

54 Meontology here means nothing but the Contemporary Zen Buddhist Philosophy of Nothingness, which is based on a radical refusal of conceiving the Being according to the category of substance, as something being identical to itself and having in itself its very foundation of being. It admits on the other hand to the category of relation, meaning that all that already exists is in a relation with the other and precisely is in a relation of mutual conditioning (inter-dependence; inter-connection). In this dynamic context everything is nothing in itself and so, according to this, it is open without limits to universal relations, which are centered on the nothing of each thing, any time in its unicity and singularity. See Carlo Saviani, *L'oriente di Heidegger* (Genova: Melangolo, 1998), pp. 25-26. For further references to Meontology see also "The Kyoto School", in *Stanford Encyclopedia of Philosophy*, https://plato.stanford.edu/entries/kyoto-school/#IdeMemWhoBelWha, First published Mon Feb 27, 2006; substantive revision Tue Apr 9, 2019.

MIMESIS GROUP
www.mimesis-group.com

MIMESIS INTERNATIONAL
www.mimesisinternational.com
info@mimesisinternational.com

MIMESIS EDIZIONI
www.mimesisedizioni.it
mimesis@mimesisedizioni.it

ÉDITIONS MIMÉSIS
www.editionsmimesis.fr
info@editionsmimesis.fr

MIMESIS COMMUNICATION
www.mim-c.net

MIMESIS EU
www.mim-eu.com

Printed by
Digital Team – Fano (PU)
March 2021